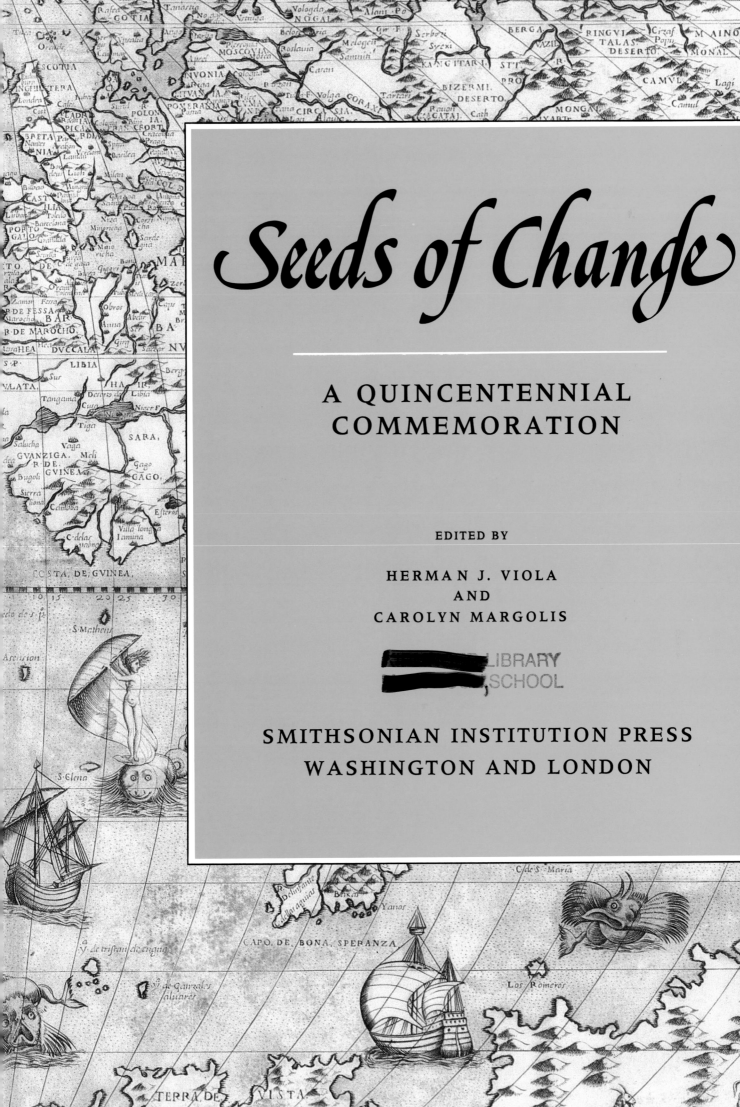

Seeds of Change

A QUINCENTENNIAL COMMEMORATION

EDITED BY

HERMAN J. VIOLA
AND
CAROLYN MARGOLIS

SMITHSONIAN INSTITUTION PRESS
WASHINGTON AND LONDON

The "Seeds of Change" exhibitions, publications, and programs
have been made possible through the generous support of

Xerox Corporation

Additional funds have been provided by the

National Endowment for the Humanities
Smithsonian Institution Special Exhibition Fund
National Corn Growers Association
The Potato Board
Arco Foundation
The Potato Museum
Beneficial Corporation

For permission to reproduce illustrations appearing in this book, please correspond directly with the owners of the works, as listed in the Picture Credits. The Smithsonian Institution Press does not retain reproduction rights for these illustrations or maintain a file of addresses for photo sources

The paper in this book meets the requirements of the American National Standard for Permanence of Paper for Printed Materials Z39.48-1984

Acquisitions Editor—Daniel H. Goodwin
Senior Editor—Jeanne M. Sexton
Editor—Jan S. Danis
Editorial Production—Craig Reynolds

Art Director and Book Design—Alex Castro
Picture Researcher/Editor—Martha Davidson
Assistant Picture Researcher—Diane Cooke
Caption Writer—Suzanne Winckler
Production Manager—Kathleen Brown
Separations—PhotoColor, Inc., Newark, Delaware
Typography—Monotype Composition Company, Inc., Baltimore, Maryland
Printing—Ringier America, Inc.
New Berlin, Wisconsin

970.01
SEE

Library of Congress Cataloguing in Publication Data

Seeds of change : a quincentennial commemoration / edited
   by Herman J. Viola and Carolyn Margolis.
       p.   cm.
   Includes bibliographical references (p.   ) and index.
   ISBN 1-56098-035-4 (cloth). — ISBN 1-56098-036-2
   (paper)
   1. Columbus, Christopher—Influence—Exhibitions. 2.
America—Discovery and exploration—Spanish—Exhibitions.
3. Indians—First contact with Occidental civilization—Exhibitions. 4. America—History—To 1810—Exhibitions.
I. Viola, Herman J.   II. Margolis, Carolyn.
E112.S45 1991
970.01'5—dc20   90-10289
                                                      CIP

Contents

Foreword

Underpinning every great exhibition are the lively minds of scholars asking questions. This book reflects some of the inquiry that supports the Columbus Quincentenary exhibition "Seeds of Change." The book and the exhibition reexamine the massive changes since the contact of the Old and New Worlds. That examination, though sometimes painful, is necessary and gives profound insight into one of the greatest events in human history.

This is not a story of the discovery of the New World by the Old World. It is a story of the encounter of two branches of humankind that had diverged from each other over tens of thousands of years of cultural development. This saga includes stark tragedy, the decimation of the hardy people of the New World by new diseases and by war and the forcible removal of at least ten million people from their African homes to serve as plantation slaves in the Americas.

This is also the story of the transfer of many new plants and animals. The horse, brought to the New World by Columbus on his second voyage, changed life for natives of the North American plains and South American pampas. With the introduction of the potato Europe was given wonderful, easily stored food that, along with improved medical care, supported a major increase in population. In a macabre parallel, corn supported an increase in the African population, thereby providing more slaves for New World sugar plantations and other servitude.

The world was never the same after the contact. With migrations from the Old World, huge, new vigorous populations flourished in the Americas and developed a powerful industrial base that became a dominant world force during our century. This success has, however, cost dearly. These new populations, with their intemperate use of American bounty, have squandered the forests and silted and poisoned the waters—and still do so—although native peoples had lived here for centuries modifying but not destroying the natural ecosystems.

During the five centuries since contact, the diversity of New World peoples and their environment of plants and animals have suffered. But in this first decade of the sexcentenary, appreciation of cultural and biological diversity has reawakened. We have accumulated knowledge of how cultures have shriveled and died, how species have been extinguished, and how our environment has been perilously damaged. It is now time to use this accumulated wisdom, born of loss, to help us to heal, restore, and diversify further.

This volume and the accompanying exhibitions are the first harvest of the Quincentenary seeds. In other books, exhibitions, and even symposia that will spring from these seeds, the National Museum of Natural History will continue, during the decade leading to the twenty-first century, to examine our human role and human responsibility in global change. By stimulating this debate, the museum not only will pursue institutional objectives but also will encourage the urgently needed redefinition of our relationship with our world and its peoples.

Frank H. Talbot
Director
National Museum of Natural History

Seeds of Change

Herman J. Viola

Every schoolchild knows that in 1492 Christopher Columbus, a Genoese seaman sailing under the flag of Spain, captained a fleet of three tiny ships and discovered a land unknown to the peoples of Europe. His was a remarkable feat despite his inability, even after three more trips to the Americas, to comprehend the true significance of his explorations. He was not alone in this lack of understanding, of course, for it took decades for the peoples of Europe to appreciate the extent of his accomplishments. No better example of this need be noted than the failure of European cartographers to call these newfound lands Columbia, in honor of Columbus. Instead, they named them for Amerigo Vespucci, a Florentine clerk with a yen for travel whose widely circulated letter *Mundus Novus,* written in 1503, publicized the discovery of the New World long before Columbus's journals were available to European readers.

Columbus did more than force the cartographers of Europe to revise their maps of the earth. His voyages of discovery were pivotal in world history. The Western Hemisphere was rapidly and profoundly transformed biologically and culturally by seeds of change—plants, animals, and diseases—that were introduced, sometimes deliberately, sometimes accidentally, by Columbus and those who followed him. Eventually the processes of encounter and exchange that Columbus initiated affected the Old World as well, altering flora and fauna, reordering the ethnic composition of countries, changing the diet and health of peoples everywhere. They continue to this day.

The voyages of Christopher Columbus initiated a continuing exchange of plants, animals, and peoples of two hemispheres. The result was a new world.

Columbus could not have sailed at a more opportune time. Affairs in Europe in 1492 were in disarray. At the head of the Catholic church, which dominated the political as well as religious life of much of Europe, was the corrupt pope Rodrigo Borgia. Bickering with the church as well as among themselves were the monarchs of England, France, Spain, and the Germanies. Peasants were crushed by a legacy of incessant warfare and excessive taxation. Intellectuals were drifting in a sea of restlessness and uncertainty, lacking the rudder of religious faith and royal authority that had characterized the Middle Ages but heeding the siren call of the Renaissance, which dared man to believe in himself, to create new art and question old gods, to seek knowledge based on facts instead of dogma.

The Renaissance was an unexpected legacy of the crusades, the failed attempt to wrest the Holy Land from its infidel occupants. Although the crusades had military and religious objectives, they produced marked and unexpected cultural, intellectual, and economic benefits for the people of Europe. Returned crusaders had been exposed to new ideas, unfamiliar technologies, strange foods. They had developed a taste for Eastern spices, precious gems, silks and satins, and other exotic attractions from the Orient. Contact with Arab civilization also inspired a revival of interest in other Mediterranean cultures, a rebirth of the classical learning of ancient Greece and Rome. The Renaissance promoted the rise of nationalism, the growth of cities, interstate commerce, a monied economy, and a merchant class. Printing presses and universities flourished as did the teaching of subjects long neglected—astronomy, chemistry, cartography, and navigation. Newly built seaworthy vessels combined with the development of new navigational aids such as the compass, astrolabe, and quadrant, sailing charts, and a rising spirit of adventure and enterprise caused Europeans to break free of physical as well as psychological boundaries.

It was then that a united Spain burst upon the world scene, unleashing forces of radical change. In addition to sponsoring Columbus's first voyage of discovery, Ferdinand and Isabella in 1492 completed seven centuries of conflict on Spanish soil with the Moorish invaders by capturing Granada. Flush with patriotic and religious fervor, the monarchs chose to expel not only the Moors but also the Jews, thereby dispersing across Europe many of the people who were to become the intellectual architects, financiers, and artisans of the global transformation begun by Columbus and continued by Spain's rivals in the decades that followed.

What Columbus had really discovered was, however, another old world, one long populated by numerous and diverse peoples with cultures as distinct, vibrant, and worthy as any to be found in Europe. Tragically, neither Columbus nor those who followed him recognized this truth. The Europeans regarded the peoples whom they encountered in North and South America more as natural objects—another form of the fauna to be discovered and exploited—than as human beings with histories as rich and ancient as their own. They could not imagine that these peoples could offer anything of aesthetic or cultural value. Only recently, in fact, have we come to realize that what Columbus did in 1492 was to link two old worlds, thereby creating one new world.

Another tragedy of 1492 was the failure of the Europeans to recognize the fragility of the American environment. They set to work despoiling the resources of the New World as quickly as they began destroying its peoples. What had taken nature thousands of centuries to create was largely undone in less than five, beginning in September 1493, when the Admiral of the Ocean Sea returned to America at the head of an armada of seventeen ships. These disgorged on Hispaniola some fifteen hundred would-be empire builders and a Noah's ark of Old World animals and plants including horses, cows, pigs, wheat, barley, and shoots of sugarcane, which was, next to disease, perhaps the most detrimental contribution of the Old World to the New.

Sugarcane merits censure because it harmed both man and the environment. With sugarcane came the plantation system and the initial assault on the tropical rain forests of the New World. Sugarcane was a labor-intensive crop that absorbed huge human resources, beyond what was needed for altering the landscape, to make large-scale production both possible and profitable. Although American Indians were readily enslaved, they just as readily died—in vast numbers from the diseases the Europeans introduced to the New World along with their plants and animals.

Consider, for example, what occurred on the island of Hispaniola, where Columbus established Santo Domingo, the first permanent colony in the New World. In neither Haiti nor the Dominican Republic, which share this island today, are there any descendants of the original Indian inhabitants. Indeed, the native peoples had disappeared by 1600. Although no one knows what their numbers were in 1492, current estimates range from sixty thousand to as many as eight million. Columbus himself remarked that "the Indians of this island . . . are its riches, for it is they who dig and produce the bread and other food for the Christians and get the gold from the mines . . . and perform all the services and labor of men and of draft animals."

If Columbus believed the Indians were the island's riches, he did little to protect Spain's fortune. Bartolomé de las Casas, the Dominican friar and polemicist, whose father and uncle had come with Columbus to Hispaniola in 1493, believed that three million natives had perished after little more than a decade of contact with the Europeans—the result of disease, warfare, forced labor, and enslavement. "Who of those in future centuries will believe this? I myself who am writing this and saw it and know the most about it can hardly believe that such was possible."

When there were no longer sufficient Indians to maintain the New World plantations, Europeans turned to Africa for labor. The exact number of Africans kidnapped and sold into New World slavery will never be known, but estimates range from ten to thirty million. Despite the enormous loss of life, both in the transatlantic passage and in the New World, that slavery entailed—perhaps the life of one slave for each ton of sugar produced—Africans not only made sugar production profitable but they also replaced Indians as the dominant ethnic group in the Caribbean. Ironically, it may have been maize, a New World food taken to Africa by Europeans, that underlaid population growth on that continent and enabled Atlantic slavers to keep the sugar, cotton, and tobacco plantations of the New World supplied with labor.

The real meaning of 1492 can be seen in Montserrat, a small Caribbean island a scant twenty miles from Antigua. When Columbus named it in 1493—after the Jesuit monastery in Spain where he had prayed a novena for a safe return from his second voyage to the New World—Montserrat was typical of Caribbean islands, a lush tropical rain forest providing shelter and sustenance to Arawak Indians.

The indigenous population and vegetation of Montserrat have disappeared. The Indians were replaced, first by Irishmen dumped there as a result of England's domestic policy and then by slaves from Africa; the rain forests were replaced by sugar plantations. Indeed, the ruins of more than one hundred sugar mills still dot the landscape. Although much of Montserrat is rain forest once again, there is a major difference from 1492. Many of the plants on the island today were introduced by its European and African occupants.

The people, of course, are also different today, and this perhaps is the most enduring legacy of Columbus. The population of Montserrat is more than 90 percent black, with the parent stock largely West African in origin. Yet, ask a Montserratian his nationality and he is likely to say, "Mon, I'm Irish!" And why not? The spirit of those early Irish residents pervades all aspects of life on Montserrat. Not without reason is it known as the Emerald Isle of the Caribbean. Many of the place names are Irish as are the dominant surnames of its black residents, many of whom speak English with a touch of brogue. Traditional musical instruments on the island include the fife and drum; one of the folk dances bears a remarkable resemblance to the Irish jig; and island residents celebrate Saint Patrick's Day with exuberant festivities. This then is the true significance of 1492. It was as if a giant blender had been used to concoct an exotic drink, but the ingredients were the plants, animals, and people of two hemispheres, and the product was really a new world.

The continuing influence of Columbus's voyages is an important part of the "Seeds of Change" story. Five hundred years ago, people gave little thought to the environment. Today, acid rain, waste management, global warming, and similar environmental issues command concern the world over. Five hundred years ago tropical rain forests seemed an inexhaustible resource and an impediment to progress. They are now disappearing at the rate of thirty-five acres a minute. Today, rain forests are considered essential to human welfare and a resource to be treasured and husbanded. Not only may rain forests have a major influence on the world's climate, but they shelter plant and animal species unknown to science. The destruction of the rain forests is likened to the destruction of a vast library whose volumes remain unread and unappreciated because the languages in which they are written have yet to be translated.

The Columbus Quincentenary should be a time of contemplation. It is a time to think upon the achievements of those first adventurers who dared to challenge the mythical monsters that had kept Europe isolated by a moat of ignorance, doubt, and anxiety, but it is also a time to reassess and evaluate our options for the future. Ours is an era when decisions have instant ramifications around the globe. Man's continued achievements offer much promise for a healthier, happier future; but technological advances often have environmental implications. The forces of change and despoliation set in motion by Columbus have not abated; if anything, they are accelerating.

As the title of an exhibition at the National Museum of Natural History at the Smithsonian Institution as well as the title of this book, "Seeds of Change" reflects the research and interests of a group of eminent scholars, each of whom has contributed an essay to this volume.

Four of these scholars deserve special recognition, for their lifework and counsel shaped the "Seeds of Change" project from the start. Foremost is Alfred Crosby, who was the first historian to understand and interpret the rapid transformation of the New World after 1492. His book *The Columbian Exchange* opened a new field of research and informed the work of countless scholars, as a careful reading of the present volume will reveal. Three other members of the core committee were William McNeill, author of *Plagues and Peoples*; Sidney Mintz, author of *Sweetness and Power*; and Henry Hobhouse of Great Britain, to whom we are indebted for our title. Hobhouse's book *Seeds of Change*, the story of the global impact of five plants—maize, tobacco, quinine, tea, and sugar—led directly to the exhibition, part of the museum's Quincentenary activities. "Seeds" is used in a generic sense to illustrate the changes that resulted when plants, animals, diseases, and people were exchanged between the Old and New Worlds as a result of Columbus's voyages of discovery.

Although literally hundreds of examples could have been chosen to represent the Columbian exchange, the scholars working on this project selected five: sugar, maize, disease, the horse, and the potato. Many will argue effectively that alternative plants and animals—tobacco, quinine, rubber, cattle, or a dozen others—were more important. Nonetheless, each of these seeds was chosen because of the human dimension in its story. Sugar led directly to the enslavement of Africans and the transformation of New World ecosystems; maize fed the Africans that provided the manpower for American plantations; the potato, like maize, was developed by American Indians and has become a basic food of people around the globe; disease, especially smallpox, measles, even the common cold, wrought havoc with New

World peoples. Exact figures will never be known, but scholars believe that 50 to 90 percent of the Indians in North and South America died of diseases introduced from Europe. Most of those who died never saw a European; the diseases radiated throughout the New World much like ripples in a pond. The demoralization and psychological devastation caused by Old World diseases also worked in favor of the European settlers in displacing the native peoples.

Obviously, the Indians of the Americas have little cause to celebrate 1492. Indeed, some Indians plan to wear black armbands in 1992, and there is rising support for a national day of mourning to honor all the Indians who died as a result of the arrival of the Europeans on these shores. Most Indians echo the sentiment of George P. Horse Capture, who contributed one of the essays in this volume: "For America's Indians 1992 means that we will have survived as a people for five hundred years."

The horse, the fifth seed of change, was one gift from the Old World that Indians came to embrace and cherish. At first amazed by these strange creatures, the Indians of North and South America eventually became some of the finest riders the world has known. Even today members of many North American tribes regard the horse as a vital part of their culture.

"Seeds of Change," both this volume and the exhibition at the Smithsonian's Museum of Natural History, is an attempt to interpret the true meaning of Columbus five hundred years after that fateful day when the Admiral of the Ocean Sea stepped ashore in the Bahamas and unwittingly changed the course of world history. As the essays in this volume show, every seed of change, whether accidental or intentional, had both positive and negative consequences. These essays examine many different aspects of the biological transformations begun in 1492. Although each essay, like each seed, is a story unto itself, taken as a whole, they reveal the larger story behind the events that followed Columbus's voyages of discovery and their implications not only for those of us alive in 1992 but for generations to come.

The Demise of the Fifth Sun

Jane MacLaren Walsh and Yoko Sugiura

The Aztecs, creators of one of America's largest and most advanced empires, believed that they understood the history of how men and women had come to what we now call the New World. According to the Legend of the Suns, the universe had been created and destroyed during four previous suns; their empire existed at the time of the Fifth Sun. They believed that the First Sun was created at a point in an Aztec calendar year equivalent to 1950 B.C. in our own calendar and that the first creation lasted 676 years.

> Those who lived in the first Sun were eaten by ocelots. . . . And they were eaten in the year 13. . . . Those who lived in the second Sun were carried away by the wind. . . . They became monkeys. . . . Those who lived under [the] third Sun . . . also perished. It rained fire upon them. They became turkeys. This sun was consumed by fire. . . . And those who lived under [the] fourth Sun . . . were swallowed by the waters and they became fish. . . . The water lasted 52 years and with this ended their years. . . . This Sun, called 4-movement, this is our Sun, the one in which we now live. And here is its sign, how the Sun fell into the fire, into the divine hearth, there at Teotihuacán. It was also the Sun of our Lord Quetzalcoatl in Tula. . . . And as the elders continue to say, under this sun there will be earthquakes and hunger, and then our end shall come. (León-Portilla 1963)

By 9000 B.C., the descendants and successors of the first migrants had reached Tierra del Fuego, and the development of cultures in the New World had begun. Among the first distinct societies were the Olmecs, who emerged about 1500 B.C. along the Gulf Coast of Mexico. Signature works of the Olmecs are the massive enigmatic heads carved from basalt.

The Aztec calendar, *La Piedra del Sol*, or **Sun Stone** (previous pages), recounts the creation and destruction of four worlds. Montezuma II (inset) presided during the Fifth Sun, an epoch also destined for collapse. Like his predecessors, he looked to the heavens for omens and is seen in this 16th-century illustration contemplating the meaning of a comet.

The Pleistocene glaciers lowered the earth's sea level between 30,000 and 12,000 B.C., thereby creating terra firma between two land masses previously separated by icy, inhospitable seas. Hunters in search of mammoth and mastodon were probably among the first *Homo sapiens* to venture from Siberia to Alaska.

It is in the nature of humankind to explain things to themselves—how the earth was populated, where people originated, how long they have lived on the earth, how much longer they have. Most societies have origin myths or creation stories, migration legends, and histories. To better understand the Aztec peoples of the Fifth Sun, we must first look at what *we* believe to be their actual origins.

The Bridge to the New World

The New World was new not only to the Europeans who discovered it in A.D. 1492. In geologic terms as well, the American continents were populated only recently. Most scientists agree that human beings, fully developed as a species called *Homo sapiens,* who had originated in Africa and had dispersed throughout the Old World, migrated to the New World at various times during the Pleistocene or Ice Age. This population movement was made possible by the formation of glaciers that lowered the sea level at certain periods between 30,000 and 12,000 B.C., allowing a land bridge to emerge between Siberia and Alaska. The basic assumption that men and women first entered the New World via the Bering Strait is widely accepted, although there is still disagreement about the specific migration routes they took and the date of their earliest appearance. Some groups of hunters may have migrated across the land bridge, called Beringia, following herds of big game—mammoths, mastodons, and bison. Others possibly followed routes across pack ice. Still other migrants may have paddled boats across the straits during the summer.

Beringia not only served as a migration route for people and herds from the Old World but also facilitated the departure of the horse and camel, which migrated to the Old World before dying out in the new. This event would have direct consequences for the New World inhabitants, since it would deprive them of the obvious benefit of large beasts of burden.

Archaeological evidence gathered from sites scattered throughout North, Central, and South America unfortunately has not provided clear, undisputed dates for the earliest occupations of New World peoples. Human populations had arrived at least by fourteen thousand years ago, and possibly much earlier. Some of the earlier radiocarbon dates, such as those gathered from sites in Mexico and South America, are still considered by many archaeologists to be problematic, however. Tlapacoya, a site near Mexico City, has radiocarbon dates of twenty-four thousand and twenty-one thousand years ago, and Peruvian sites have yielded dates as early as twenty thousand years ago. Whatever the exact time of their arrival, once in Alaska, small groups of hunters made their way south along the coast and through ice-free corridors to the northern Great Plains. From there they gradually penetrated other regions of the American continents. By 9000 B.C., a date accepted by most archaeologists, the New World was populated from Alaska to Tierra del Fuego, the southernmost tip of South America.

By the end of the Ice Age, around 10,000 B.C., gradual climatic warming produced environmental changes that profoundly affected the natural resources of the two American continents. The global warming that has recently been predicted may have similarly dramatic effects on the planet. This early period of warmth may have contributed to the disappearance of mammoths and other large game in the Americas and caused a radical change in vegetation. As a consequence, early populations, called Paleo-Indians by archaeologists, were forced to elaborate new subsistence technologies, which involved a greater dependence on the hunting of small game, fishing, the gathering of shellfish, and the foraging for plants, wild grasses, nuts, seeds, fruits, and vegetables. Paleo-Indians eventually became more sedentary, making them more capable of exploiting particular environments more thoroughly.

The Birth and Growth of Societies

In the course of human dispersal over the span of two continents, different groups developed specific responses to the enormous diversity of environmental conditions. Some settled in extremely hostile natural settings where resources were scarce, necessitating seasonal migration in search of food. Others found conditions favorable enough to obtain abundant foodstuffs, thereby permitting more permanent settlements. With the passage of time, the more sedentary people became familiar with the life cycles and reproductive mechanisms of the plants they gathered and the animals they hunted. They eventually began to cultivate the plants to produce better, more resistant varieties. The intentional experimentation of early Native Americans, in conjunction with accidental mutations and other natural genetic change over many generations, gradually improved the quality and availability of preferred vegetable foods. The change from total reliance for survival on hunting and gathering to intensive foraging and occasional cultivation of specific plants marked the beginnings of agriculture in the New World. It would be many centuries, however, before permanent village life based solely on agriculture would make its appearance in the Americas.

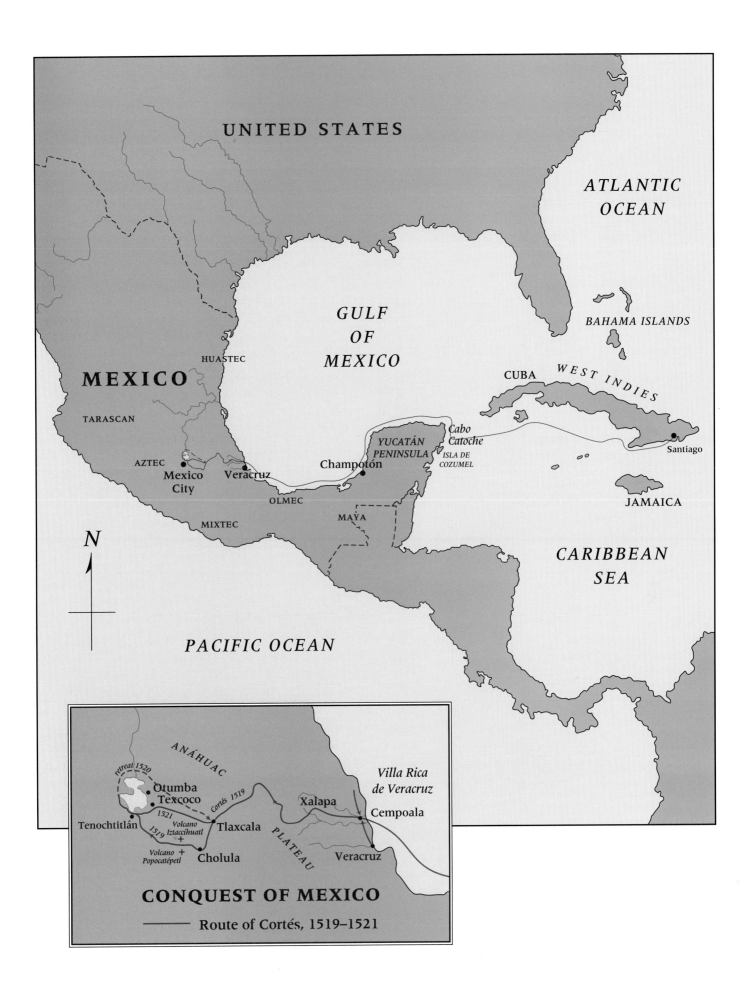

UNITED STATES

ATLANTIC OCEAN

GULF OF MEXICO

BAHAMA ISLANDS

MEXICO

HUASTEC

CUBA

WEST INDIES

TARASCAN

AZTEC

Mexico City

Veracruz

Champotón

YUCATÁN PENINSULA

Cabo Catoche

ISLA DE COZUMEL

Santiago

OLMEC

MIXTEC

MAYA

JAMAICA

CARIBBEAN SEA

N

PACIFIC OCEAN

ANÁHUAC

retreat 1520

Otumba
Texcoco

Cortés 1519

Villa Rica de Veracruz

Xalapa

Cempoala

Tenochtitlán

1521

1519

Volcano Iztaccíhuatl

Tlaxcala

PLATEAU

Veracruz

Volcano Popocatépetl

Cholula

CONQUEST OF MEXICO

——— Route of Cortés, 1519–1521

21

As a 20th-century Maya farmer and 16th-century Andean field workers show, in certain corners of the New World the harvesting of corn has continued through millennia little changed in particulars.

The historical and cultural complexity reflected in the several hundred distinct linguistic and cultural groups scattered over North, Central, and South America at the time of European contact requires more profound analysis than is possible in the space allotted to this essay. Such an enormous topic as the New World on the eve of European discovery obviously requires the selection of but a few emblematic groups to illustrate the wide diversity of cultures, as well as the amazing development and complexity achieved by native peoples. Cultural groups on both continents amassed large bodies of knowledge and degrees of advancement, but two regions in particular—Mexico/Central America and the Andean region of South America—realized particularly noteworthy achievements. The Olmec, Maya, Toltec, and Aztec cultures in Mexico and Central America, and the Chavín, Moche, Wari, and Inca of the Andes excelled variously in metallurgy, astronomy, mathematics, architecture, city planning, road building, hydraulic engineering, literature, and agricultural technology, even while lacking some fairly important tools. To be more precise, they developed highly complex societies in the absence of the wheel, beasts of burden, and iron implements available to people of the Old World.

By the time of European contact, other regions of the American continents had been the locus for the development of highly advanced societies which had reached a level of social complexity and organization comparable to that of sixteenth-century Spain. Numerous regions of North America were inhabited by groups organized into villages and chiefdoms, such as the Pueblos of the American Southwest. In addition, most archaeologists would agree that by A.D. 1000 North America would produce at least one state-level society, with its capital at Cahokia, in present-day Illinois. In Mexico and Central America a number of states flourished before the advent of Europeans during the sixteenth century. Notable among these were the Aztec of Tenochtitlán, the Mixtec of the valley of Oaxaca, and the Maya of the Yucatán peninsula and Central America. The principal South American empire encountered by Europeans was the Inca of the Andean high plateau.

Mesoamerican Societies

To illustrate the complexity and sophistication achieved by Native Americans before the advent of Europeans, we have selected as a case study the middle region located between the two great land masses of North and South America. This region, called Mesoamerica, is appropriate for a more detailed analysis since it not only achieved great heights in technological and social development but also was the first high culture encountered by the Spaniards, about twenty-five years after Columbus's first voyage. The term *Mesoamerica* is one used by archaeologists and historians to describe a region of high cultural attainment encompassing much of present-day Mexico (from a point about one hundred miles north of Mexico City) to Costa Rica in Central America.

The great Mexican states began as villages scattered throughout Mesoamerica. Several thousand years after the early peoples of this area had begun to experiment with the cultivation of plants, village life, based mainly on agriculture, evolved in numerous regions of the Americas. Village life need not be exclusively supported by the cultivation of plants, as there are many examples of permanent settlements based solely on efficient hunting and foraging, such as those found along the northwest coast of North America. It is a fact, however, that agricultural settlements were the first major step toward the formation of complex societies in Mexico.

After a long process of domestication, the cultivation of corn began in Mexico around 3500 B.C. By 3200 B.C. the technology arrived in the Peruvian high plateau, where it did not have a great impact on native Peruvian societies, since these groups had been cultivating a number of other plants for many centuries. Although in much of North America corn was not grown until around 500 B.C., in the eastern portion of the continent several native crops were domesticated between 2000 and 1000 B.C. The emergence of village life in this region would be delayed until approximately A.D. 200, however. Archaeological evidence from various sites in central Mexico indicates that by 2000 B.C. the basic Mexican diet of maize, beans, squash, chili, amaranth, and avocados was well established. Within a few centuries of this date, agricultural villages had spread throughout Mesoamerica.

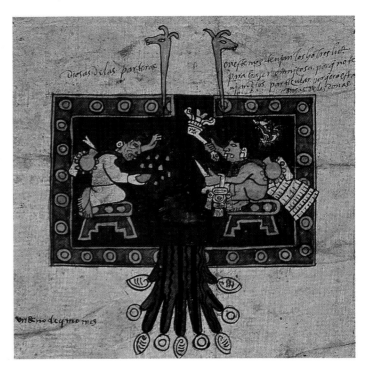

The potency attributed to corn is seen in the Aztec myth in which the first human couple cast kernels of maize to divine their future.

The traditional diet of Mesoamerican groups has unique nutritional properties that have been fully appreciated only in the twentieth century. Corn supplies carbohydrates, squash and beans are sources of vegetable protein and other nutrients,

If the pursuit of agriculture gives rise to villages, the mercantile instinct gives birth to great cities. By means of its vast trading network, Teotihuacán attained dominion throughout Mesoamerica. By the 5th century A.D., the city had reached its zenith, with a population of perhaps 200,000. In the 8th century, however, its inhabitants abandoned Teotihuacán for reasons that still baffle archaeologists. Nahuatl-speaking tribes, who wandered through its ruins many centuries later, gave names to the city and its splendid structures, such as the Pyramid of the Sun. Teotihuacán means Place of the Gods.

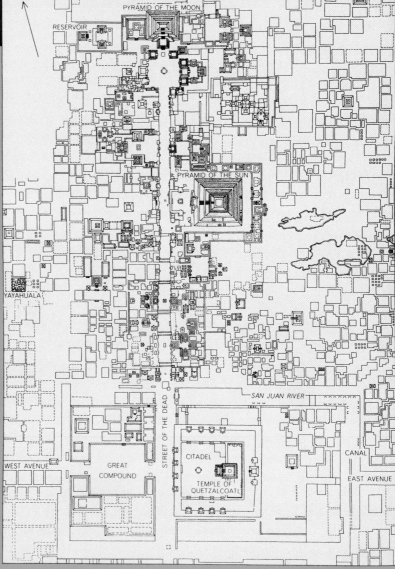

avocados provide fats and oils, and chilis have many essential vitamins. Futhermore, corn eaten in combination with beans provides lysine, which is absent if maize is consumed by itself. Lysine increases the dietary protein. Ancient Mexicans added calcium to their diet by soaking corn in limewater.

The ancient Mexican method of planting corn, beans, and squash together was another phenomenon unique to the region. These crops were always cultivated in the same field, allowing the climbing bean and squash plants to support themselves on the cornstalk, while aiding in the retention of nitrogen, thereby keeping the soil fertile. The attainment of this early, profound knowledge of the cultivation and manipulation of plants provided the foundation for all subsequent Mesoamerican high cultures. Agriculture supported the essential stability of these early societies and pervaded almost every facet of life in ancient Mexico, from the political and economic institutions established to the pantheon of gods worshiped.

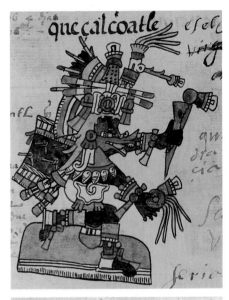

The Olmecs

Soon after the appearance of permanent agricultural village settlements in Meso-america (at approximately 1500 B.C., or some 150 years before the reign of Tutankhamen in Egypt), the Olmec culture emerged as an important element in southern Mexico. Some archaeologists have referred to the Olmec as the mother culture of ancient Mexico, and, indeed, many elements of this early, highly advanced culture are found in later societies. The sophistication and artistic attainments apparent in Olmec sculpture and ceremonial centers led scholars to believe that they represented a much later phenomenon than we now know them to be through radiocarbon dating. It is still unclear from archaeological evidence, however, just how these Olmec groups emerged along the Gulf Coast as an already extremely advanced culture.

Without large draft animals, wheels, or iron tools available in the Old World, the Olmec and later Mesoamerican cultures constructed large, elaborate ceremonial centers requiring time, labor, and organization on a massive scale. The size of these centers, the creation of monumental sculpture beautifully executed by Olmec craftsmen, and the presence of numerous specialized artisan trades indicate the existence of a complex and centralized society.

Between 1200 and 600 B.C. the spread of Olmec influence throughout Mesoamerica is evidenced in archaeological finds by the presence of the unique Olmec style of pottery, finely modeled ceramic figurines, and masterful stone sculpture at sites in Oaxaca, Guerrero, Morelos, the Valley of Mexico, and as far south as El Salvador. This wide diffusion was probably due to an extensive trade network. The Olmecs, as the Mesoamerican mother culture, may also have been the originators of the ball game unique to that region, the long-count calendar, a rudimentary writing system, and certain key religious ideas embracing the all-important deities of rain, fire, corn, and fertility.

In ancient Mexico, as in other regions of the Americas, agriculture was closely tied to a knowledge of astronomy. The Mesoamericans, in particular, seemed fascinated with the heavens, plotting the movement of the planets and creating lunar, solar, and various ceremonial calendars to mark the passage of time and commemorate important events.

Mesoamericans venerated a pantheon of deities, some from the time of the Olmecs. The goggle-eyed, fanged Tlaloc (bottom) governed rainfall and hence figured in the rites of harvest and fertility. Quetzalcoatl (top), often depicted as a feathered serpent, was god of the morning and evening star, a patron of priests, and creator of the calendar and of books. Because Montezuma mistakenly associated Quetzal-coatl with Hernán Cortés, the god played a role in the collapse of the Fifth Sun and the ulti-mate demise of the Mesoameri-can world at the hand of the Spanish conquerors.

South American Societies

The historical development of native cultures took a somewhat different turn in South America. While there is some disagreement, recent archaeological evidence seems to indicate that the beginning of complex societies there was based on the efficient exploitation of marine resources, not agriculture. The social and cultural complexity attained by societies in this area is reflected in large ceremonial centers built along the Peruvian coast, since, as previously noted, massive building projects require the organization of a substantial labor force. It is important to realize that these coastal centers flourished some time around 2000 B.C., before the advent of agriculture and ceramics. Later settlements were established farther inland, where intensive agriculture, assisted by irrigation, was possible around 1800 B.C. The technological advancement evidenced by these later agricultural centers whose inhabitants possessed knowledge of specialized crafts, such as metallurgy, indicates that the initial pace of development in South America, especially in the Andean region, was somewhat accelerated when compared to developments in Mesoamerica. There, centers such as these would not appear until about 1200 B.C. In North America such centers were not in evidence until about A.D. 200.

At approximately the same time that the Olmec culture flourished in Mesoamerica (1200–600 B.C.), a parallel phenomenon was taking place in the Andean region. At Chavín de Huántar in the Peruvian high plateau, a unique style of pottery and architecture was elaborated, and by approximately 850 B.C. the stylistic features characteristic of Chavín culture seem to have spread over a large part of the Andes.

The Mayas of southern Mexico and Guatemala built spectacular ceremonial centers, produced beautiful pottery and ornamental objects, and developed a sophisticated system of writing. They used the concept of zero a millennium before Europeans did. In many respects the Mayas represented the climax of Mesoamerican refinement and erudition. But in the 8th century A.D., at about the same time as the demise of Teotihuacán, their centers were also abandoned.

26

While agriculture at Chavín was still supplemented by hunting, gathering, and fishing, archaeological remains indicate that a large number of cultivated plants had already been added. Besides squash, beans, and chili peppers, new highland plants, such as the potato, the sweet potato, and quinoa, became part of the Andean diet.

Chavín's importance lies in its establishment of an extensive and highly elaborated religious cult and the dissemination of its influence over a large area. Archaeologists have accounted for its rapid growth and wide cultural influence in much the same manner that they attempt to explain the ascendancy of the Olmecs. Trade, directed by a central authority at Chavín de Huántar, connected the various regions, which included the coast and the tropical rain forest east of the Andes.

Militarism, like mercantilism, imprinted Mesoamerican cultures. The Toltecs of Tula were particularly noted for militancy. They arose in the wake of Teotihuacán and held sway from the 8th to about the end of the 12th century. Huge stone effigies of fierce warriors evoke the intensity of these empire builders. Though the Toltecs incorporated many motifs of Teotihuacán, their art and architecture never achieved the grace and refinement of their predecessors.

Early Mesoamerican States

At approximately 600 B.C., about two hundred years before the Greeks built the Parthenon in Athens, the Olmecs and related societies were eclipsed by other cultures developing in the valley of Oaxaca and the central highlands of Mexico. It was in these regions that the first Mesoamerican states emerged. Large, important ceremonial and urban centers, such as Cuicuilco and Teotihuacán in the central Valley of Mexico, Monte Albán in Oaxaca, Kaminaljuyú and Tikal in Guatemala, and numerous other lowland Maya sites, give ample evidence to the phenomenon of emergent statehood in Mesoamerica.

Teotihuacán, located at the northeastern edge of the Valley of Mexico, began as a village before the birth of Christ. It became the most important city in all of Mesoamerica, and its political, economic, and cultural influence was felt in varying degrees from perhaps as far north as the American Southwest to at least as far south as Guatemala in Central America. Its hegemony was extended by long-distance trade rather than conquest, possibly by colonization in some cases and perhaps by the collection of tribute. Teotihuacán—an enormous cosmopolitan urban center that was apparently planned as it grew—was unique in the New World. It was organized into *barrios* or neighborhoods where different occupations were practiced and groups from many regions of Mexico resided. The name Teotihuacán was given to the center by wandering, Nahuatl-speaking tribes who passed through the city many centuries after it had fallen into ruins. The Aztec word means "Place of the Gods," for the grandiose ruined city must have astounded these people who would eventually found their own metropolis nearby. The Aztecs called the two largest structures in the city the Pyramid of the Sun and the Pyramid of the Moon. The wide avenue that connected all the temples and plazas they called, somewhat lugubriously, the Street of the Dead. On one important pyramid at the southern end of the avenue were tenoned the heads of that culture's two most important deities—the feathered serpent, Quetzalcoatl, and the goggle-eyed, fanged mask of Tlaloc, the rain god. These gods, who play an extremely important role in the subsequent development of Mesoamerican culture, seem to have been present in one form or another since the time of the Olmecs.

Urban planning in Teotihuacán attained its zenith about the fifth century A.D., when the population, according to some archaeologists, may have reached two hundred thousand. The splendor of this metropolis was aided by a trade monopoly of certain natural resources and manufactured products, along with the control of local agricultural production and distribution of goods within the valley of Teotihuacán itself. Numerous satellite communities provided additional resources. Advanced agricultural technology involving massive irrigation and terracing projects made the intensive cultivation of the region feasible. The central administration emanating from Teotihuacán then efficiently directed the distribution of cultivated and manufactured goods.

The fall of the great city of Teotihuacán in the eighth century A.D. marked a change in political structures throughout Mesoamerica and apparently coincided with the collapse of other sophisticated state-level societies, such as that of the Mayas of the Classic period. The Maya culture in southern Mexico and Guatemala flourished during the early centuries of the first millennium A.D. The Mayas developed a sophisticated and, until recently, enigmatic system of writing. They elaborated various counting and calendrical systems that employed the concept of zero about a thousand years before Europeans would make the same discovery. They built great ceremonial centers, such as Palenque, Tikal, Copán, and Uxmal. This particular phase of Maya culture seemingly disintegrated, however, at about the same time as the abandonment of Teotihuacán. There are many hypotheses about the causes of the so-called collapse of the Classic Maya world. Some focus on natural catastrophe, others on political or military confrontations, still others propose the possibility of internal strife and rebellion caused by the stress of overpopulation. At present there is no consensus as to the cause of the demise of so many important ceremonial centers.

Andean States

At the time Teotihuacán, Monte Albán, and the cities of the Mayas in the south were flourishing, new states were forming in the Andean region—the Mochica civilization on the north coast of Peru and the Nazca culture on the southern coast are prominent examples. The Moche formed a complex and highly structured society in which specialized artisans developed an advanced metallurgy, enabling them to produce some of the finest gold, silver, and copper ornamental objects in the New World. Archaeological evidence indicates that organized teams of laborers were recruited from Moche communities for public works. This system of recruitment to effect public good was much like that employed by the later Incas. It also seems apparent that, in comparison with Mesoamerica, warfare was a much more prevalent feature of life in these early city states.

In the highlands near Lake Titicaca, the Bolivian city of Tiahuanaco began to be erected around 400 B.C., flourishing until sometime after A.D. 1000. The most outstanding feature of this great city is its architecture. The builders of Tiahuanaco constructed their temples of enormous stones that were carefully worked and tightly fitted together without mortar. The city quickly expanded its political domination throughout the Andes. Unlike its much larger Mesoamerican counterpart, Teotihuacán, Tiahuanaco carried out this territorial expansion by means of military conquest, which ensured its rulers control over production and distribution of goods within divergent ecological zones. This vertical control of resources, from coast to highlands, seems to have been a characteristic pattern of Andean empires.

Between A.D. 1000 and 1450, various states developed in the Andean region including the kingdom of Chimu, the Chancay culture, the Ica-Chincha, and the kingdom of Cuzco. These states had broken away from the more centralized

At the same time that Teotihuacán and the Maya cities of Mesoamerica were flourishing, other cultures were forming in South America. Though different in details, these cultures also developed into complex societies, used trade and warfare to extend their power, and built grand cities and ceremonial centers. One of these was Tiahuanaco, which flourished in the Andean highlands near Lake Titicaca from 400 B.C. to 1000 A.D. According to one Inca origin myth, the first Inca, Manco Capac, Son of the Sun, emerged from the waters of Lake Titicaca and traveled northward to a fertile valley where he founded Cuzco. Contemporary Indians at Lake Titicaca (left) offer a sacrificial llama for the prospect of bountiful crops.

authority of the older Wari state. By A.D. 1430, the people known as Inca to the Spaniards, since that was the designation used for their supreme leader, held control over an enormous region of South America. The Inca empire, known as Tawantin-suyu, had its capital at Cuzco and covered an area of some four thousand kilometers, from northern Colombia to central Chile. The great Inca highway system, much of it inherited from the earlier conquered states, provided a superb communications network.

The Toltecs

In Mexico, after the collapse of Teotihuacán in the eighth century A.D. and as yet several hundred years before the Aztecs would gain ascendancy in the central valley, the Toltecs made their appearance on the Mesoamerican stage. Although the origin and basic composition of the Toltec empire remains somewhat clouded, it clearly grew quickly, extending its control and economic influence over much of northern Mesoamerica. Its dominance eventually reached the great Maya center of Chichén Itzá in the Yucatán peninsula. Many hypotheses have been proffered to explain its rapid expansion. Militarism, control over irrigation in the valley of Tula, and monopoly over the production and distribution of obsidian, which was essential to the manufacture of tools and weapons, have all been suggested as the key component of growth.

The Toltec capital at Tula in the modern Mexican state of Hidalgo, although much fabled in Aztec legend, was in fact a rather unimpressive place. The distinction or size of their capital notwithstanding, within a very short time the Toltecs had subjugated a large part of ancient Mexico and incorporated numerous cultural groups, directly or indirectly, into their sphere of influence.

The city of Tula and the Toltec people themselves became the stuff of legend for the Aztecs. They considered these empire builders to be unparalleled architects, inventors, artisans, and statesmen. In fact, the word Toltec seems to have been for Aztecs synonymous with a cultured and educated person. In the fifteenth century A.D., the emperor Itzcóatl ordered a rewriting of Aztec history to establish the Aztecs as the rightful heirs of the Toltec legacy. In Aztec myth and legend a central figure in Toltec history was a priest of the god Quetzalcoatl, whose name was Ce Acatl Topiltzin Quetzalcoatl. Ce Acatl, which means "one reed," denotes the year of his birth. The priest-ruler Topiltzin, instrumental in the establishment of the Toltec capital at Tula, was remembered as the embodiment of truth and knowledge. According to legend, Quetzalcoatl built palaces of precious jade and turquoise at Tula, established a code of laws, and fought against the Toltec custom of human sacrifice, eventually running afoul of political intrigue. Topiltzin is associated very closely with the god Quetzalcoatl and is, in fact, often confused with him in these legends. After he was disgraced by his rival Tezcatlipoca, "Smoking Mirror," Topiltzin was driven from Tula. Migrating south and eastward, legend had him founding cities in Cholula and Xochicalco and, finally, gaining sovereignty over Chichén Itzá in Yucatán. One account told of his sailing eastward and promising to return one day.

The Aztecs demonstrated supremacy over their conquered neighbors by demanding tribute in such valuables as animal furs, food, fabric, and bird skins. Their social order was a strict hierarchy of classes. Netzahualcoyotl, king of Texcoco (inset), was a poet and philosopher as well as a builder and ruler—a worthy example of Aztec nobility.

The Rise of the Aztecs

In the fourteenth century A.D., when the Aztecs, along with other ethnic groups, arrived at the shores of the lakes in the central Valley of Mexico, according to their own history and legend, their primary god Huitzilopochtli, "Left-handed Hummingbird," ordered them to settle on an island where they would find an eagle perched on a cactus devouring a serpent. The eagle is the emblem of the war god, Huitzilopochtli, and the serpent is that of the old god Quetzalcoatl. The symbolism is clear. After numerous battles with already established states that, despite Aztec legend, had actually forcibly relegated the newcomers to the small island in the lake, the Aztecs defeated the Tepanecs of Atzcapotzalco and became the main power in the Valley of Mexico. In less than two hundred years they built the most powerful and extensive empire in Mesoamerica. They demanded tribute from their conquered neighbors in the valley and took control over the surrounding *chinampas*, the famous "floating gardens" of Mexico.

Aztec society was tightly stratified and contained many hereditary classes, such as the priesthood, the nobility, the military, certain classes of merchants, commoners, and slaves. There were, however, means for achieving some class mobility, chiefly through the military. The social structure was organized around the *calpulli*, twenty corporate groups probably derived from the community's original clans. Each calpulli appointed one chief for civil and religious affairs and, almost always, a second chief for war. Since agriculture was the basis of life in ancient Mexico, the calpulli controlled the land that supported its members. Warfare brought new lands and riches in the form of goods and slaves. Successful warriors were granted lands and people to work them. This system of rewards was much like that of the Spaniards, who gained land in Spain at approximately the same period through the reconquest

from the Moors. The Spaniards would eventually repeat this tradition in Mexico. In fact, a century before the *encomienda*, the Spanish system of land grants and indentured servitude, was initiated in Mexico, the Aztecs were in the habit of appropriating entire village populations, moving them into more controllable regions, and forcing them to work on state construction projects. Conquered peoples were forced to pay tribute to the Aztec overlords in quantities of finished goods, such as textiles, pottery, and other craft articles. They also paid in raw materials—jade, gold, and silver and other items considered precious, such as tropical bird feathers. In addition, tribute payers were required to supply human beings for slavery or sacrifice. Considering the enormous payments extracted from conquered peoples, it is not difficult to imagine the resentment that groups like the Tlaxcalans must have harbored toward the Aztecs.

The two main Aztec temples in the center of Tenochtitlán were dedicated to the ancient rain god, Tlaloc, and the tribal god, Huitzilopochtli. The latter, according to Aztec belief, demanded continual sustenance in the form of human hearts. The sacrifice of living beings, cruelly dispatched by having their hearts cut out of their chests, was a constant in Aztec daily life. The blood of sacrificial victims was thought to be a means of feeding the gods and thus sustaining all creation. According to legend, more than five thousand people were sacrificed at the coronation of Montezuma II to mark the event. Some say the main pyramid was inaugurated with the sacrifice of twenty thousand.

Aside from territorial expansion, sacrifice was one of the main motivations for warfare, which was carried out for the purpose of obtaining victims. "Flower wars," as they were called (blood and flowers seem to be metaphorically the same in Aztec writing), were completely staged, choreographed events. Usually they were fought with subjugated cities, although occasionally defensive allies were the combatants. The duration was agreed upon beforehand and the purpose was to gain captives. Once the requisite captives were obtained, both sides would call a truce.

As the two worlds stood face to face, artists from each hemisphere rendered images of the alien that bore the stamp of the maker's own culture. An Aztec artist drew a Cortés that looked as Mesoamerican as Doña Marina, or Malinche, his Nahuatl-speaking counsel, while a European artist portrayed Montezuma as a Greco-Roman warrior.

The Return of Quetzalcoatl

On the eve of destruction of this large New World empire, the Spaniards and Aztecs were blissfully ignorant of each other. In the year 1519, Hernán Cortés set out from Cuba with eleven ships and 550 men from Spain. He brought with him an additional 200 islanders from Cuba, several blacks, and a few Indian women. He also had on board the fleet sixteen horses. Setting sail on 18 February 1519, he had hopes of great riches and dreams of enduring glory.

On the island of Cozumel off the coast of Yucatán, Cortés met with a Spanish castaway who would provide invaluable assistance to his efforts. Jerónimo de Aguilar had been shipwrecked some eight years earlier, being taken as a slave by the people of Yucatán. During his servitude he had become fluent in Yucatec Mayan. As the Spanish fleet rounded the peninsula, navigating the waters of the Caribbean and crossing into the Gulf of Mexico, they landed near the town of Potonchán, now called Champotón, in the state of Campeche. There, Cortés would have a second stroke of luck—the gift from the chief of the woman called Malinche, whose Nahuatl name was probably Malintzin but whom the Spaniards would baptize and rename Doña Marina. She "was a person of the greatest importance and was obeyed without question by the Indians throughout New Spain" (Díaz 1956). Originally from Coatzacoalcos on the Gulf Coast, Malinche had been sold into slavery by merchants of Xicalanco, allies of the Aztecs, to the Mayas of Potonchán. Doña

33

Marina was fluent in both Mayan and Nahuatl, the language of the Aztecs. Almost from the moment he landed, through the interpretation of Malinche and Aguilar, Cortés could understand the speech of nearly everyone he encountered, giving him an enormous advantage over the native peoples he met. Eventually Malinche learned Spanish and became Cortés's most trusted adviser.

From Potonchán the Spanish fleet made its way up the east coast of Mexico and landed in a port they called the Villa Rica de Vera Cruz. Here, because of dissension among his troops, many of whom wished to return to Cuba, Cortés made a bold decision. He unloaded his entire army, all of his servants, supplies, and horses, and set fire to ten of his eleven ships. The last ship was sent back to Cuba with the dissenters. There was no turning back now, but Cortés had by this time heard many tales of the fabled city of Montezuma and had even met with Aztec ambassadors bearing gold and gifts of great artistry. He must have been certain that his dreams of glory were about to come true.

In August, Cortés left the Totonac city of Cempoala on the Gulf Coast where he had been welcomed, and the army marched inland toward the Aztec capital. On the last day of the month they came into the territory of the fierce Tlaxcalans, enemies of Montezuma. Bernal Díaz de Castillo, a soldier in Cortés's army, described their first encounter with the Tlaxcalans. "Two armies of warriors approached to give us battle. They numbered six thousand men and they came on us with loud shouts and the din of drums and trumpets." This number eventually, according to Díaz, swelled to forty thousand, but the fighting was perplexing to the Spaniards. "We noticed that many of the strongest among them crowded together to lay hands on a horse." It seemed that the Tlaxcalans thought these horses and riders were one great and terrifying creature, and they hoped to capture and sacrifice it. The Tlaxcalans were defeated in early September and later joined the Spaniards in an alliance against Montezuma. The Tlaxcalans were ancient enemies of the Aztecs, had fought numerous wars with them, and were happy to supply Cortés with an army of some twenty thousand warriors.

All along his route Cortés was visited by ambassadors of Montezuma, who brought incredible objects masterfully crafted of jade, gold, copper, and feathers. The emperor mistakenly believed that these gifts would dissuade the invader from continuing his journey to Tenochtitlán. In fact, they spurred him on.

The myth of Quetzalcoatl had determined Montezuma's understanding of the Spanish landing at Veracruz. Since Quetzalcoatl, in one version, had sailed eastward and Cortés had come from the sea, Montezuma believed that the god had returned to reclaim his kingdom. Coincidentally, the year 1519 was also Ce Acatl, or 1-Reed, in the Aztec calendar. Bernardino de Sahagún, the Franciscan who wrote a history of these events in 1585, noted that among the first presents Montezuma sent Cortés were ornaments from the Temple of Quetzalcoatl. According to Sahagún, Montezuma was supposed to have told his ambassadors, "Our Lord Quetzalcoatl has arrived, go and receive him . . . these jewels that you are presenting to him on my behalf are all the priestly ornaments that belong to him."

As the Spaniards made their way toward the fabled city of Tenochtitlán, over the high mountains surrounding the Valley of Mexico, traversing a path between the towering volcanos called Popocatépetl and Iztaccíhuatl, their first view of the great city startled and amazed them. Their astonishment was eloquently recorded by the soldier Bernal Díaz some forty years after the event. "During the morning, we arrived at a broad Causeway and continued our march towards Iztapalapa, and when we saw so many cities and villages built in the water and other great towns

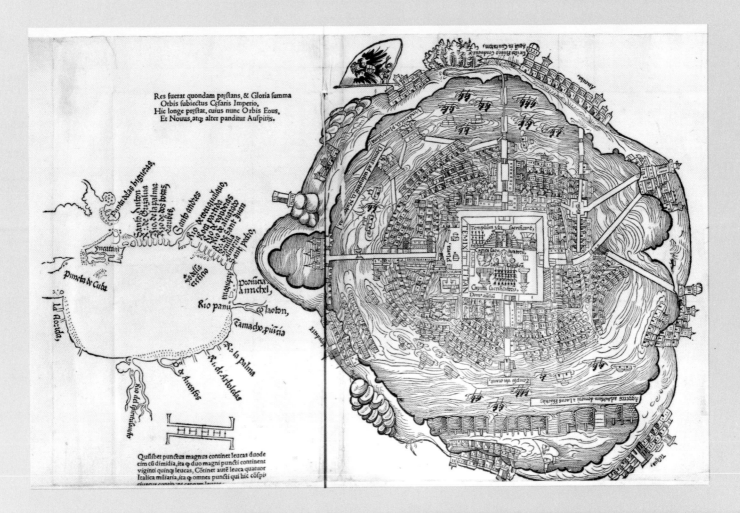

Cortés and his men were aston-
ished by their first sight of Tenochtitlán, the island city of
glimmering spires, painted
buildings, and verdant gardens,
which extended over several
square miles of a valley that
teemed with wildlife. Bernal
Díaz later wrote that "some of
our soldiers asked whether the
things that we saw were not a
dream." In 1524, Cortés penned
a diagram of Tenochtitlán, the
oldest known map of what is
now Mexico City (above).
Among the many exotic sights
were the *chinampas*, raised beds
of vegetables and flowers that
appeared to the Spaniards to be
floating gardens.

on dry land and that straight and level Causeway going towards Mexico, we were amazed and said that it was like the enchantments they tell of in the legend of Amadis, on account of the great towers and cues [temples] and buildings rising from the water, and all built of masonry. And some of our soldiers asked whether the things that we saw were not a dream."

The Chinampas of Tenochtitlán

This seeming mirage, Tenochtitlán, which covered an area of some ten square miles, several times larger than sixteenth-century London, was one of the wonders of the world. The high towers and painted buildings sparkled in the sunlight. The city was situated on an island in the center of a lake, connected to the mainland by a series of broad causeways, supplied with fresh water by means of a huge aqueduct and surrounded by chinampas, in a valley teeming with wildlife. In these extraordinarily productive chinampas, the Aztecs cultivated an enormous variety of vegetables and flowers. They only appeared to float, however. The Aztecs formed their gardens artificially by digging ditches in the marshy lakeshore to drain the water and piling up the fertile mud to form the field. Some archaeological evidence indicates that this highly productive agricultural technique may have originated at a much earlier time, but it was during the Aztec reign that the chinampa system became the principal source of their food supply. It is thus easy to understand that the production of chinampas was carefully planned and controlled by the central government. In addition to the chinampas, the surrounding mountains were covered with agricultural terraces, which were irrigated by fresh water brought by the aqueduct. They supplied the city with other varieties of fruits and vegetables.

"Let us return to our entry to Mexico," wrote Bernal Díaz. Tenochtitlán was situated on one of two islands, the other was occupied by its sister city Tlatelolco, with causeways connecting the two cities to the mainland and other surrounding towns like Tláhuac, Texcoco, and Xochimilco. A huge dike, constructed during the rule of Montezuma I, under the guidance of Netzahualcoyotl, the poet-king of Texcoco, separated the brackish water of the largest lake from those surrounding the islands. The writer Francisco de Garáy described in detail the effect of the masterfully engineered dike. "As the lakes of fresh water to the south poured their surplus water into the lake of Mexico through the narrows of Culhuacan and Mexicaltzingo, those waters spread through the western lake, the Lake of Mexico, and completely filled it. . . . In this way the basin of fresh water was converted into a fish pond and a home for all sorts of aquatic fowl. Chinampas covered its surface, separated by limpid spaces which were furrowed by swift canoes, and all the suburbs of this enchanting capital became flowery orchards."

The central sacred precinct of Tenochtitlán was larger and more grandiose than that of Tlatelolco. The square was the religious and administrative center of the empire. It was dominated by the enormous pyramid with twin temples dedicated to Huitzilopochtli and Tlaloc, with smaller pyramids to Quetzalcoatl and his rival Tezcatlipoca. A series of wooden racks filled with the skulls of sacrificial victims stood to one side of the round pyramid to the god of wind, Ejecatl. In all there were more than seventy buildings within the enormous court. In the second letter written to the king of Spain, Cortés described the central plaza, "the principal one, whose great size and magnificence no human tongue could describe, for it is so large that within the precincts, which are surrounded by a very high wall, a town of some five hundred inhabitants could easily be built. All round inside this wall there are very elegant quarters with very large rooms and corridors where their priests live. There are as many as forty towers, all of which are so high that in the case of the largest there are fifty steps leading up to the main part of it; and the most important of these towers is higher than that of the cathedral of Seville'' (Pagden 1986).

The profound admiration of Mexico's conqueror is apparent in his lengthy descriptions of the culture he had encountered. ''These people live almost like those in Spain, and in as much harmony and order as there, and considering that they are barbarous and so far from the knowledge of God and cut off from all civilized nations, it is truly remarkable to see what they have achieved in all things.''

The Market of Tlatelolco

Tlatelolco, sister city of Tenochtitlán, was the site of a cornucopian market. Its profusion of merchandise, as well as its order and efficiency, greatly impressed the Spaniards.

Cortés and his men were greeted with kind if guarded hospitality, treated to great riches, and escorted on many royal tours throughout the island cities, which they compared to Venice. Bernal Díaz could not contain his amazement when he described Tenochtitlán's sister city, Tlatelolco. Here he was especially impressed by the great market. ''We were astounded at the number of people and the quantity of merchandise that it contained, and at the good order and control that was maintained, for we had never seen such a thing before. The chieftains who accompanied us acted as guides. Each kind of merchandise was kept by itself and had its fixed place marked out. Let us begin with the dealers in gold, silver, and

precious stones, feathers, mantles, and embroidered goods. Then there were other wares consisting of Indian slaves both men and women. . . . Next there were other traders who sold great pieces of cloth and cotton, and articles of twisted thread and there were cacahuateros who sold cacao." He goes on to list the merchandise: ropes and sandals, skins of wild animals, vegetables and herbs, fowls, rabbits, deer and young dogs, "every sort of pottery made in a thousand different forms from great water jars to little jugs, these also had a place to themselves." He also remarked upon the honey, lumber, blocks and benches, firewood, *amatl* (bark) paper, tobacco, ointments, dyes, salt and stone knives, axes of copper, brass, and tin, and gourds and painted jars. "I could wish that I had finished telling of all the things which are sold there, but they are so numerous and of such different quality and the great marketplace with its surrounding arcades was so crowded with people, that one would not have been able to see and inquire about it all in two days."

The market with its carefully marked divisions, its "fixed places," speaks volumes about Aztec society, its complexity, sophistication, centralized polity, the enormous variety of craft specialists it produced, and the division of the society into classes of nobility, commoners, and slaves. The market was in a sense an Aztec discourse, the means by which this society defined and talked about itself. The variety of goods sold in the market also reflects the many and diverse regions with which Tenochtitlán traded. Trade networks had been established throughout the empire for many years, and long-distance trade sent merchants far outside the imperial domain. They traveled as far south as Central America and as far north as the Pueblos of the American Southwest. The son of an Aztec feather merchant, who had accompanied his father on journeys, was the first to tell the Spaniards tales of the seven cities of Cíbola. Aztec trade was carried out by a hereditary class of merchants, called *pochteca*, who often traveled in long caravans protected by soldiers and the power of the emperor. During Montezuma's reign the pochteca had become rich and powerful. Some trade was state supported and, therefore, had definite political overtones, since pochteca often served as spies, ambassadors, and agents of the emperor. Apparently pochteca always traded at market places within towns. Because they often traveled great distances they usually dealt in high-value, low-bulk items. Many historians believe that trade preceded tribute in the formation of this empire. Traders in search of more varied merchandise traveled farther and farther afield. They were often followed by conquering armies.

Sunset

The great lord Montezuma, by then fearful that the end of the Fifth Sun was upon him, was described by Bernal Díaz as "about forty years old, of good height and well proportioned. . . . He had good eyes and showed in his appearance and manner both tenderness and, when necessary, gravity. He was very neat and clean and bathed once everyday in the afternoon. He had many women as mistresses, daughters of Chieftains, and he had two great Cacicas as his legitimate wives. . . . The clothes that he wore one day, he did not put on again until four days later." Cortés wrote, "Touching Mutezuma's [sic] service and all that was remarkable in his magnificence and power, . . . I have not yet been able to discover the extent of the domain of Mutezuma, but in the two hundred leagues which his messengers traveled to the north and to the south of this city his orders were obeyed . . . that his kingdom is almost as big as Spain" (Pagden 1986). Bernal Díaz also wrote many pages describing Montezuma's zoo, the buildings that housed birds and animals, and their frightening cries in the night. He was amazed at the number and variety of people who inhabited Montezuma's homes—the weavers, gold and silversmiths, feather artisans, dancers, jugglers, and other entertainers in the court of the Aztec emperor.

Montezuma II, ruler of an empire not yet two centuries old, did not survive the winter of the year Hernán Cortés entered his land. After being held captive by Cortés, according to the Spanish chronicles, he was stoned to death by his own people who were angry at his refusal to lead them against the invaders and their leader, perhaps because he still believed Cortés to be Quetzalcoatl. The Aztec version of the event recorded that his death was by strangulation at the hands of Spanish soldiers.

Montezuma's successor, his brother the mighty Cuitlahuac, died of smallpox within four months of his ascendancy. He fought bravely against the Spaniards, but many facts of Aztec life would favor the European conquest. Even the rules of the flower wars would play into the hands of the conquistadores. Given the Aztecs' less deadly approach to warfare, combined with European firepower, the frightening vision of the horse and the devastation wrought by disease, it is not difficult to explain how several hundred Spaniards in league with about twenty thousand Tlaxcalans could have vanquished a nation of nearly a million people.

The last Aztec emperor was Cuauhtémoc, a nephew of Montezuma. He led a final bold assault against the Spaniards and their Tlaxcalan allies, but the smallpox epidemic so ravaged his troops that he was forced to surrender. For his valor in the face of torture and death, romantically portrayed in this late-19th-century painting by Leandro Izaguirre, Cuauhtémoc remains heroic to all Mexicans.

Cuauhtémoc, Montezuma's nephew, the last of the Aztec emperors, led the final assault against the invaders but surrendered because of tremendous loses due to the smallpox epidemic that raged in Tenochtitlán in 1521. The valiant Cuauhtémoc, still heroic to all Mexicans, was hanged by Hernán Cortés while the Spaniards prepared to invade Honduras.

Malinche, whose assistance to Cortés was invaluable, is considered to have been a traitor. The word "Malinchista" is still used by Mexicans to define one who betrays his own people. Hernán Cortés, planning to return to Mexico to spend his final days, died in Spain in 1547 after a brief illness. Modern Mexico celebrates 12 October, the day Christopher Columbus arrived in America, as "Día de la Raza," or the beginning day of the formation of a new race of people.

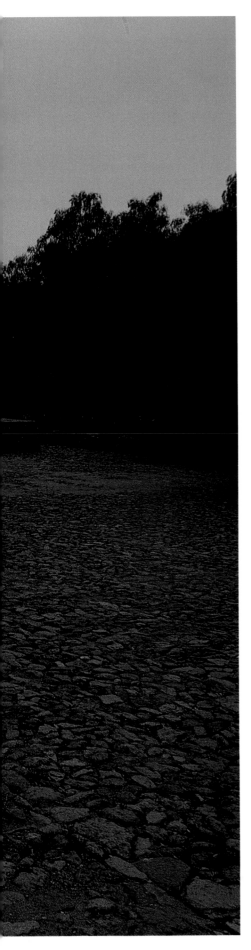

In two short years the Spanish conquerors destroyed an empire that marked the zenith of more than thirty centuries of civilization in Mesoamerica. The immediate consequences of the conquest were many and palpable. The city of Tenochtitlán-Tlatelolco was burned, the causeways destroyed, the dikes broken, and the population decimated many times over by disease. Within twenty years of Cortés's entry into the Valley of Mexico its ecology had been drastically altered. The Spaniards cut down enormous numbers of trees for fuel and construction, plows cut deep into the fertile chinampas, cattle and sheep grazed the land almost bare, and the water used for irrigation was diverted to supply power to the numerous Spanish mills, thereby destroying the cultivated terraces. The population of the Valley of Mexico in 1500 has been estimated at between 1,500,000 and 3,000,000 people; by 1600 there were approximately 70,000.

The Legend of the Suns, which had told of the consumption of the four previous worlds by ocelots, wind, fire, and water, prophesied the destruction of the Fifth Sun by earthquakes and hunger. The terrible destruction wrought by the Spaniards, the roar of guns and cannons, and the rumble of galloping horses may well have caused the Aztec earth to shake. The siege of Tenochtitlán lasted eighty-five days, with fierce fighting rarely abating. Hunger and disease were rampant, and even Bernal Díaz feared that the end of the world was at hand. "We were attacked by the enemy in such numbers that both on land and water we could see nothing but men and they raised such cries and yells that it seemed that the world was sinking." All the while the battle raged, the city was cut off from food and a smallpox epidemic went unchecked. After nearly fifty days of fighting, Bernal Díaz wrote, "Indians in the city were dying of hunger and . . . they came out by night to search among the houses . . . seeking for firewood and herbs and roots for food."

In the end, the Fifth Sun of the Aztec universe was eclipsed by the power of Spanish guns and the devastation of European disease. The poets of the Aztec nation mourned the loss of their world:

Broken spears lie in the roads;
we have torn our hair in our grief.
The houses are roofless now, and their walls
are red with blood.

Worms are swarming in the streets and plazas,
and the walls are splattered with gore.
The water has turned red, as if it were dyed,
and when we drink it,
it has the taste of brine.

We have pounded our hands in despair
against the adobe walls,
for our inheritance, our city, is lost and dead.
The shields of our warriors were its defense,
but they could not save it.

(León-Portilla 1962)

41

American Food Crops in the Old World

William H. McNeill

Columbus and the innumerable discoveries that followed his venture across the Atlantic changed many things for the inhabitants of the Old World, but for most people what mattered most was not the new information about the lands, peoples, plants, and animals of the earth that came pouring into Europe after 1492, nor was it the gold and silver treasure that made the Spanish government so powerful for a century and more. Instead it was a change that historians have often overlooked: the spread of American food crops to Europe, Asia, and Africa.

These crops included maize, potatoes, sweet potatoes, tomatoes, peanuts, manioc, cacao, as well as various kinds of peppers, beans, and squashes. All of them were totally unknown outside of the Americas before the time of Columbus. If you imagine the Italians without tomatoes, the Chinese without sweet potatoes, the Africans without maize, and the Irish, Germans, and Russians without potatoes to eat, the importance of American food crops becomes self-evident. Worldwide, the latest available figures compiled by the Food and Agriculture Organization of the United Nations show wheat, rice, maize, and potatoes to be the four chief staples of human diet. The harvest for the two American crops, maize and potatoes, totalled 788 million metric tons in 1986, or 78 percent of the total 1,010 million metric tons for wheat and rice. Their share of that addition to the world's food supplies constitutes by far the greatest treasure that the Old World acquired from the New.

Yet because American crops spread slowly and were often introduced by poor, illiterate farmers who did not keep records of their experiments, finding out exactly when the peoples of the Old World began to grow maize, potatoes, or some other New World crop is very difficult. Historians have only recently begun to pay serious attention to the question, so information remains sketchy even though the importance of the spread of American food crops throughout the world is plain and incontrovertible.

From its native ground in Mesoamerica, maize dispersed to all corners of the world (previous pages). New World food crops brought far greater treasure to the Old World than the gold and silver that first caught the attention of Spanish explorers.

The first question to ask is why should farmers give up familiar routines and crop rotations to make room for strange plants that looked very different from what they already knew and required rather strenuous cultivation during the growing season to keep down weeds? Even more to the point: why start to eat something unfamiliar that might be poisonous and that had to be prepared differently from the foods already tried, tested, and available?

In most circumstances the answer to such questions is obviously negative. As long as familiar foods were available in suitable quantity and enough land was accessible for cultivating established crops in traditional ways, farmers had little or no incentive to experiment with anything as strange and risky as the new American crops often, in practice, turned out to be. For that reason, change came slowly. Even after some experimenters in a particular region discovered advantages in raising something strange and new, others held back until they encountered difficulties and hardships with their established ways of farming.

To be sure, difficulties and hardships were chronic in all parts of the Old World. Crop failures meant hunger, perhaps even famine; and irregularities of the weather could be counted on to create crop failures from time to time. But, of course, American crops were also liable to the vagaries of the weather, so it took a more systematic, ongoing crisis to persuade cultivators to change over to new crops. Population growth, putting pressure on available land and creating a pool of underemployed labor that could usefully be put to work hoeing fields of corn or potatoes during the growing season, was the usual trigger for bringing in American field crops.

The reason is this: maize and potatoes had a fundamental advantage over the different sorts of grain that Old World farmers already knew. With suitable growing conditions, they produced more calories per acre—sometimes very many more. Take the north European plain for example. Throughout that region, extending from the coast of the North Sea to the Ural Mountains, rye was the only grain that could be depended on to ripen in the short and often rainy summers that prevail there. But potatoes thrived in such a climate and could ordinarily produce about four times the number of calories per acre that rye did. This meant that across the vast plain of northern Europe four times as many people could live on the produce of the soil when they learned to eat potatoes instead of rye bread.

The advantages of raising the new crop were even greater than this remarkable ratio suggests because potatoes could be planted on the fallow fields required for successful cultivation of rye. To begin with, therefore, the new crop did not reduce

Northern Europeans, such as the harvesters pictured opposite, relied primarily on rye, the only grain that dependably ripened in the short and rainy summers. But this climate was equally suited for potatoes. The potato, native to the highlands of Peru, had sustained Andean cultures and inspired their crafts, such as the Chimu-style pottery vessel (center). By the end of the 16th century, Basques along the northern coast of Spain were cultivating the tuber. The potato's first record in European literature appeared in 1597 in John Gerard's *Herball* (right).

Le Noble est l'airaignée et le Paisan la mouche.

"The more one has, the more one wants" is the epigram on this 17th-century illustration. In Europe, noblemen and governments extracted a generous portion of the peasants' produce in rent and taxes. Grain, because it had to be harvested all at once and then stored in barns, was especially difficult to conceal during times of war from pillaging soldiers (opposite). By contrast, potatoes could be left in the ground over winter and removed for daily consumption, an economic and nutritional advantage for peasants who began to cultivate them.

production of grain in the slightest. Instead, it occupied fields that had previously produced nothing but self-seeded weeds.

That, indeed, was the reason for fallowing. Fields planted year after year with rye (or any other grain) became so clogged with weeds that harvests began to fail. By plowing a weed-infested field in early summer, the unwanted plants could be plowed under before their seeds for the next year had formed. This cleared the field quite effectively, so the next year a new crop of rye (or some other grain) could be planted with little competition from weeds. Sometimes, European cultivators fallowed in alternate years: more often by the eighteenth century they used a three-year rotation, whereby grain was planted two years followed by fallowing.

Potatoes and other row crops, including maize and sweet potatoes, had to be hoed two or three times during the growing season to clear out weeds. This had almost the same effect as fallow plowing, for in a well-hoed field weeds were killed before they formed seeds, thus clearing the way for grain in the following year.

The drawback was that hoeing is a far slower way of controlling weeds than plowing. But the addition to the food supply was spectacular and made sense wherever extra hands were available for the extra work.

Hence population growth was prerequisite for large-scale adoption of the new crops; and of course population growth also created an urgent need for the extra food that American crops could provide. The two thus fitted together like hand in glove, so that when the modern growth of population set in after about 1750, American food crops came into their own, at first as a supplement and then in some places as a successor to older, less labor-intensive and less nutritious crops.

To be sure, in most other parts of the earth, American crops had a smaller advantage than potatoes did in northern Europe. Exact results varied with climate and soils. Maize yielded more calories per acre than wheat in climates that were warm and wet enough to ripen the ears of corn, but it fell short of the caloric yield of rice paddies. Not surprisingly, therefore, rice held its own wherever it was grown. But in rice-growing regions, American crops could and often did occupy slopes where water was unavailable or where fields could not be made exactly level to hold the standing water that rice requires.

In competition with wheat, maize suffered from two handicaps. It needed more water to ripen, and it lacked certain amino acids essential for human nourishment. As a result, an exclusive diet of maize, however rich in calories, brought on a crippling deficiency disease known as pellagra. Potatoes, on the contrary, provided an adequately balanced diet for human beings and required minimal supplement—except for variety.

Potatoes had another advantage, which in fact triggered their initial acceptance in Europe. Ripe grain must be harvested and then stored in a barn, where it constituted a convenient target for tax and rent collectors in peacetime and for plundering soldiers in time of war. European peasants had learned to live with rent and tax collectors, but wartime requisitioning threatened disaster because hungry soldiers were likely to take everything. Even in the eighteenth century, when military requisitioning was more or less legalized so that peasants and landlords got chits of paper entitling them to payment for grain the soldiers seized, governments were almost always slow to pay up, and poor peasants could starve before officials got around to settling the accounts.

Potatoes, on the other hand, could be left in the ground through the winter and dug only as needed for daily consumption. Soldiers usually could not take the time to dig a field to get their food, and they certainly would never do so if stores of grain were ready and waiting in neighboring barns. Anyone with enough potatoes in the ground could survive the most ruthless wartime requisitioning. Even if all the grain was taken, food remained at hand to tide over the crisis. When this became clear, European peasants hastened to plant the new crop as a kind of insurance against the disasters of war.

The potato was native to the altiplano of Peru, where it provided the principal food for the Incas and their subject populations. Shortly after the Spaniards conquered Peru in 1536, Spanish ships operating in Pacific waters off the coast of Peru and Chile began to use potatoes as a cheap food for sailors. But since men and goods going to Spain usually crossed the isthmus of Panama by caravan, so bulky a food as potatoes got left behind. But once in a while, when a ship left the Pacific and headed for home around the Horn or through the treacherous Strait of Magellan its store of potatoes might last all the way to Spain.

In this entirely unrecorded fashion, the new food eventually reached the Old World. Before the end of the sixteenth century Basque sailors' families along the Biscay coast of northern Spain became the earliest European population to make room in their gardens for the new crop. They used it as it had been used along the Pacific coast of South America, as shipboard food. Fishermen, operating off the coast of Ireland from northern Spanish ports, before 1650 transmitted potatoes to the Irish, who then established an entirely new style of subsistence farming on the basis of potatoes alone.

Once potatoes came ashore in Europe, learned botanists, interested in novelties from the Americas, discovered the recent import (again in unrecorded ways). It

Vincent van Gogh's *Planting Potatoes* (top) resembles drawings of Inca laborers at the same task. The ancient Peruvian food became a mainstay of the European peasant diet because potatoes produced more calories per acre than standard Old World crops like rye. In Ireland, where the potato became virtually the sole source of food, the population, particularly rural laborers, was devastated when the potato blight struck in 1845–46. Thousands died of starvation; thousands of others fled to the Americas.

entered the literary record for the first time when John Gerard published his *Herball, or generall historie of plantes* in 1597. Gerard took special pride in his discovery and used a woodcut of a flowering potato plant as the frontispiece of his book. He praised the food value of the tubers and even recommended a meal of potatoes as a stimulus to sexual potency. Tomatoes, nicknamed "apples of love," had the same reputation when they were introduced to Europeans. There may even have been some truth in the idea for both tomatoes and potatoes have a stock of vitamins that grains lack, so vitamin-deprived Europeans may have benefited from eating even small quantities of the new foods. But a short-lived vogue among the upper classes soon faded when the humble potato proved to be an ineffective aphrodisiac. On the other hand, tomatoes, with their handsome red color and higher vitamin content, retained their reputation as "apples of love" down to my grandmother's time.

The literary record tells us nothing about how potatoes spread to the gardens of ordinary people from the original lodgment along the coast of northern Spain. Spread they did, but, except in Ireland, they remained a relatively unimportant garden vegetable until peasant cultivators saw how useful it would be to have more potatoes on hand when military requisitioning threatened their grain stocks. This happened first in what is now Belgium, when Louis XIV's wars ravaged the land in the 1680s. Potatoes then spread across Germany and Poland in the eighteenth century, becoming important in southwestern Germany during the War of the Spanish Succession (1700–1713) and reaching eastward into Prussia and Poland during the Seven Years' War (1756–63). The Revolutionary and Napoleonic Wars (1792–1815) brought the potato to Russia and intensified its cultivation throughout the whole north European plain. Indeed, potato acreage increased during every subsequent European war, including World War II. That was because, given the soil and climate of northern Europe, no other crop produces as many calories per acre; and when food gets short, extra calories become irresistible.

The advantage was counterbalanced by a difficulty. Potatoes do not last in storage nearly as well as grain. Carryover from one year to the next is impossible, since stored potatoes start to sprout and then to rot. As a result, a population depending wholly on potatoes risks real disaster in case of crop failure. That is what happened to the Irish in 1845–46 when a fungus arrived from America (on fast, new steamships) and destroyed the fields of potatoes upon which they had become dependent.

Ireland was, indeed, the first European land in which potatoes became really important. As elsewhere, war triggered the shift to the new crop. Between 1649 and 1652, Cromwell's Roundheads conquered the whole of Ireland, and his government decided to make the island safe for English Protestantism by settling army veterans on Irish soil, while confining the native Irish to the westernmost province of Connacht. This created a severe crisis for the thousands of Irishmen who were uprooted from their homes and driven into the rain-soaked western part of the island. Grain could not ripen there, and pastureland was insufficient to support the refugees. Survivors found a solution by cultivating potatoes, brought ashore by Basque fishermen at places where they were accustomed to drying their catch before returning home.

Once the Irish learned how to cultivate the new plant, and discovered that a whole family could live on a single acre of potato land, they were able to undercut the army veterans that Cromwell's government had planted in other provinces of Ireland. The Irish could afford to work for English landlords (who remained in possession of most of Ireland until the twentieth century) by offering their labor at much cheaper rates than Englishmen, who insisted on eating bread, were willing to do. Ireland was thus restored to the Irish in the course of the eighteenth and early nineteenth centuries, but only at the cost of abject poverty and an almost total dependence on a diet of potatoes.

Ireland in fact developed a two-tiered society and economy. Landlords hired Irish laborers to produce beef and other commodities for sale, usually in England. But for most of the population, wages only slightly modified a subsistence economy; rural laborers simply channeled their income into the rent for a bit of land on which they planted the potatoes they needed to feed themselves. When blight struck in 1845–46, the great majority of the Irish had absolutely no reserve of food. Hundreds of thousands died before public relief could be organized. Other scores of thousands emigrated to America and elsewhere beyond the seas. Back home, survivors began a slow, angry climb back towards political sovereignty and the mixed farming that prevails today, in which cattle, hogs, and horses matter more than potatoes.

The exotic potato (above) and the even more luscious-looking tomato (opposite) acquired a reputation in the Old World as aphrodisiacs. Instead, these nutrient-rich foods enhanced the diet of the vitamin-deprived Europeans.

On the Continent and in England, potatoes never displaced grain growing and mixed farming. Accordingly, the blight of 1845–46 did not create outright famine, as in Ireland, although failure of the potato crop did create (or at least exacerbate) the food shortages of the "Hungry Forties," which were long remembered by Europe's poorer classes. In 1847, dryer summer weather checked the blight, and eventually sprays and blight-resistant varieties forestalled repetition of the massive crop failures of 1845–46.

As population mounted in Germany and elsewhere across the north European plain, potatoes ceased to be only a fallow field crop. With other new crops like sugar beets, they began to encroach on rye fields, and the poorer classes began to eat more and more potatoes and less and less bread. But outright dependence on a single food that had characterized the Irish before 1845 never arose on the European continent. Even the poorest German, Polish, and Russian farmers were able to supplement their diet of potatoes with other foods—especially cabbages, beets, and bread. Nevertheless, throughout northern Europe, potatoes dominated the diet of the poor in the nineteenth and twentieth centuries. This in turn allowed the industrialization of Germany to take place on the basis of domestic food supplies. German farms could feed the massed populations of the new industrial towns with potatoes, as they could not have done with bread, simply because potatoes produced so many more calories per acre.

Before the 1880s, when railroads and steamships brought American grain to the European market in quantity, this was the only way the growing German population could have been fed. Hence it is no exaggeration to say that the swift rise of industrial Germany was the greatest political monument to the impact of American food crops on Europe—and on other continents as well, for World Wars I and II were among the consequences of that rise. The extraordinary growth of Russian population and power in the nineteenth and twentieth centuries was based on the same superiority of potatoes to rye as a food base for an industrializing society; and the significance of Russia in our world scarcely needs argument.

If one looks for a measure of the importance of American food crops in Old World history, this is it. The surge of population and spread of industrialization in northern Europe, with resulting shifts of power since 1750, simply could not have followed their actual course without the nourishment provided by expanding fields of potatoes. No other single American crop played such a decisive role on the world stage; but maize in southern Europe and in Africa, together with sweet potatoes in China, also transformed the lives of millions of people.

In Mediterranean climates, the hot, dry summers did not suit any of the American food crops. Consequently, long-established agricultural practices, featuring the cultivation of wheat, vines, and olives, remained unchanged. But with a little extra watering garden-grown tomatoes would ripen abundantly. Tomatoes therefore were eventually able to add an important ingredient to Mediterranean diets, since their vitamin content nicely supplemented the nutritional value of the established staples. It is not accidental that Italy today produces almost half as many tomatoes as all of North America, while Europe as a whole raises more tomatoes than any other continent. Italian cooking without tomato sauce is hard to imagine, but exactly when and how tomatoes became important in Italy and other Mediterranean countries seems to be one of the questions historians have not yet explored.

In better-watered parts of southern Europe maize (called corn in the United States) played a role rather like the role of potatoes in the north. It did well in mountain valleys from Spain to the Balkans, wherever summer rainfall was sufficient to ripen the ears. It also prospered in the Po valley and in the Danube plains, where temperature and rainfall were well suited to its needs. But exactly how maize spread from Spain, where it arrived with Columbus, is difficult to discover.

Wars did not matter nearly as much as they did in the diffusion of potatoes, for maize has to be harvested and stored in barns like any other grain. The people who started to cultivate the new crop did so in large part because they found that they could escape paying taxes and rents in kind on their maize fields, for the simple reason that landlords and city folk did not want anything to do with such stuff. As a result, the spread of maize was not recorded. Only after the new crop was already prominent enough to attract the attention of travelers (and eventually of tax and rent collectors too) do written records reveal its dispersion.

This was the situation in the Veneto of northern Italy and in the Romanian provinces of the Ottoman empire by about 1650. In both these areas poor peasants learned to live on cornmeal mush, eventually beginning to suffer from pellagra as a result. A two-tiered society like that of Ireland developed, for these same peasants, subsisting on plots of maize, also raised crops and livestock for their landlords to sell in town.

In other parts of the Balkans, however, maize became the staple grain of free mountain villages. These communities, where sheepherding and mixed farming prevailed, also began to spring up about 1650 and increased in importance for the next two hundred years. Beans and a variety of tree crops—plums and nuts especially—supplemented maize; and there were no landlords to demand a share

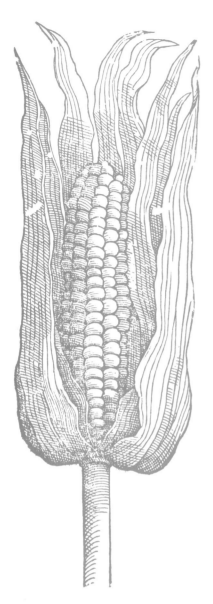

of the harvest. Indeed, these communities probably formed around summer camping grounds, established by shepherds, who from time immemorial had pastured their flocks on high mountain meadows every summer and wintered them in the plains. When Greeks, Serbs, and Vlachs found that the new maize crop allowed them to live all year round in high mountain valleys, where they were safe from the twin scourges of the plains—malaria and Turkish oppression—the political and economic balance of the Balkans began to shift.

Eventually, these villages became the cradle of Greek and Serbian national independence. Population growth in the mountains during the eighteenth century compelled the villagers to seek new ways to make ends meet. Casual labor in towns and at harvesttime in the plains was one resort, and expanding caravan trade was another. But the politically significant alternative was guerrilla attack on the Turkish landlords of the plains. This was what provided the skill and fighting manpower for the Greek War of Independence (1821–28) and remained a factor in subsequent Greek-Turkish conflict through World War I.

Serbian history was a bit more complicated, for Serbs, on emerging from their mountain refuges, found extensive empty lands to occupy in the Morava valley. There they pioneered in exactly the same way that Scotch-Irish settlers were doing at the same time in Appalachia, by relying on maize and hogs in a heavily forested frontier land. Then, when Turkish authorities tried to make them pay rents for the lands they had brought under cultivation, armed revolt (1803–15) established the local Serbian autonomy that eventually became full independence.

Thus one may say that what potatoes did for Germany and Russia between 1700 and 1914, maize did for mountain Greeks and Serbs in the same period of time. In each case, a new and far more productive food resource allowed population to surpass older limits, and larger populations in turn provided the basis for the enhanced political and military power attained by the four peoples involved. Similarly, what the potato became to the Irish, maize became for Romanians and for some northern Italians—the staff of life, but a treacherous one. For in these diverse parts of Europe the two American staples created dense populations of poverty-stricken subsistence farmers whose labor sustained their landlords' commercial farming while, in return, they only got rights of access to the small plots of land they needed for their sustenance.

These striking contrasts obviously depended on how the new crops fitted into preexisting social and agricultural routines. Extra calories could be a blessing or a curse, depending on what the larger populations thus supported were able to do with their lives. But taking Europe as a whole, it seems clear that American food crops were an essential resource for the nineteenth-century surge of numbers, wealth, and power that raised European nations so far above the rest of the world. The labor force that sustained Europe's intensified urban activities—industrial, commercial, administrative—could not have been fed without them. The flood of emigrants who peopled the Americas and other lands overseas could not have survived infancy without the extra calories that came from potatoes and maize.

The principal historical impact of the American food crops, I suggest, was that they undergirded Europe's rise to world dominion between the eighteenth and twentieth centuries. No other continent of the Old World profited so greatly. That was because Europe's climate, and especially its comparatively abundant rainfall, fitted the needs of the American food crops better than anywhere else, except China; and in China rice was so productive that the new crops had less to offer than potatoes and maize did in Europe.

Every continent and every people was profoundly affected by Europe's expansion, but more direct and local impacts of American food crops were only spotty. Climate was critical. The principal American food crops needed rain to ensure satisfactory ripening, as the traditional grains of the Middle East and India did not. Wheat, barley, millet, and sorghum all flourish under semiarid conditions. As long as sufficient rain falls during their early growth, a few weeks of drought will not hinder the ripening of the harvest. Indeed rain coming too close to harvest can hurt the crop, both by encouraging fungi and other infestations and by beating down the standing grain so that it becomes difficult to cut.

In climates where a rainy season gave way to months of drought, American crops were therefore of little value. Only if they could ripen during the rainy season were they worth growing. But since the rainy season in the Middle East came in winter, when vegetable growth was very slow, the American crops required irrigation at ripening time if they were to prosper. This meant, in effect, that they were limited to gardens; and since older irrigated crops yielded almost as abundantly as the newcomers from America and provided more balanced nutrition than maize, Middle Eastern peoples, like those of Mediterranean Europe, had little or no incentive to make much use of the new crops.

The monsoons of India, with alternating seasons of rain and drought, also limited the value of the American food crops for that country. In India, however, the rainy season came in summer, and thirsty crops like maize and potatoes ought therefore to ripen successfully in many parts of that subcontinent. However, as FAO figures show, maize, potatoes, and tomatoes all remain unimportant in India. Peanuts are the only American food crop that Indian farmers have found attractive, but, even though India's peanut harvest amounts to almost a third of the world total, it still remains trivial by comparison with the two staples of Indian agriculture—wheat and rice. Why the Indian maize crop totals less than an eighth of the Chinese maize crop seems hard to explain, since the caloric advantage maize has over other cereals (except rice) ought to count in India as much as in China or any other heavily populated land. Potatoes, on the other hand, require a cooler climate than India's, so their almost total absence from the Indian landscape is geographically determined.

China and southern Africa are the two parts of the Old World where American food crops have something like their importance for Europe. China's potato harvest in 1986 was more than twice as great as that of North America and almost a quarter as great as Europe's world-leading total. Maize in China was almost equal to Europe's total harvest and 28 percent of North America's world-leading total. China's peanut harvest, likewise, was second only to that of India and more than three times as great as that of North America. Obviously, these American staples are important in China today, but the New World crop that outweighs them all for the Chinese is sweet potatoes. Indeed, in 1986 China raised 80 percent of the world's sweet potatoes according to FAO statistics, leaving all the rest of the world far, far behind.

Chinese records attest the early arrival of all of these American food crops. Maize, for example, was known in the southwestern frontier province of Yunnan in the 1550s. How it arrived there is unknown, perhaps from across the Burmese border. Other American food crops reached China by sea and caught the attention of officials and writers of local gazetteers at various times during the sixteenth century. For example, peanuts were praised by an agricultural writer as early as 1538, and in 1594 the governor of Fukien, on the southern coast, touted sweet potatoes as an answer to a widespread failure of other crops in his province in that year.

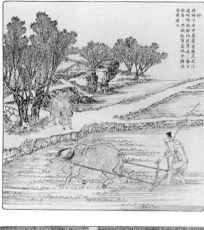

China was receptive to such New World produce as corn, sweet potatoes, peanuts, and tomatoes because its peasantry, long inured to the physical demands of growing rice, did not flinch at the arduous task of cultivating American crops. These crops still play a considerable role in the Chinese diet, providing about 37 percent of the country's food supply.

Regular contact between China and America was established when the Spaniards occupied the Philippines in 1565 and started up a transpacific trade featuring exchange of Mexican silver for silk, porcelain, and other Chinese wares. But the new American food crops had all made an initial lodgment in China before that date, very soon indeed after the Spanish from the east and the Portuguese from the west first penetrated Far Eastern waters.

Chinese agriculture was, of course, already very highly developed when the new crops arrived. In particular, the labor-intensive style of rice paddy farming made hoeing American food crops look easy by comparison with the stooping that rice required for transplanting and harvesting. One great obstacle to their acceptance that had to be overcome in other parts of the Old World therefore did not apply in rice-growing regions of China.

Another factor facilitating the introduction of the new crops was that in many parts of China multiple cropping already prevailed. Throughout southern China and in parts of the Yellow River valley as well, the growing season was long enough to allow a second crop to mature after the first had been harvested. Many and varied cropping patterns thus arose, and it was not difficult for Chinese peasants to fit in one or another of the new American crops by way of experiment when they first became available.

All the same, China's vastness and the normal conservatism of farmers who have inherited a satisfactory system of agriculture meant that the spread of the new crops was gradual. At first, maize was important mainly on the southwestern frontier, where the initial capital investment of building rice paddies had not yet been made. Maize there served as a very satisfactory pioneer crop for land being cleared from the forests, just as it did in North America and in Serbia in the same period of time.

Sweet potatoes, on the other hand, quickly established themselves on some of the steeper hillsides in rice-growing districts of south China where even Chinese patience could not profitably construct level paddy fields. This, too, meant extending fields onto previously forested slopes, and in some cases inviting destructive erosion. But Chinese peasants were usually capable of checking erosion by trapping the runoff and then carefully channeling the precious water into their paddy fields below. They were already familiar with the elaborate social arrangements local water management required. Rice paddy cultivation dictated cooperation among all the families involved in bringing water to the fields; and rules for deciding among rival claimants to the vital water and for constructing and maintaining the necessary dikes, terraces, and water conduits were already of long standing in China before the sweet potato arrived to enlarge the country's food resources by making previously forested hillsides productive in a new way.

In the course of the eighteenth century, the Chinese more than doubled their number, thanks in considerable part to the new resources the American food crops put at their disposal. But, unlike the situation in Europe, where a comparable growth of population was accompanied by dramatic new developments in commerce and industry so that new urban careers opened for a larger and larger proportion of the population, in China the great majority of people remained on the land. Urban technologies and jobs grew comparatively slowly.

As a result, rural population pressure began to provoke peasant rebellions in the late eighteenth century, and disorders became massive in the mid-nineteenth century, when the Taiping Rebellion (1850–64) resulted in the deaths of some thirty million. Even after this enormous bloodletting, simmering rural discontent, together with foreign aggression and the persistent ineffectiveness of the government, kept China in turmoil until 1949, when widespread peasant support brought the Communist party to power.

The rural poverty and overpopulation that fueled China's long travail probably provoked further expansion of the American food crops. Much is obscure, and historians have scarcely begun to search the records for information about when these crops became important in particular parts of the country. One recent study, nonetheless, shows that maize arrived in the Wei valley of north China in the late eighteenth century, when refugees from disorders in the south squatted on marginal lands in the hills. But maize did not find lodgment in the fertile lowlands of the Wei valley until the 1860s and 1870s when prolonged outbreaks of violence upset the older regime on the land. Unlike the situation in most other parts of the earth, in the Wei valley lowlands war-induced depopulation prepared the way for the introduction of maize, for its cultivation required less work in the fields than the crops it displaced.

Overall, it seems clear that American food crops made a substantial difference in China—not all of it positive, since the massive population growth the new crops helped to sustain provoked difficulties from which the country has yet to recover. But keeping people alive is hard to deplore, and contemporary agricultural statistics (measuring crudely by tonnage) show that American food crops in China contribute something like 37 percent to the country's food supply. With a population of more than a billion, this in turn means that sweet potatoes, maize, potatoes, peanuts, and tomatoes (listing only the most significant) have vitally affected the lives of more people in China than in any other country of the world—by far.

In Africa, as in China, important new food crops arrived from the New World very soon after the European discovery of America. For example, maize was being grown in West Africa by 1550, and an ambiguous Portuguese text may attest its presence as early as 1502. Maize reached the coast of East Africa by 1561, but little

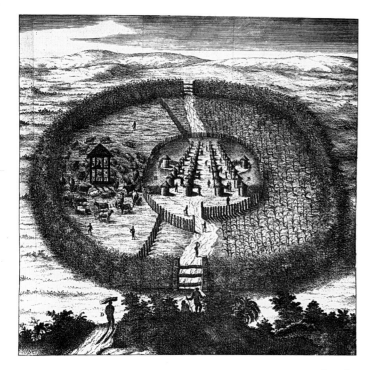

is known about how rapidly it penetrated the interior, since foreigners seldom ventured far from the African coast. Sometimes the new crops were slow to arrive even in places where they are important today. This was the case in southern Africa, as we shall soon see; and when Europeans first penetrated Uganda in 1861, maize was not yet there.

The difficulty arises from the fact that in Africa as elsewhere cultivation of maize and other American crops was undertaken by local people who made no records; and the handful of casual visitors who first recorded the presence of American food crops did so only haphazardly. Hence no coherent account of the spread of American food crops in Africa can be hoped for. A few general remarks about circumstances that affected the way the new crops fitted into older agricultural practices is about all historians can offer, unless or until local researches in oral traditions and pollen analysis of suitably stratified sites make the facts more apparent.

In general, African agriculture was very hospitable to experimentation with new crops. A garden style of cultivation prevailed, mingling different plants in the same field and using hoes to cultivate the ground. It was therefore easy to plant a few seeds or roots of a new food plant along with older, familiar standbys. The rigidity of European open-field agriculture, which required everyone to plant the same crop in a particular field so that the cycle of the year would not be interrupted, was completely absent. As a result it is not surprising that historians have found early reports of the use of American food crops scattered widely along Africa's coast.

Such early notices do not mean very much, because the new crops had to prove their value before Africans could begin to rely on them as staples. In this connection, Africans confronted a serious obstacle. Most of the continent is too dry for the

American crops to flourish, and in the areas of tropical rain forest, where it rains almost every day, the abundance of water was counteracted by other difficulties. In particular, even when the heavy work of clearing the tropical forest had been accomplished, the soil could not sustain cultivation year after year due to leaching by the heavy rains.

The effect of these conditions was to make it impractical for most African farmers to adopt the American crops as staples of their diet anywhere north of the equator. Instead, millet, sorghum, and manioc retained their place as the principal food crops for tropical Africa. Millet and sorghum were far more drought-resistant than maize, but they yielded less per acre. Manioc needed water but had the advantage that when locusts or some other insect pest destroyed its leaves, the plant regenerated from the root, whereas maize could not survive a locust attack.

Nevertheless, in some locations the new crops did outproduce the older staples of African agriculture. In particular, American crops turned out to be valuable in southern Africa, since enough rain fell in many regions to allow maize and sweet potatoes to mature successfully—at least in most years. In contemporary Africa, therefore, it is in Angola, Zambia, Zimbabwe, Mozambique, and the Union of South Africa that African farmers depend mainly on American crops for their nutrition.

This, however, is a rather recent phenomenon. Until the twentieth century, the open grasslands that dominate much of the landscape of southern Africa were more hospitable to pastoralism than to agriculture. Then in the nineteenth century, bloodthirsty wars launched by Shaka Zulu (reigned 1816–28), followed by a series of no less bloodthirsty wars between Europeans and Africans, depopulated vast regions of southern Africa. In the twentieth century, rapid population growth soon restored these losses, while the new colonial governments favored white settlers and landowners and made the old pastoral and tribal life impossible. Africans of the region therefore settled down to farming and made maize their staple because it was by far the most productive crop available to them.

Yet the situation in southern Africa is very unstable. Relatively frequent droughts are a recurrent threat to this new style of farming. Far more serious are problems of soil erosion, which, combined with a continually rising population, put unbearable pressure on the land. The end of European colonial rule after World War II did nothing to solve the difficulty; while in the Union of South Africa, where whites continue to rule, their effort to confine black Africans to specified rural homelands and urban ghettos promises nothing but trouble ahead as growing numbers, straitened resources, and mounting anger collide with the privileges whites seek to reserve for themselves.

Some other parts of Africa also face ecological disaster from population pressure on the land, accentuated by swift and sudden resort to new American crops. In the Ivory Coast, for example, commercial production of cacao, an American tree from whose fruit chocolate and cocoa can be derived, boomed after World War II. Peasant entrepreneurs cut down the rain forest to plant cacao trees, thus inviting all the unfortunate consequences of wholesale deforestation. Even at best, dependence on variable world market prices is an uncomfortable position for peasant farmers to find themselves in; and in the Ivory Coast this commercial vulnerability is compounded by the ecological vulnerability of cacao plantations that in effect are mining the soil of nutrients accumulated when the natural rain forest still prevailed. Under the circumstances, the comparative prosperity that the Ivory Coast enjoyed in the recent past seems unlikely to continue for very long into the future.

An illustration from an 18th-century English travel book about inland Africa (opposite, top) and photograph of Beti tribesmen ca. 1920 demonstrate the hop-scotch progress of corn across sub-Saharan Africa. The development of American crops on the African continent has been patchy compared to that in Europe and China. Northern Africa is too arid, while the rain forest soils in tropical areas are too fragile for long-term success with corn.

It is always easy to predict disaster and quite impossible to foresee what human ingenuity may devise when real crisis hits, as it well may do in much of Africa, where extremely rapid population growth has upset all older ecological relationships. If so, American food crops are sure to play a part, and perhaps an enhanced part, in whatever solution Africans find for their difficulties, since the superior caloric yields of maize and potatoes over other staple crops, except rice, remain an enduring reality.

So far, at least, American food crops have done rather less for Africa than they did for China. In 1950 one authority suggested that the caloric yield from maize and sweet potatoes was 28 percent of the calories Africans got from their older staples of millet, sorghum, and manioc. If this sort of ballpark guesswork is on target (and there is no way to be sure) then the new American crops are less important overall for Africans than for the Chinese, who, according to FAO statistics, derived 37 percent of their food supply (measured by weight) from American crops. Moreover, African agriculture is far more unstable ecologically than China's ancient system of water and land management, and the African continent suffers from more than its share of public health hazards as well.

In Africa, therefore, American crops helped to alter older balances between humans and the environment, especially in southern parts of the continent, but the result is far more precarious than in Europe or China, where the new American crops also allowed populations to rise enormously but did so by fitting into preexisting agricultural systems without disrupting ecological balances as radically as has happened in Africa.

Ecological considerations are, perhaps, the right note on which to conclude our consideration of the impact of American food crops on the Old World. All sorts of other ecological upheavals resulted from the European discovery of America. The most drastic affected the New World and Oceania. These previously isolated lands experienced massive invasions from Eurasia—all the way from European sailors and settlers with their domesticated animals and plants to the array of weeds, pests, and disease organisms that Old World peoples had learned to live with. The Americas and Oceania had little to offer in return, for their ecological systems, being more isolated, had evolved less rapidly than the Eurasian ecosystem and were therefore vulnerable to the invaders.

But the superior caloric yield of maize and potatoes did constitute an advantage that led, as we have seen, to their widespread adoption in suitable Old World environments. Accordingly, these two crops, with a few other less important ones like sweet potatoes, peanuts, and tomatoes, altered Old World ecological relationships more profoundly than any other import from America. Reverberations of their spread still resound throughout Eurasia and Africa, since the modern surge of population, sustained in large part by the new crops, is still going on, with drastic but unforeseeable ecological results. That, in a nutshell, is what the American food crops meant for the Old World.

New World, Vineyard to the Old

Henry Hobhouse

VITIS VINIFERA L.
Die weintragende Weinrebe.

The wine vine, *Vitis vinifera,* is an Old World native as far as is known. A variety of this, *V. silvestris,* occurred or was taken all over the Greco-Roman world before the Christian era. East Atlantic islands like the Canaries, the Azores, and Madeira were the first wine colonies of the Renaissance. Wine production was already important when Columbus passed through the Canaries in September 1492. He took cuttings with him on the first voyage, but whether they came from Spain or the Canaries, we do not know. Like the crew members left behind, the wine vines planted on the second voyage, on Hispaniola, also perished, as did the sugarcanes.

Cortés planted several strains drawn from the Estremadura by his father, a petty landowner who supplied the conquering son with innumerable cuttings, from apples to yarrows (the apples did better than the yarrows). Mexico was, and is, inferior wine country. New World vine production that first impressed the Spanish was in Chile and Peru. The first good Peruvian vintage was in the late 1550s; the Chilean in the 1580s. Export started within twenty years from both countries, but jealous Spanish merchants at home persuaded the bureaucracy to make colonial export of wine, and much else, illegal. Wine production subsided to a level no greater than was necessary to look after the needs of Spanish settlers. At a later date, wine

production, again for local consumption, began in Argentina, Uruguay, even in southern Brazil. None of it was, until recently, very good wine. Though Argentina and Chile can now make wine to meet the world trading standards, the finest wine in the New World probably comes from California.

California has played a crucial role in the wine production not only of the United States but also of Europe. The oldest wine-producing area north of the Rio Grande, California makes nine-tenths of American wines today and most of those American table wines that can be compared, without derision, with fine wines from France, Italy, or Germany. The Californian trade was also responsible for the three worst pests to afflict the vine, pests against which precautions have to be taken even today.

The European vine, *V. vinifera,* does not occur naturally outside the Old World. This vine was brought by priests from Mexico to California in 1564, and it is probable that small quantities of sacramental wine were made around what is now San Diego and Los Angeles from 1600 onwards. The Franciscans introduced what was later called the mission grape in 1767, and small quantities of surplus wine were used to refresh travelers and other mundane consumers from the early 1800s, long before many Anglo-Saxon Americans arrived in California. The wine trade had to wait for Amer-

icans and others from the East Coast to establish the vineyards in their present dominant position in the San Francisco area.

There were false starts. In 1824, a Frenchman, Jean Louis Vignes, planted three hundred acres of vines near what is now the railroad station in downtown Los Angeles. This was unsuccessful on account of sea fogs, which are the essential half, of course, of the smog that blights the area today. In most years the wine was inferior, so Vignes distilled it into brandy, always, before transport became cheap and easy, more marketable than wine. Vignes traded brandy northwards to Monterey and southwards to Lower California. In 1849 the gold rush established San Francisco as the center of gravity in the new state, admitted to the Union the following year. The miners and the traders, the harlots and the laborers demanded wine, and within a few years, vineyards had been established in the Sierras, Sonoma, and Napa Valley. The wine was not very good. It did not have to be. In a boom, people will drink anything.

The great figure in the advance to quality was a Hungarian, Agoston Haraszthy de Mokcsa, who in 1840 settled in Mission Valley, north of San Diego. He planted European vines, which he had imported directly. The grapes failed to ripen because of summer fog. He moved himself and his vines to Crystal Springs, south of San Francisco, where the

same grapes failed to ripen for the same reason. He moved to Sonoma in 1857. Before his death in 1864, he had established the Buena Vista cooperative, imported and tried nearly seventy varieties of European grape, written a standard work on grape culture and wine making, proved that vines from European grapes could be grown in California without irrigation, and (by sending American vine cuttings to Europe) unwittingly caused nearly as much damage as the Civil War—five billion dollars.

An early import of grapes into Europe from California introduced white mildew, a fungus, about 1851: this was called oidium. The leaves of affected vines withered and drooped, the grapes were poor in taste, and the wine made from such grapes had to be drunk within twelve months, however careful the winemaker. In France, production of all wine fell by a quarter, in Germany by a third, in Italy by half. Madeira altogether ceased to make wine between 1852 and 1860. Production of fine wine was nearly eliminated throughout the world. In Europe, generally, wine production was reduced by more than two hundred million liters a year, at a time when a liter was worth about one dollar wholesale in today's value, and the pest was not conquered for nearly twenty years. The total loss was nearly four billion dollars in today's money.

In the end, the cure proved to be cheap and simple. Flowers of sulfur, distributed around the vines, prevents the mildew. Before, however, this remedy was identified, many expedients had been

followed, and one attempt at a cure for oidium introduced a far worse pest into Europe, Africa, and Australia. Haraszthy suggested the import into Europe of *V. riparia* and *V. rupestris,* American vines resistant to oidium. They are also hosts to the aphid known as phylloxera, from Greek words meaning dry leaf. The leaves, when attacked by this aphid, turn yellow and dry and die. Without leaves no plant can live or produce grapes. If some grapes are produced, the immature pinheads do not swell; at harvesttime they remain hard and small. Oidium reduces the quality and quantity of wine, but phylloxera devastates. There is *no* wine. Oidium caused a loss of two hundred million liters for twenty years, but phylloxera was responsible for a loss of five times that quantity for twice as long.

California was wholly planted with European rootstocks when phylloxera appeared from the East, by ship or covered wagon. However it traveled, the scourge of the aphid was as serious in the 1860s and 1870s in California as in any country in Europe. Taken accidentally to Europe about 1860, phylloxera did as much damage as the War between the States, but worldwide. In France, production halved. By 1890, the pest had reached every country in Europe, North and South Africa, and Australia. Wine, which had been in surplus in the 1860s, started to rise in price as it became more and more difficult and expensive to produce. The cure took nearly forty years to discover and perfect.

Before an aphid can be controlled, its life cycle must be known. Aphids of roses or cereals are migrants, moving in vast waves in dry weather, on the wind. They are destroyed, in nature, by heavy rain or by ladybirds or other predators. Nowadays, they can be controlled by insecticides for up to a month at a time, but in the latter half of the nineteenth century no insecticides were available. The control parasite for the aphid phylloxera is a mild mite called *Tyroglyphus phylloxera.* Unfortunately, when imported into France, *Tyroglyphus phylloxera* found other sources of food, and the aphid and the mite lived together in perfect peace. This is proof, if proof were needed, that man's use of biological controls, so beloved of theoretical ecologists, breaks down in practice. The deliberate movement of insects is no more successful than the deliberate transfer of plants, and for the same reason, that no one can predict the side effects.

Sulfur was found wanting; drowning the vineyard was found ineffective; an intensely poisonous chemical, carbon disulfide, was found too expensive. In the end, the cure came from the same source as the disease, America. The idea was to use the American species that are phylloxera resistant, but which produce indifferent wine, as rootstock and to graft the superior European species, *V. silvestris,* in various forms, as the cultivar. Today, every vine of consequence in the world is a graft of European cultivars onto an American rootstock, which confers the characteristic immunity to phylloxera to the rest of the vine. This particular technique of grafting took forty years to develop successfully and led in the meantime to specially grafted apples, pears, oranges, apricots, peaches, and so forth.

Few, very few, prephylloxera vines are left in the world. There is only a tiny area of ungrafted vines in Europe, out of which prephylloxera wines are still made. Extreme snobs affect the claim that the wine produced from ungrafted stock is far purer than the vast majority of wine produced on the scions.

California was also responsible for another great pest of the nineteenth century, the blue mildew, *Peronospora.* This causes leaf drop; the grapes never mature but remain sour and soft with a high acid content, since without efficient leaves the plant cannot turn carbon dioxide into sugar. This mildew was, in fact, controlled within five years of its appearance. Spraying with copper sulfate (Bordeaux mixture) was instituted as a method of control as early as 1880, and the blue of the vineyard became as much a part of France before 1914 as the blue of the poilu's uniform.

California was wiped out as a wine producer by phylloxera and had barely recovered when Prohibition struck in 1919. Prohibition did many things for America, encouraging gangsters, disrespect for the law, and the consumption of cheap and nasty alcohol. But it also produced a boom in legal wine making. By a deliberate concession in the Volstead Act, each householder was allowed to make two hundred gallons of wine a year at home. Of course, many made much more, and, when Prohibition came to an end in 1933, wine making at home increased rather than diminished, probably because of straitened finances during the Depression. Vast areas in California were planted with grapes to produce juice for the home vintner to make into wine or for the consumer to drink unfermented. A favorite speculation was to plant with Thompson's seedless, a grape with four markets. It could be sold fresh for the table, or dried into raisins, or pressed into juice, or made at a winery into a strong (at more than 16 percent alcohol), unsophisticated, and unsubtle drink for winos. This was the position at the end of World War II. Only a few, a very few, Californian wines were mentioned in the same breath as the best products of Europe.

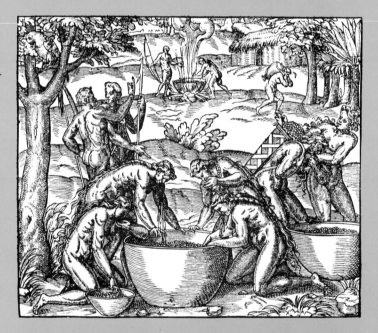

New World peoples had their own intoxicating beverages. This 16th-century illustration shows an important step in the process of making maize beer. The workers are chewing the grain, then spitting the masticated pulp into the brew to enhance fermentation.

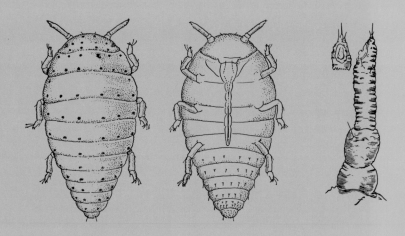

Biological and economic chaos sometimes follows the inter-continental travel of organisms. Wine vines prospered in the New World. In the 1850s California grapes brought a ruinous mildew called oidium to Europe. American vines resistant to oidium were then imported, but these cuttings carried the even more devastating pest phylloxera (bottom left). In the path of phylloxera, whole vineyards had to be uprooted (top left).

The Napa Valley (above) became one of the centers of the wine industry in California. The Beringer brothers (right) established their winery there in 1876. Modern wine making, especially in California, is increasingly the result of mechanization in the vineyard and chemistry and bioengineering in the laboratory, an approach to vinification that ignores Old World traditions.

Old and New in the Worlds of Wine

"The 1989 vintage in most of France was of a quality able to look that of 1929 in the eye, and it is unlikely that the current century will see another vintage to equal either." No doubt, but the 1929 vintage was handled in a manner that medieval vintners would recognize, while the 1989 vintage was often made with almost revolutionary methods. The changes in method over the intervening half century have occurred because of the need to meet the requirements of the top end of the market, crude financial realities, and, above all, the corrosive influence of inflation. Neither war, nor revolution, nor unstable government, has mattered as much to the winemaker as inflation, whose malign arithmetic has altered method and brought chemistry to the aid of the industry.

Nearly everyone is aware of developments in field mechanics since 1929—tractors substituted for horses, implements for men, trucks for carts, tanker trucks for railway flat cars loaded with wooden barrels. But the net effect of these mechanical improvements in productivity (perhaps a factor of three) is dwarfed by the contribution of the biochemist (a factor of two in the field, four after harvest). It has been estimated that the 1989 harvest, grown, picked, crushed, fermented, husbanded, and bottled by the methods of 1929, would cost seven times more, in real terms, than it already does, and that is only to the end of the first eight months. To keep the 1989 harvest for drinking twelve or more years later would cost, who knows? Inflation, whatever can be done to defeat it in the field, still rules in the cellar. There is little modern commercial sense in aiming at a vintage that will be drinkable only in fifteen to twenty years' time.

The need to beat inflation has meant that tannin is out, together with acidity, the bitter taste. Unfortunately these characteristics of young, immature wine are the very qualities that make the wine memorable twenty, thirty years later and give it keeping quality, flavor, the incredible fullness of a great red, which no other drink on earth can leave in the mouth. The great problem of the fourth quarter of the twentieth century is how to combine the virtues of an old, mature wine with the need to produce the same in half the traditional time. The manipulators are involved at every stage, from the field treatment of vines, the picking of grapes, the fermentation of must, through the disciplines of the cellar, to meet the basic requirements: to control costs in such a way that a fine wine can be produced at a price which is not only credible but which also leaves a fair margin of profit.

The prospect of standard wines of quality being made anywhere in the world, out of grapes grown anywhere in the world, and sold to anyone in the world who can afford the cost is no longer a dream (or a nightmare) but a projection of what is already current procedure. For this chemical revolution winemakers are indebted to California. This large state, inhabited by more people than any other in the United States, produces more ingenuity as well as more gross income, more winners of Nobel prizes, and more clever inventions than most sovereign nations. A state that can conceive of at least one new religion a month for most of this century is not going to be defeated by the more mundane problem of how to vanquish cost-price squeezes in the vineyards.

In order to stay competitive with less expensive European producers, and to meet—some would say anticipate or even form—modern taste, some California wineries have developed the no-hassle method of vinification. This, briefly, is to ferment at a very low temperature, using yeasts (containing enzymes) that operate in a high concentration of inert gases, so that of the sugar in the grape juice more can be turned into alcohol and less into carbon dioxide. Alternatively, it is now possible to ferment immature grapes into bland, drinkable wine, without risk, without trouble. Either way, there is little strong taste in the must, and taste, if necessary, can be added later. All the grapes can be machine-gathered on any convenient day, regardless of the maturity of the grape, or indeed of

its sugar content, and the whole of any area of a vineyard can be cleared, like a cornfield, at a tenth of the cost of hand-harvesting. The no-hassle fermentation technique was essential to the process. Without chemical control of the complex enzyme-sugar-alcohol chain, mechanization in the field leads only to inferior wines.

Californian wines are not inferior. To compete, Europeans have had to charge more for the same quality, or to emphasize the virtues that the Californians cannot claim. Europeans engaged in the enterprise of selling the idea of Old World tradition in competition with New World advantages call it marketing and use every trick in the book. Territory, grape type, and strict rules of vinification are called into play. At best they are probably likely to be defeated by the manipulation in the laboratories. At worst, and if public taste follows the pattern of the seventies and eighties, Europeans are likely to have to imitate the Californians. Some European wine producers already flatter the Californians by importing their techniques. Others have invested in the Californian industry, both for direct profit and as a way to acquire know-how. Privately, no European quality wine producer would dare denigrate the success of modern Californian viniculture.

Nor can there be another example of a natural product of the very highest quality being achieved within forty years. Today, Californian wines are a tribute to the know-how, ingenuity, and faith of a few hundred people determined on an end that most Europeans would have claimed was impossible in 1950. What was probably equally unforeseen by the most optimistic Californian oenophile in 1950 was that California would become, by 1990, the source and reservoir of modern methods, both in the field and in the winery.

From a marketing as well as a manufacturing point of view, Californians have made much of single variety wines. The law is such in California that a varietal wine must since 1983 be made from 75 percent of the declared grape. Cabernet sauvig-

non, a red wine variety high in tannin and body, has been spread all over the world by vegetative means (cutting and layering, not seed). The variety is believed to have altered virtually not at all since Roman times. Today it is naturalized from Chile to Bulgaria, from Australia to Azerbaijan. This is a variety probably used in the Burgundy and Bordeaux areas two thousand years ago, and probably the most widespread of all red wine grapes. Though the cabernet sauvignon vines have to reach a certain age for the resulting wine to have subtlety (the roots must get deep into the subsoil in order to produce the micro-flavors) and plenty of sun is essential for good yields, the grapes are small and the yield lower than is the case with other red wine varieties. Yet a wine made of 75 percent cabernet sauvignon grapes cannot be bad wine, as, indeed, people all over the world have successfully proved.

Cabernet sauvignon and its cousin, cabernet franc, also have a biochemical advantage in Italy, California, Australia, and other countries. Rich, al-luvial, flat (and therefore cheaply worked) land planted with cabernet vines still produces quality, not quantity, giving the lie to the Burgundian saying: "If your land weren't so poor, it would not be so rich." Cabernet turns rich soil into a bankable proposition in fine wine producing. Many, not all, other varieties on the same flat, easily mechanized land would produce dull wines. In marketing terms, more and more wines of quality will in the future probably identify themselves by grape rather than territory of origin or soil type.

The future of wine making is exciting in its possibilities. Thanks to genetic engineering, we are within sight of breeding enzymes that will produce wines of a particular taste, from any old grape juice anywhere in the world. New Zealand grape juice could be shipped to Hamburg and turned into burgundy; Argentine juice could be shipped to New Orleans and turned into bordeaux; Israeli juice could be shipped to Göteborg and turned into hock, champagne, or chianti; the permutations are endless.

There is already much in evidence:

- Americans in the early 1960s started spraying vines with synthetic *Botrytis cinerea* to produce noble rot at exactly the right time.
- Nearly all food and perfume flavors are now synthesized by the petrochemical industry. Almost any smell can be bought, in powder or liquid form, for a few pennies, from the taste of anchovy to the scent of Zara. Thousands of tons are used annually by the food industry. How soon in wine?
- World-famous perfumes can be imitated in smell-alike forms, for about 1 percent of the cost of the real product. So effective are the imitations that, once on the skin, they are undetectable. Only a spectrographic analysis will reveal all. What about cheap wine?
- Enzymes are now being built to block/unblock certain precursors to disease in plants, including vines.
- Genetic engineers have successfully tailored high-sugar, low-fiber carrots, celery, and peppers, each about the size of a walnut, designed to be sold as snacks in competition with candy. Grapes can be given more or less sugar.
- Grass and cereals have been rearranged to reduce their propensity to freeze. Thus barley and ryegrass can be ripened in the Arctic. The grape season could be extended by a month or more.

Thanks to the skills of the genetic engineer, the enzyme synthesizer, and the biochemist, the trade is presented with the answer to the problem of too many of the wrong sort of bottles chasing too few drinkers. Much better to give the drinkers a rational answer to many problems: give them what they never knew they wanted—grapes grown in the cheapest, sunniest places, wine made near the consumers and to their taste, products tailored to requirements—a triumph for the theories of Adam Smith and the practices of the marketing men. We are a long way down this road.

Metamorphosis of the Americas

Alfred W. Crosby

Chimalpahin Cuauhtlehuanitzin, one of our best sources of information on Mexico in the years immediately before and after the Spanish conquest, was an Indian historian whom the invaders trained in the reading and writing of the Roman alphabet in the sixteenth century. His writings (in Nahuatl) inform us that the year 13-Flint before the invasion was a grim one in the Valley of Mexico. There was sickness, hunger, an eclipse of the sun, an eruption of some sort between the volcanoes Iztaccíhuatl and Popocatépetl, "and many ferocious beasts devoured the children." But 13-Flint, Chimalpahin makes clear, was an exception in what was an era of triumph for the Aztecs. They, who within recorded memory had been wanderers from the savage north, now exacted tributes of food, gold, quetzal feathers, and human hearts from vassal states all the way from the remote dry lands from which they had emerged to the rain forests of the south and east. The stiff-necked Tarascos, at the cost of perennial war, retained their independence, as did—precariously—the anciently civilized Mayas, and there were a few others who survived in the chinks of the Aztec empire. Otherwise central Mexico lay under the hegemony of the Aztecs.

Lord Ahuitzotl, who was ruler of the Aztecs in 13-Flint, used the legions and wealth under his command to improve and adorn his capital, the incomparable Tenochtitlán. He built a new aqueduct to bring fresh water to its scores of thousands of inhabitants. He rebuilt and reconsecrated the gigantic temple to the Aztec tribal deities, Huitzilopochtli and Tezcatlipoca. He did not—how could he have?—see in the strange events of 13-Flint portents of the end of his empire and of his world.

Ahuitzotl (inset, previous page) ruled over an empire of great wealth and military strength, but it proved to be vulnerable to the Spanish invaders and their Old World arsenal of livestock, weaponry, and pestilence. The war between the two worlds was more than a religious, political, and cultural conflict. It transformed the biota of the Western Hemisphere.

The Spaniards' ships disgorged wheat, clover, chick peas, grape vines, melons, onions, radishes, fruit trees, horses, pigs, cattle, sheep, goats, burros, and pathogens—the most deadly of which was the smallpox virus. Perhaps half the Aztecs and other peoples of Mesoamerica died from the disease, while those who survived bore disfiguring scars.

A decade later, in 10-Rabbit, his nephew Motecuhzoma Xocoyotzin, known to us as Montezuma, succeeded him as leader of the Aztecs. His subjects numbered in the millions, and, so far as he or they knew, the empire had no equal in power and riches under the sky. Montezuma made plans to rebuild the great temple once more, higher and more extravagantly than any of his predecessors.

Reports drifted in from the eastern coast of pale, hairy visitors in boats "like towers or small mountains." There were only a few of them, and invaders traditionally came from the north, as had the Aztecs themselves, not from the east and never from the sea. Gods, however, might come from the sea.

In the year 1-Reed the visitors came to invade and to stay forever. The invaders proved to be humans, not gods, but they were incomprehensibly alien and powerful. They had light skin and much hair on their lips and chins, and some of them had yellow hair. They dressed in metal and brought weapons of metal. They had huge animals allied with them. The invaders had at their sides dogs bigger and fiercer than any seen before: "The color of their eyes is a burning yellow; their eyes flash fire and shoot off sparks." They had, also, man-animals that ran faster than any man and were more powerful than any creature the Aztecs had ever known. Then these creatures divided, and the Aztecs saw that the invaders had "deer to carry them on their backs wherever they wish to go. These deer, our lord, are as tall as the roof of a house."

Most hideous of all the invaders' allies was a pestilence, a *hueyzahuatl,* that swept all the land immediately after the Aztecs, quickened by atrocities, turned on the invaders, killing half of them as they fought their way out of Tenochtitlán. The pestilence spared the invaders but was a thing of agony, disfigurement, and death for the peoples of Mexico. There was no defense against it nor cure for it. Sahagún learned how it struck in the month of Tepeilhuitl and

spread over the people as great destruction. Some it quite covered on all parts—their faces, their heads, their breasts, and so on. There was a great havoc. Very many died of it. They could not walk; they only lay in their resting places and beds. They could not move; they could not stir; they could not change position, nor lie on one side; nor face down, nor on their backs. And if they stirred, much did they cry out. Great was its destruction. Covered, mantled with pustules, very many people died of them.

A third, a half—no one knows how many—of the Aztecs and the other peoples of Mexico died.

Then the invaders and their human allies, the Aztecs' former vassals and enemies, diminished by the epidemic but emboldened by the presence of the invaders, fought their way down the causeways and across Lake Texcoco into Tenochtitlán. Seventy-five days later, on the day 1-Serpent of the year 3-House, the siege of Tenochtitlán ended. Aztec poets expressed the grief of those who, somehow, had survived:

Weep my people:
know that with these disasters
we have lost the Mexica nation.
The water has turned bitter,
our food is bitter.

The invaders' chief, Hernán Cortés, ordered that stones from the temple of which Lord Ahuitzotl had been so proud should be gathered up, and that a Christian cathedral should be made of them in the center of what had become, by his victory, Mexico City. The vanquished learned that the ominous year 13-Flint was more properly designated as the year 1492 of a deity both more imperialistic and more merciful than Huitzilopochtli or Tezcatlipoca, and that Tenochtitlán had fallen in the year 1521, not 3-House.

The fall of Tenochtitlán in the year 3-House was the worst discrete event in the Aztecs' history. Worse, however, was this: 3-House was the beginning of the worst century of their history. Their civilization suffered massive amputations and survived at the root only by accepting alien graftings in the branch, as the conquistadores and the friars replaced their ancient noble and priestly classes. There were advantages that came with the defeat: an alphabet, a more supple instrument for expression than their own logo-syllabic system of writing; the true arch to replace the corbel; tools with an iron edge that did not shatter like an obsidian edge when it struck the rock hidden in the leaves. But the magnitude of the change, good and bad, was almost greater than the mind could encompass or the heart endure. The metamorphosis was more than political or religious or intellectual or technological; it was biological. The biota of Mexico—its *life*—and, in time, that of the entire Western Hemisphere changed.

If Lord Ahuitzotl had returned to Mexico (now New Spain) a hundred years after 13-Flint he would have found much the same as in his lifetime. He would have recognized the profiles of the mountains, all the wild birds, and most of the plants. The basic and holy food of his people was still maize. But he would have been stunned by the sight of plants and creatures he had never seen or dreamed of during his days on earth. Alien plants grew alongside the old plants in Mexico, and its 1592 fauna, in its large animals, was as different from that of 1492 as the native fauna of Zimbabwe differs from that of Spain.

The invaders had brought in wheat and other Eurasian and African grains; peach, pear, orange, and lemon trees; chick-peas, grape vines, melons, onions, radishes, and much more. A Spanish nobleman come to America could require his *indios* to furnish his table with the foods of his ancestors. Along with the Old World crops had come Old World weeds. European clover was by now so common that the Aztecs had a word of their own for it. They called it Castilian *ocoxochitl,* naming it after a low native plant that also prefers shade and moisture.

Of all the new sights of 1592—the cathedrals, the fields of wheat, wheeled vehicles, brigantines with sails and lounging sailors on Lake Texcoco where there had once been only canoes and sweating paddlers—nothing could have amazed Ahuitzotl more than the new animals: pigs, sheep, goats, burros, and others. Now there were cattle everywhere, and ranches with more than a hundred thousand each in the north. Now there were thousands upon thousands of horses, and they were available to any European (and, despite the law, the Indian, too) with a few coins or the skill to rope them. The horsemanship of the Mexican vaquero was already legendary on both sides of the Atlantic.

During Lord Ahuitzotl's lifetime the best way to move four hundred ears of maize in Mexico was on the bent back of a man, and the fastest means to deliver a message was by a runner. Now the bent man loaded four thousand ears onto a wheeled wagon pulled by a burro, and the messenger vaulted onto a horse and set off at several times the fastest pace of the fastest sprinter.

But Lord Ahuitzotl was an Aztec, an *indio,* and what would have put a catch in his breath a century after 13-Flint was not so much the new animals, for all their number, but his own kind of people, in their meager number. War, brutality, hunger, social and family disarray, loss of farmland to the invading humans and their flocks, and exploitation in general had taken their toll, but disease was the worst enemy. The *hueyzahuatl* of 1520–21, like the fall of Tenochtitlán, may have been the worst of its kind, but, more important, it was the beginning of a series of pestilential onslaughts. The worst of the worst of the times of *cocoliztli* were 1545–48, a time of bleeding from the nose and eyes, and 1576–81, when, again, many bled from the nose and windrows of Indians fell, but few Spaniards. If Lord Ahuitzotl had returned a century after his death, he would have found one for every ten or even twenty *indios* who had lived in his time.

Some of the survivors were *mestizos,* children of European men and Indian women. The mestizo, with his Indian skin and Visigothic eyes, proffering a cup of cocoa, a mixture of *chocolatl* and Old World sugar; the wild Chichimec on his Berber mare; the Zapotec herder with his sheep; the Aztec, perhaps the last of the line of Ahuitzotl, receiving the final rites of the Christian faith as he slipped into the terminal coma of an infection newly arrived from Seville—in so many ways New Spain was *new,* a combination, crossing, and concoction of entities that had never before existed on the same continent.

The transformation of Tenochtitlán into Mexico City began when Hernán Cortés replaced the Great Temple, dedicated to the Aztec gods Tlaloc and Huitzilopochtli, with a Christian cathedral.

To understand the complexity of that concoction, we have to look far back in the history of our planet, farther back than Europeans of the age of exploration could imagine. They believed that God had created the world a cozy six thousand years earlier, a colossal underestimation that forestalled comprehension of the causes of the differences between biotas on opposite sides of the Atlantic. Columbus and his contemporaries had no inkling that two hundred million years ago the continents

of the earth were parts of one immense world continent in which physical contiguity minimized the development of biological diversity. That is to say, the world's land biota, though it varied from one region or even neighborhood to another, was more homogeneous than at any time since, because true geographical isolation was very rare, except for oceanic islands.

Then slow and unimaginably powerful tectonic forces tore the supercontinent into several, eventually six, masses and shouldered them to the positions where they were in 1492, where they are today, with a few centimeters difference. During the interval of more than 150 million years the dinosaurs disappeared, birds appeared, and mammals advanced from minor status to dominance over most of the terrestrial globe. In the large Eurasian-African mass, most of the species of mammals that are most widely distributed in the world today originated or evolved into their present forms. In the other land masses, life evolved divergently, and thus Australia's biota is very different from Eurasia-Africa's.

Columbus wrote of the West Indies that the trees were "as different from ours as day from night, and so the fruits, the herbage." He was so surprised by the differences in the plants, and animals too, that he even claimed the rocks were different.

In Africa a few geological eras ago arboreal mammals with binocular eyesight and prehensile hands and feet moved down from the trees and out on to the grasslands. The toes of some of them shortened and the palms of their feet flattened and rose into arches for walking, and two of their ten fingers developed into thumbs. They developed bigger and better brains to compensate for the puniness of their teeth and claws and their slowness in pursuit and flight. They learned how to live and to hunt in teams, how to make and use tools, how to make clothing, how to control fire, and how to teach their young these skills. Their numbers increased; they began to migrate, first throughout Africa-Eurasia and even into the blue shadows of the retreating glaciers, and then to Australia, and across from Siberia to Alaska and the Western Hemisphere.

That was, for the geologist or paleontologist, barely yesterday, but for the anthropologist or historian it was a long time ago. The most recent common ancestor of Native Americans, whose ancestors crossed from the eastern extreme of Eurasia into America, and of Europeans, who sailed from the western extreme in 1492, lived tens of thousands and perhaps even more years ago. The Tainos and Spaniards who met in the Greater Antilles were products of physical and, more significantly, of cultural evolutions that had been diverging for a very long time. The Tainos reached out to feel the Spaniards "to ascertain if they were flesh and bones like themselves." For the Spaniards, the Tainos were the most exotic people they had ever met, with their hair not tightly curled like the Africans' "but straight and coarse like horsehair." Columbus wrote of them that "the whole forehead and head is very broad, more so than any other race that I have ever seen." They did not have the wheel or wheat or rice or iron or bronze. They did have a few trinkets of gold.

The contrasts continued to astonish Native Americans and Europeans after the latter reached the mainland. And no wonder: these two peoples had migrated in opposite directions around the world and for millennia before they met each other. The duration of their period of separation ensured that not only their physical appearance but their cultures had developed divergently. In the crude test of confrontation, one would be likely to have, at least for the short run, material advantages over the other. History makes clear that it was the Europeans who had the edge.

The metamorphosis of the Americas inspired subjective, dreamlike interpretations from both worlds—such as the scene of Peruvian Indians harvesting wheat, pastoralized by a Spanish artist (opposite), and the nightmarish portrait of a weapon-wielding, man-headed horse, rendered by a vanquished Aztec.

But to exploit their advantages, they had to get them across the Atlantic. Europeans could no more have successfully invaded the Americas from Europe in the sixteenth century than the Allies could have invaded Normandy from North America in 1944. Large offshore bases were essential in both cases, the British Isles in the latter, the Greater Antilles in the former. The Allies needed the British Isles as a center from which to gather intelligence about the mainland and as a storage, training, and staging area. The conquistadores needed the Antilles for all that and—much more importantly—for the seasoning and propagation of their biological allies.

Except for the Tainos and bats, the only land mammal in the Greater Antilles in 1492 was the hutia, a tasty rabbit-sized rodent. There was a profusion of birds and many reptiles, including the large, extravagantly ugly but tasty iguana. The Tainos, whom Columbus noted as "very unskilled with arms" and fit to be servants and even slaves, were numerous, at least three million on Española (Hispaniola) alone, said an eyewitness.

Columbus returned to Española and the Antilles in 1493 with seventeen ships; twelve hundred men; seeds, cuttings, and stones for wheat, chick-peas, melons,

A new mixture of peoples—Indian, European, and African—was a result of the Columbian exchange, and a new racial caste system stratified Mexico in place of the old Aztec social order.

onions, radishes, salad greens, grape vines, sugarcane, and fruit trees; and horses, dogs, pigs, cattle, chickens, sheep, and goats. That he also brought weeds, vermin such as rats, and germs is certain: there was no such entity then (or now) as a sack of truly clean seed, an absolutely clean ship, or a horse, pig, or man without microorganisms in its feces, fluids, and breath.

European crops, though they eventually prospered in both Americas, did not thrive in the tropical Antilles; the conquistadores were obliged to substitute the Taino staple, manioc, for wheaten bread. But their livestock did well, some fabulously well, in the Antilles, where the large carnivores were rare, where there were no local equivalents of rinderpest or hoof-and-mouth disease, and where, at first, the quantity of nourishment was immense and its quality splendid. Most of the imported animals prospered, most notably for the purposes of Cortés, Pizarro, and the like, the horses, cattle, and swine. They increased so fast that soon the backcountry of the Antilles swarmed with feral livestock. When the time came for launching invasions of the mainland, good mounts, pack animals, pork, beef, and hides were cheap—free, if you were willing to go get them yourself. Cortés did not invade Mexico with horses emaciated from weeks crossing the Atlantic, but with horses fresh from Cuba. Hernando de Soto traveled amid herds of hundreds of succulent pigs, all probably descendants from the eight Columbus brought from Spain to Española in 1493. The masters of America's first *haciendas* did not begin with bulls too weak to mount cows too frail to carry calves to full term, but with healthy beasts selected from the avant-garde herds of the Antilles.

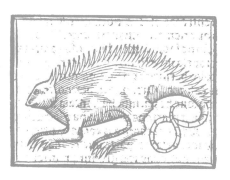

The ugly but tasty iguana, a reptile native to the Antilles.

The conquistadores' most powerful ally of all, the smallpox virus, also incubated in the Antilles. Smallpox had been a common affliction in the more densely populated regions of Europe in the Middle Ages, but it was not commonly a killer. Then, around 1500 it added to its ease of transmission a tendency to kill its hosts. It was so common in the cities facing west across the Atlantic that nearly all urban children caught it and were soon dead or immune—either way, no longer media for its propagation. Not for two more decades did chance provide the virus with a way to cross to the Americas. However it came, either by means of a few smallpox scabs in a bale of waste cloth or the serial infection of a few immunologically virgin hidalgos from rural Castile who decided to gamble their futures in the colonies, it arrived not long before or after Christmas of 1518.

It seared through the Tainos like a fire driven through dry brush by the wind they called *hurakán*. Their number had been falling precipitously since the 1490s, and now came the worst single blow of all. Bartolomé de las Casas recorded that the smallpox left no more than one thousand alive on Española "of that immensity of people that was on this island and which we have seen with our own eyes."

Within thirty years of Columbus's first landfall in the West Indies those islands contained all that the conquistadores needed for the successful invasion of the mainland: considerable numbers of their ambitious selves, livestock in cheap abundance, and at least one highly infectious and deadly disease to which almost every adult invader was immune and for which Native Americans were kindling. This team of invaders conquered the Aztecs within two years of first penetrating their empire. In the following decade the same team, pushing south from the Spanish settlements in Central America, achieved an equally dramatic conquest of the Inca empire. There were no more such magnificent conquests because there were no more such empires in the Western Hemisphere; but whenever the Spaniards—Soto, Coronado, Valdivia—made their spectacular *entradas* into unknown lands, and wherever they founded permanent settlements—Buenos Aires,

Guatemala City, Florida's Saint Augustine—their successes were as much due to their biological allies as to their abilities. The feats of the conquistadores seem to us, four and five centuries later, superhuman precisely because they were just that—the triumphs of teams that included more than humans.

The reputations of the conquistadores and their Portuguese, French, Dutch, British, and Russian equivalents need no more burnishing than historians have already afforded them, but the other large creatures of the invading team have been relatively neglected. In the long run, such species as chickens, sheep, and goats were crucially important, particularly for the Native Americans, but let us focus on the imported organisms that were most important in the short run, particularly to the invaders: pigs, cattle, horses, and pathogens.

First, the noble swine who accompanied the conquistadores were not the pampered, paunchy Neros of our barnyards, but the lean, fast, tusked boars and sows of medieval Europe. They were intolerant of direct sunlight and high temperatures, but there were shade and wallows in plenty in the American tropics. More food was immediately available for these omnivorous beasts in the areas first settled by Europeans in the Americas than there was for any other immigrant animal. In the Antilles they rooted the Tainos' manioc tubers and sweet potatoes out of the ground, stole their guavas and pineapples, gobbled lizards and baby birds—everything went down their maws. Within a few years of their debarkation in Española they were running wild there in numbers *infinitos.* Swine explosions of commensurate magnitude took place in the other islands of the Greater Antilles.

The invasion team so successful in Mexico—conquistadores, livestock, and disease—was equally invincible in South America. Pizarro encounters the Inca emperor Atahuallpa in the 16th-century illustration (above); (opposite) a looted pre-Columbian graveyard near Lima in 1973.

Pigs adapted similarly everywhere in continental America. In New England they thrived on the shellfish they rooted out of the tidal flats; in Virginia they did "swarm like Vermaine upon the Earth." In the open pampas the sun was hostile, but they adapted and went wild along the watercourses; and in Brazil, according to a visitor in 1601, "they beginne to have great multitudes, and heere [pork] is the best flesh of all." Much of the meat in the first European colonists' diet, from Nova Scotia to Patagonia, was American green turtle or venison or other game, but after that it was usually pork—plentiful, tasty, nourishing, cheap in the market and free to the hunter.

Cattle do not have the swine's sensitivity to sunlight and heat, but neither are they as good at crawling under logs as pigs nor are they omnivorous. In other words, they were not as ready to seize the opportunity for independence in so wide a variety of American environments as pigs. Jungles, for instance, are not to their liking, and they often require a period of several generations to adapt to hot, wet grasslands. On the other hand, they were agile, swift, and formidably equipped for survival. They were more like their Pleistocene ancestors or Texas longhorns than upholstered Guernseys and Holsteins.

The Spanish cattle took to the meadows and savannas of the Antilles like Adam and Eve returning to Eden. The cows were soon dropping calves two and three times a year, and the first American bulls were massively bigger than those back in Spain, a report confirmed by modern archaeology. In 1518 Alonzo de Zuazo

informed his king that thirty or forty strays would grow to three or four hundred in as little as three or four years. Feral cattle were roaming the hinterlands of Española by the 1520s and, soon after, the other Antilles. Stray men could and did live off these stray herds. When these humans became pirates, they were called buccaneers, a name probably derived from the wooden grate, the *boucan*, on which they smoked their wild beef.

In the next chapter, Bennett and Hoffmann recount in detail the prodigious propagation of cattle throughout the Western Hemisphere, a story mirrored in several respects in the drama of the horse. Columbus brought horses, essential to almost every European endeavor in the Americas, across the Atlantic in 1493. Many

Agile, omnivorous, and readily adaptable, swine spread from Nova Scotia to Patagonia "like Vermaine upon the Earth." By comparison, the horse fared less well on the ocean crossings and was less tolerant to New World conditions, especially the hot, humid, tropical lowlands. The equine population exploded, however, on the pampas (opposite) and the other temperate grasslands of the Western Hemisphere. On these vast expanses, the horse inspired the birth of colorful and original regional cultures—from American Indian warriors to vaqueros, gauchos, and cowboys.

1. *Pont de Liane, ou Bejuques.* 2. *Tarabite pour passer les Animaux.* 3. *Tarabite pour passer les Hommes.*

of these large animals, awkward to care for and difficult to feed properly on shipboard, died during the crossings, and the West Indian environment was not ideal for them; but by 1501 there were twenty or thirty on Española and two years later no fewer than sixty or seventy. Horses, good ones, were available when the conquistadores set off for the mainland. They were slow in adapting to the tropical lowlands of the continents but achieved population explosion when they reached the temperate grasslands of the Western Hemisphere.

At the end of the sixteenth century the horses roaming free in Durango were beyond possibility of counting. Taken to New Mexico and California, beyond the great deserts, by Spanish explorers and settlers, they inspired the covetousness of the northern Indians, who rustled them and traded some to Indians further north. That process repeated itself until horses reached Alberta by mid-eighteenth century. When the Aztecs first saw horses they called them deer; the Mayas called them tapirs; and Indians to the west of the Great Lakes called them moose. Mounted upon these wonderful animals, the Indians moved on to the plains to live off the buffalo and became light cavalry nonpareil. They were the last Native Americans north of Mexico to wage war against the invaders from the eastern ocean.

On the pampas the drama of the horse of Mexico was matched and surpassed. As in North America, Indians swung up onto their backs and moved into the grasslands to live off the herds of wild quadrupeds, which here were not indigenous buffalo but exotic horses and cattle. Native American resistance on the pampas would not be broken until the nineteenth century, at approximately the same time as the Great Plains Indians were defeated. The differences between the new kings of the great grasslands of the Americas—vaqueros, gauchos, cowboys—were not discernible at more than a few hundred meters, nor were the differences between their lightly tamed mounts.

The impact of the animals the Europeans brought with them on the Americas transformed whole ecosystems. For example, cattle and horses were so numerous on the pampas early in the seventeenth century that there were reports that they were destroying the ground cover. That is quite plausible, considering their density and the fact that, in time, Eurasian and North African grasses and forbs took over much of the pampas, a usurpation which could have taken place only along with

the destruction of the native flora. Similar usurpations took place in Mexico and Texas in the first post-Columbian centuries.

The first Euro-Americans paid little attention to the impact of the smaller creatures they brought with them, but it may have been as great as that of the larger animals, even as great as that of the close-cropping sheep and goats. Old World rats swarmed in and around European colonies from Quebec to Patagonia, decimating the native small animals and minor flora and enhancing the importation and spread of disease. Imported domestic cats and dogs threw off their allegiances to humanity and went wild everywhere the environment allowed, living off whatever creatures they could pounce upon or drag down. Nothing, however, that crossed from the Eastern to the Western Hemisphere made as much difference in the first or any other post-Columbian century as disease.

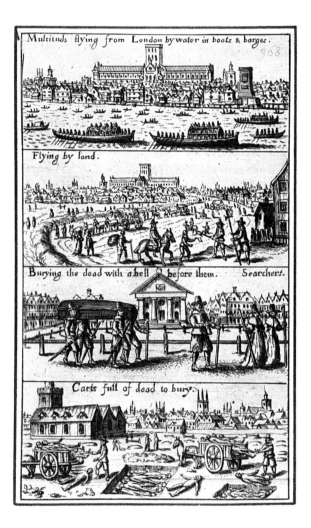

Cities in the Old World had long experience with formidable epidemics, but diseases such as smallpox, measles, and influenza were unknown in the New World.

Native Americans are not native to the Americas, if by the adjective you mean in possession of a pedigree that goes back forever in association with a particular geographical region. Tapirs qualify as native Americans, but Indians are descendants of immigrants from Asia who crossed through the Arctic into the Western Hemisphere a phylogenetically short time ago. Human beings are not native to the Americas, nor are their direct ancestors and near relatives, the chimps, gorillas, and such.

This has not only zoological but great historical importance, because it means there could have been no microorganisms or parasites adapted and predisposed to preying on humans when those clever bipeds came down through the glaciers into America. These immigrants were not free of infections, of course. They brought some infections with them, but not those informally known as the "crowd diseases." The Proto-Indians were hunters and gatherers and traveled and lived in small bands, not crowds. The microorganisms of diseases like smallpox or measles disappear in small populations of hosts. These viruses have no animal hosts to circulate among while not circulating among humans; they quickly die outside living bodies; and they race through small populations, either killing or producing permanent immunity as they go. That is, they swiftly burn up all their fuel and disappear like a forest fire that has run out of trees. As for the germs of long-lasting infections like tuberculosis or syphilis, the Proto-Indians could have and doubtlessly did bring some in that category with them, but perhaps not as many as you might think. The Proto-Indians came as nomads through the climatically hostile Arctic, where the chronically ill could not have lasted for long: they either died or were, for the sake of the band, left behind to perish.

To put it in a nutshell, a medical officer in Alaska at the end of the Pleistocene epoch would have given most of these Asian immigrants a clean bill of health. They were entering a Western Hemisphere free of specifically human infections, but not a totally wholesome Eden. A few American microorganisms and parasites managed in the brief interval (i.e., thousands, but not millions of years) between the first entry of humans into the Americas and the appearance of Christopher Columbus in the West Indies to adapt to living in and off the newcomers. Chagas' disease, for instance, is natively American. But most of what were in 1492 and have since been the leading causes of morbidity and mortality among the world's communicable diseases were not present in the Western Hemisphere.

The world's leading infections were the by-products of the rise of agricultural and pastoral peoples in not the Western but the Eastern Hemisphere, where humans began living in dense, often sedentary, and usually unhygienic concentrations before even the most advanced American Indians. Many Eurasians and Africans lived, as well, in close proximity with their livestock, exchanged infections with their herds, and, one might almost say, cultivated pathogens and parasites.

There is much debate about which historically important infectious diseases were present in the Eastern but *not* in the Western Hemisphere at the beginning of 1492. A truly definitive list may never be made, but most paleopathologists, epidemiologists, and scholars who have perused the early records of Europe's first American empires agree that the list should include smallpox, measles, whooping cough, bubonic plague, malaria, yellow fever, diphtheria, amoebic dysentery, and influenza. The list should probably be longer, but this one is long enough to indicate what

devastation the arrival of Europeans could visit upon an immunologically naive population.

The densest populations of the Eastern Hemisphere from China and Java to western Europe and Africa (the natives of the last two never long out of contact with America after 1492) were also the sickest, especially the city dwellers. They caught all the endemic or commonly epidemic infections long before advancing to adulthood, hence the name given to many historically significant infections, the "childhood diseases." Those who survived had efficiently adapted to their environments, and they often had long and productive lives. Children who died were quickly replaced by means of what was, over the years, a very high birth rate.

When the Europeans and Africans carried their diseases to America, "virgin soil epidemics" followed, infecting the great majorities of all populations at risk and killing adults as often as children. These epidemics were as effective in breaking resistance to the invaders as the air raids on civilian targets were intended to be in World War II, but were not. That is to say, they slaughtered great numbers, especially in the centers of population where the leadership elites lived; they paralyzed normal economic, religious, and political functions; and they terrorized the survivors.

We cannot be sure when the first post-Columbian virgin soil epidemic detonated in America. The decline of the Antillean Tainos in the first quarter century after 1492 seems to have been steeper than can be attributed to Spanish brutality. The swarms of pigs certainly provided a medium for an influenza epidemic, but the early chroniclers did not mention one, and whether anything as explosive as an influenza epidemic could have escaped their attention is doubtful. The fact is that the record does not mention any unambiguously epidemic infection until the end of 1518 or the very beginning of 1519.

The Spaniards in Española, where that infection struck first, identified the disease as smallpox. Bartolomé de las Casas said it was from Castile. It rarely affected the Europeans but devastated the Indians, killing one-third to one-half, a death rate not far out of line with what the population at risk in European ports—that is, the children—suffered. The affliction quickly spread throughout the Antilles, reaching Cuba just late enough for the Cortés expedition to the Mexican mainland to embark without it. In the next year a following expedition to Mexico included a man who carried smallpox. He infected the household in Cempoala where he was quartered, and the infection "spread from one Indian to another, and they, being so numerous and eating and sleeping together, quickly infected the whole country."

This, America's first recorded pandemic, spread far beyond the Antilles and Mexico. It rolled ahead of the Europeans and reached the lands of the advanced peoples of South America before the conquistadores' invasion of the fabulous Inca empire. It slaughtered the Inca's subjects, killed the Inca himself, disrupted the succession, and set off a civil war. The people whom Pizarro conquered were the survivors of one of the worst periods of their history. How much further south and east the smallpox spread we can only guess, but if fire spreads in tinder, then why would this infection have stopped at the far boundaries of the Inca empire?

To the north of Mexico the record on the subject is blank, but again we must grant that there was little reason for disease not to have spread. A decade after the fall of the Inca empire a veteran of Pizarro's invasion of Peru, Hernando de Soto, led an expedition on a long maraud through what is now the southeastern part of the United States in search of other Tenochtitláns and Cuzcos. He found hierarchical societies, village complexes, dense populations, pyramid temples, but nothing as attractively lootable as Mexico or Peru. He also found evidence of the passage of epidemic disease. In Cofachiqui, somewhere in present-day Georgia, he came upon recently emptied villages and large funereal houses filled with the drying cadavers of people who had perished in an epidemic. What he saw in Georgia may have, should have, reminded him of what he had seen in Peru.

Onslaughts of the new diseases swept over the Native American peoples throughout the sixteenth century and for all the generations since. It may be that we distort reality if we try to count epidemics, plucking them up out of the surmounting tide of infection, but for the sake of getting some idea of the dimensions of the flood, let us take the chance. About fifty epidemics swept through the Valley of Mexico between 1519 and 1810. Peru underwent twenty between the arrival of the

Spaniards and 1720, Brazil perhaps forty of smallpox alone between 1560 and 1840.

The epidemiology of England's beginnings in America was similar to Iberia's. When Sir Francis Drake raided Saint Augustine in the 1580s, he brought an epidemic with him. The local Florida Indians "died verie fast and said amongest themselves, it was the Inglisshe God that made them die so faste." Another (conceivably the same) epidemic swept the coastal tribes of Carolina and Virginia before the end of that decade, "the like by report of the oldest men in the countrey never happened before, time out of mind." The Pilgrim settlement to the north at Plymouth was preceded by an epidemic that began in 1616 and, said contemporary sources, killed 90 percent of the coastal Indians.

The material effect of these tidal waves of infection is one that we can at least crudely apprehend even at a distance of many years. The psychological effect—that is to say, the interpretations the invaders and the invaded placed on these epidemics—is not as apparent to people like ourselves, who blame infections on germs, not on the supernatural. Consider for a moment a statement made by an early nineteenth-century clergyman on the precipitous decrease of New England Indians since the first coming of the English: "Must we not ascribe it to the sovereign pleasure of the Most High, who divides to the nations their inheritance; who putteth down one and raiseth up another?" Both invaders and the invaded may have found this idea plausible.

And on and on to the present day. Alaska's and Canada's most remote Eskimos and Indians and South America's last tribes of hunter-gatherers and horticulturalists have been decimated by tuberculosis, measles, and influenza within living memory. Ninety-nine percent of the native people of Ungava Bay in northern Quebec came down with measles in a brief period of 1952, and about 7 percent died, even though some had the benefit of modern medicine. In 1954 measles broke out among the Native Americans of Brazil's Xingu National Park: the death rate was 9.6 percent for those who had modern medical treatment and 26.8 for those who did not. In 1990 the Yanomamos of the borderland of Brazil and Venezuela were decreasing rapidly under the attack not only or even primarily of the encroaching gold miners, but of malaria, influenza, measles, and chicken pox. The best ally of the invaders continues to be disease.

An avalanche of exotic organisms from the Eastern Hemisphere has been pouring onto the shores of the Americas for five hundred years. It continues, altering the ecosystems in all parts of the Western Hemisphere and the fates of Americans of every ethnicity and generation. The more recent immigrant organisms have often, like the wheat and peach trees that arrived in the sixteenth century, had positive effects. The Far East's soybean, for instance, has become a major crop and source of nourishment in the Americas since World War II, but the nastiest newcomers, like the Japanese beetle and Dutch elm disease, are the ones that get the most attention. Kudzu, a vine introduced from the Far East about a hundred years ago, was a decorous sort of a plant until the 1930s; since then it has been spreading

The English pillager Sir Francis Drake, aptly called El Dragon, brought an epidemic to the coast of Florida when his forces invaded Saint Augustine in the 1580s.

cancerously through the Gulf and southern Atlantic states. The notorious "killer bees," aggressive African bees first released in Brazil in 1957, have spread in spite of every effort to hold them back and in 1990 were nearly at the border of the United States. Flying Asian cockroaches, newly arrived, infest Florida. Significant and infamous above all recent imports is the AIDS virus, which probably first appeared in the Western Hemisphere in the 1970s. By sea and by air, by mammoth container ship and by jet aircraft, by diplomatic pouch and by impromptu encounter, the homogenizing process accelerates.

Native Americans often object to the name "New World," a European term for the lands of the Western Hemisphere. They point out that those lands were familiar to them long before Christopher Columbus was born, and their argument is one the rest of us owe respectful consideration. But we all are justified in the use of the title for the Americas since 1492. Until Columbus found his way across the Atlantic the biota of the two sets of continents on either side were markedly different, the products of what, through time, had usually been divergent evolution. Since then the biota of both, most undeniably of the Americas, have in significant part been the product of revolution, that is, the abrupt addition and explosive propagation of exotic species from the lands on the other side of the waters that Columbus crossed in 1492. The great Genoese navigated, administered, crusaded, enslaved, but above all he mixed, mingled, jumbled, and homogenized the biota of our planet.

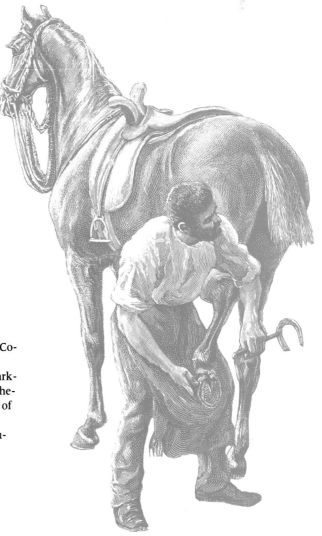

A century after the arrival of Columbus, the landscape of the New World was already remarkably changed. There were cathedrals, orchards of fruit, fields of wheat, wheeled vehicles and burros to pull them, and thousands of horses free for the taking.

Ranching in the New World

Deb Bennett and Robert S. Hoffmann

Introduction: Ranch Ecology

Through the medium of television, nearly every American knows what a cow pony is; the word brings to mind a tough, wiry horse, which, though it might have been worth less money than the saddle slung upon its back, was nevertheless vital to the weather-hardened man of the plains who rode it. Yet this romantic image tends to obscure the real roots of the cow pony (and the cowboy), which are overwhelmingly Iberian. And just as Iberian colonizers brought horses and horsemanship to the New World, during the centuries preceding the Encounter Spain itself had learned much about horsemanship and livestock handling from invaders, first the Romans and later the Moors. In truth, the American cowboy and his pony never existed in the isolation to which legend assigns them, for they were an integral part of the distinctive, imported agrarian ecology that we call ranching. The macroorganic components of ranch ecology include not only men, women, and horses but also cattle, sheep, goats, hogs, and the plant species these animals consume. Because they found New World foods unpalatable, the soldiers, dons, and padres who came west to the New World during the sixteenth century imported as many items as possible of what, to them, was a staple diet. A less obvious but equally significant import was the Spanish concept of ranching with its characteristically Iberian forms of land use.

In all of western Europe, no land is so suitable as Spain for grazing herds of hoofed mammals. By the time they arrived in America, many of the Iberian colonists were already accustomed to the cattleman's life on the open range. Techniques that Americans think of as their own, such as periodic roundups, branding, and cattle drives, were all invented in medieval Iberia. At the same time, no land but Spain had so many excellent horses, and they were owned and ridden not only by the nobility but by nearly everyone. Mounted on the horses on which their lives depended, Spanish soldiers and cattlemen lived and tended their herds along a troubled frontier, ever on the lookout for raids by mounted Moorish enemies—enemies replaced in the New World by mounted Indians.

Iberian ranching evolved not only from climate and soil but also from the importation to Spain in the first century B.C. of Roman law, custom, and breeds of livestock. The basic physical plant of the ranch, consisting of walled and tile-roofed, adobe-brick buildings surrounded by wooden corrals, surrounded in turn by pastureland, was established in Iberia with the construction of the first Roman villas.

More than fifteen hundred years of ranch tradition thus lay behind the outlook of the Spanish colonist, and it is no coincidence that Spain was able to colonize successfully those areas and latitudes of the New World ecologically most similar to it and most suitable for ranching. Spreading north and south from the Mexican tropics, Spaniards encountered the three great grasslands of the New World: the Argentine pampas, the Venezuelan llanos, and the Great Plains of North America, stretching from northern Mexico through the central United States and southern Canada.

The cowboy and the cow pony have come to constitute a New World icon (previous pages), but the source of this indelible American image is rooted in medieval Iberia. *La Era,* by the Mexican artist Diego Rivera (left), portrays a landscape with an even more ancient lineage. The *estancia,* with its walled compound enclosing corrals and adobe buildings, is the New World equivalent of Roman villas first constructed in Iberia more than 2000 years ago.

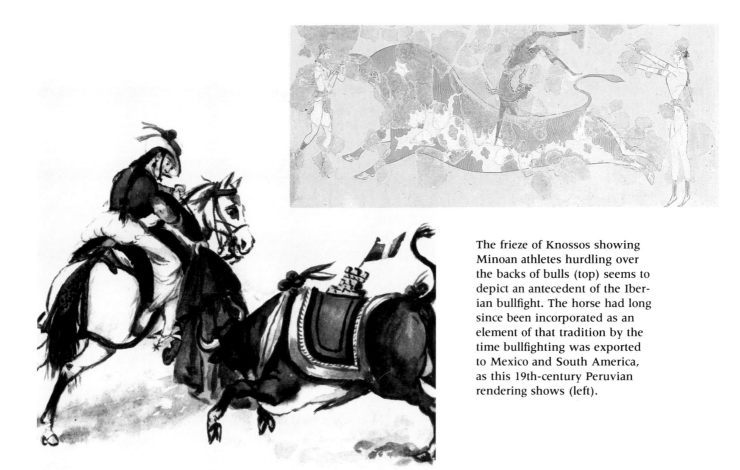

The frieze of Knossos showing Minoan athletes hurdling over the backs of bulls (top) seems to depict an antecedent of the Iberian bullfight. The horse had long since been incorporated as an element of that tradition by the time bullfighting was exported to Mexico and South America, as this 19th-century Peruvian rendering shows (left).

Ecologically, the three grassland areas were not equally suited to raising livestock. The llanos had a tropical climate characterized by alternating seasons of scorching heat and inundating flood; grass there, although abundant, was of lower nutrient quality, and thus the yield of cattle is lower. Sheep ranching has been successful in drier areas such as the Chaco of Argentina, Paraguay, and Bolivia and New Mexico and the Great Basin in the United States. In tropical and subtropical climates of the New World, such as in the Caribbean and most of Brazil, hogs did best, while in the temperate grasslands of the Argentine pampas and the North American Great Plains, cattle became king. While the avarice of gold-hungry conquistadores is legendary, greater fortunes were made both in the Caribbean and on the mainland by ranchers whose life-style better harmonized with the ecology of the land they had claimed.

Cattle

The wild ancestors of domestic cattle *(Bos taurus)* appear to be the aurochs *(Bos taurus primigenius)*, large cattle with elegantly curving long horns shaped like those of Spanish cattle and their descendants, the American longhorns. Aurochs once roamed open forest habitats of the temperate zone of North Africa, Europe, and southwestern Asia eastward to China. Cattle were probably first domesticated in southeastern Europe or southwestern Asia. Few other events in history have held such far-reaching significance for human culture as did this, for oxen made plowing possible, and thus fostered the development of agriculture. When the Celts came westward to Europe in the second millennium B.C., they brought docile cattle bred for draft, milk, and meat.

While use of cattle for practical purposes predominated in Asia and Celtic Europe, the ritual use of cattle is equally ancient, and cattle sacrifice was once practiced by many civilizations. The Minoans of Crete produced the famous frieze of Knossos, which shows athletes leaping over bulls. Among all the bull-worshipping cultures that contributed to the cultural development of Iberia, this one is of special importance for it was probably the source of the still-extant bullfight ceremonies of southern France, Iberia, Mexico, and South America.

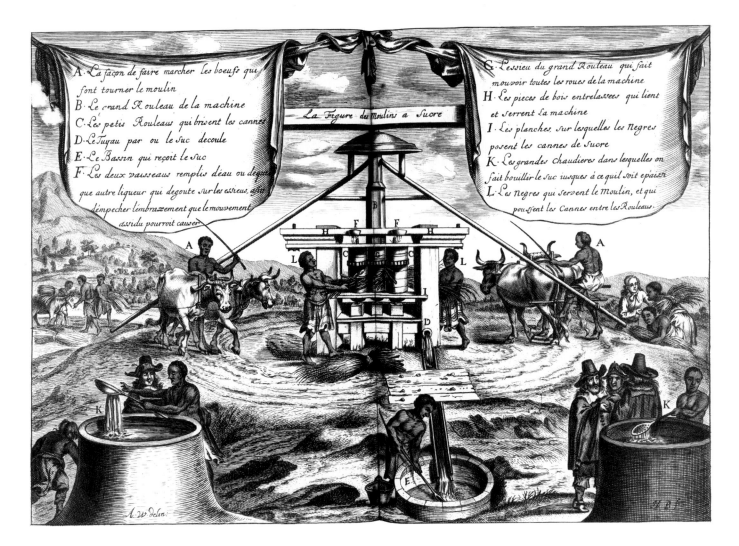

Cattle, working in tandem with African slaves, were widely used in the production of sugar, which was the chief colonial export in tropical regions of the New World.

In seafaring expeditions westward, the Greeks brought bull rituals to Iberia, and probably also cattle. The Celts brought dairy cattle. Thus when the Romans invaded Iberia in the second century B.C., both fighting cattle and the tamer milk-beef variety were already being herded.

On his second voyage in 1493, Columbus brought cattle from Spain and the Canary Islands to Santo Domingo (Hispaniola). The spotted, self-sufficient, all-purpose Castilian range cow formed the backbone of the ranching complex that the Iberians brought to the Americas. Fast and lean, Spanish range cattle would make a poor showing at the stockyards today, but they were the breed of choice in a variety of climates and against a variety of predators from the cougars of the upper Missouri, to the vampire bats and piranhas of the Venezuelan llanos, to the jaguars of the Río de la Plata. The most useful characteristic of Spanish cattle was their ability to "rustle" or find forage under difficult conditions. Long-legged and hardy, they could stand long walks between water holes. Good grazers, they made efficient use of feed, but the cows did not waste energy producing milk beyond the needs of their own calves.

Despite their preference for temperate savanna climates, in the early decades of the Encounter period Spanish cattle did very well even in the tropical Antilles. In the 1520s the chronicler Fernández de Oviedo reported many herds of five hundred on Hispaniola and even some of eight thousand.

In all tropical climates of the New World the chief export product throughout the colonial era was sugar. In sugar-producing areas, the most important use of cattle was to haul the cane from the fields and to power the sugar mills, and this continued to be important despite the importation of slaves from Africa. In tropical areas where cattle productivity was low, slaughter of cattle that could be used for work was forbidden. But where cattle yields were high, the export of hides often equaled or even exceeded that of sugar.

Cattle raising also dovetailed with another favorite Spanish industry: mining for precious metals. Brazilian *vaqueiros* marketing to mines at the headwaters of the São Francisco River organized long drives during the late seventeenth century. Since cattle drives had already been practiced for centuries in Iberia—although on a smaller scale—it is not surprising that these first Brazilian roundups and trail drives were similar to those which occurred later in Mexico, California, Texas, and the central Great Plains.

Early Importations to the Mainland

From Cuba in 1521 Gregorio Villalobos and Hernán Cortés brought cattle to Mexico for breeding purposes. Within a decade, scores of cattle ranches had been established in the central Mexican plains and valleys and even along the hot Gulf Coast. As supply went up, prices went down; the price of beef in Mexico City dropped 75 percent between 1532 and 1538.

The greatest herds developed in the savanna of northern Mexico—the southern-most extreme of the Great Plains. Nueva Vizcaya was colonized in 1562, but feral cattle propagating in great numbers had preceded European colonists. In 1586, two *estancias* of the region branded a total of 75,000 calves. Peralta reported about 1579 that some ranches in the north owned 150,000 head of cattle, and that 20,000 was considered a small herd.

Outside of Mexico, the only major site of importation was Brazil; in this case, the cattle originally came from Portuguese-held islands such as the Madeiras. In Brazil, two separate cattle-raising regions developed, one along the São Francisco River and one in the *sertão* south of São Paulo. The first cattle brought to Brazil were evidently imported to the Bahia area at the mouth of the São Francisco by Martim Afonso de Sousa between 1531 and 1533. Ships in 1549 brought, along with Brazil's first captain-general, Jesuit priests and more cattle directly from Iberia. The Jesuits soon established themselves as cattle breeders, foreshadowing efforts the Franciscan brothers were to make in North America two hundred years later. Soon Bahian cattlemen began to move southward along the coast, crossing the São Francisco River. By 1625, they were ready to advance westward into the valley of the São Francisco, an expansion further prompted by the Dutch, who captured

Mexico became the major supplier of cattle to the far-flung grasslands of the New World. After 1540, cattle imported from Mexico to Peru spread onto the Argentine pampas, which proved to be the most productive cattle-grazing land on earth. By 1600 some 45 ranches had been established on the llanos of northern South America, and by the 1680s the first cattle ranches were operating north of the Rio Grande in what is now Texas.

Recife and Pernambuco in 1630, forcing Portuguese refugees to flee southward along the coast.

What they found in the south was Brazil's second great grazing ground, the *sertão*. There, men of the *mameluco* class, of mixed Portuguese and Indian ancestry, became the first *vaqueiros* and introduced cattle from São Paulo northward into the upper São Francisco valley. By the beginning of the eighteenth century in Brazil, *fazendas* of the *sertão* and upper São Francisco could claim herds of as many as twenty thousand head.

Expansion from Mexico

While cattle imported to Brazil generally remained there, Mexico became the major cattle-exporting country of the hemisphere. The first significant grazing area south of Mexico is the Venezuelan llanos. In 1548 a Spanish stockman passed through the llanos with a small herd. By 1600, some forty-five ranches had been established in the tropical grasslands. Already during the period from 1620 to 1665 hides accounted for 75 percent of the total value of Venezuelan exports to Spain, the harvest of some 140,000 head of cattle that grazed the llanos. By the early nineteenth century, the cattle had increased to an estimated 4.5 million, only to be decimated during the Venezuelan War of Independence. Throughout the rest of the nineteenth and twentieth centuries, the Venezuelan cattle industry has undergone further fluctuations, with a nineteenth-century high of 12 million. The cattle population of the Venezuelan llanos is today only about 4 million head, a reflection of difficult environmental conditions and the steady deterioration of the plant productivity of the grasslands. Fences, wells, windmills, and tanks are currently being introduced into the region to foster the propagation of tropically adapted Zebu, Santa Gertrudis, Charbray, Brangus, and Beefmaster cattle. Zebu cattle relish kudzu, the fast-spreading subtropical forage vine (an ecological disaster elsewhere) introduced into the region during the 1950s.

From Mexico, herds of cattle were also taken to Peru, arriving in Lima before 1540. From Peru, they spread south into Chile, and from there they wandered into the Argentine pampas where the productivity of cattle has been the greatest in the world. By 1619, Governor Gondra of Buenos Aires reported herds of more than 240,000. In succeeding decades, cattle continued to push south toward Patagonia. Eyewitness reports of the size of the Argentine herds bring to mind the North American plains, "blackened by buffalo." By the end of the eighteenth century, these myriads of cattle produced an export of one million hides annually.

Mechanization and the importation of heat-tolerant breeds, such as the Zebu and Santa Gertrudis, have modified many of the details of ranching, but the roundup is a task that appears little changed from its ancient roots in Iberia. The work still demands the expertise of the vaquero and his horse.

The Spread of Cattle North of Mexico

It is very unlikely that cattle or horses became established in the region north and east of Mexico as a result of Spanish expeditions of Soto and Coronado, which penetrated the interior during the first half of the sixteenth century. The modern Mexican states of Chihuahua, Coahuila, Durango, and Zacatecas constituted the best cattle-raising region of New Spain, and from there New Mexico and Texas were initially stocked.

In 1598, seven thousand head of cattle were driven from northern Durango to New Mexico as part of Juan de Oñate's colonization. Settlements founded on the Rio Grande from 1659 to 1682 established the first ranches in what is now Texas. In the next century, cattle became common throughout the Mexican borderlands, and by the 1830s, cattle had even been driven from central California to northern Oregon.

Starting about 1685, extensive Spanish settlements began to be established in California, Arizona, and eastern Texas. Ranching there began with the Catholic missions, and during practically the entire Spanish colonial occupation, the largest herds were of mission cattle. The Texas longhorns were first developed on these missions as selected strains of the old Spanish-Mexican stock. Due to a lack of men to herd them, many cattle became feral, beginning in south-central Mexico in the sixteenth century and spreading over the next hundred years to Texas and New Mexico. "Black cattle" continued to be listed as a game species in Texas until their extirpation shortly after World War II.

The era of cattle driving on the Great Plains began shortly after the Civil War, but the range remained open for only another forty years. The closing of the range at the turn of the twentieth century put an end to long cattle drives and fundamentally altered the ecology of ranching in North America. Prior to 1884, no purebred cattle, barbed wire fences, or windmills existed in northern Mexico. While Mormon colonists in Mexico probably were the first to use windmills and barbed wire, their widespread acceptance was promoted in the region by large landowners, such as George Hearst, owner of a million-acre ranch and one of the first to stock Herefords.

Between 1910 and 1923, during the period of the Mexican Revolution, the range cattle business in northern Mexico effectively came to an end. With rampant economic and social instability, soldiers and bandits ate the cattle, while drought and ecological degradation of pastureland thinned the yield. In desperation the ranchers shipped their stock out to the United States, where heavy demand fueled by World War I provided an insatiable market. All this set the stage for the present era, in which the ranges have been restocked with graded cattle and purebreds (chiefly Hereford whitefaces), whose purity of blood has been preserved by extensive use of barbed wire fences.

In dusty drives across the open range, cowboys herded longhorn cattle northward through the Great Plains from Texas to the green pastures of the Dakotas and Montana or to railheads in Kansas. Although the trail drive period lasted only 40 years, it gave rise to many legends of the "wild West." *The Stampede* is one of many works by Frederic Remington, whose paintings and sculptures immortalize this brief but very colorful period in American history.

Sheep and Goats

Various species of wild sheep were once widely distributed in the Eastern and Western Hemispheres. The domestic sheep *(Ovis aries)* is the smallest herding animal associated with ranching, and, along with the goat, it probably was the first hoofed species to be domesticated. Like goats and cattle, sheep are cud-chewing ruminants who possess no upper incisors, so they crop grass closely and make very efficient use of what they consume. Sheep can survive on much drier, scantier forage than horses or cattle.

Except in the drier and hillier parts of the New World, cattle became the primary ranch stock; yet in Renaissance Iberia sheepherding predominated. Range sheep resembling the Spanish churros were probably first bred in southwestern Asia and brought to Iberia some two thousand years ago. Today they are found in these two areas and—a surviving remnant of once-huge Mexican herds—in New Mexico. Long-legged like the wild mouflons, churros have thick, shaggy underfur which yields a long-staple wool that mats easily.

History, husbandry, and geography conspired to bring another breed—the wooly merinos—late to Iberia: developed by the Romans, later exported from Italy to Africa, they were finally brought to Spain by the Moors near the end of the twelfth century. So important were the merinos to the Renaissance Spanish economy that for centuries the export of live merinos from Spain or its territories was strictly forbidden. The sheep first taken to the New World by the conquistadores therefore were not "woollies" but shaggy churros. This proved a good thing. Although despised in Spain, churros adapted much more readily to the semiarid pastures of the New World. Range-hardy, they endured long drives to market without becoming footsore. Able to substitute morning dew and succulent plants for drinking water, churros could withstand drought better than the inbred merinos. While merino herding demanded seasonal drives to follow tender green pasture, churros could

Nuestra Senora de la Soledad in California was one of many missions that the Catholic Church began to establish in the 17th century in Texas, Arizona, and California. Though their primary purpose was to convert Indians, the padres also taught the Indians how to handle livestock and in so doing extended Iberian-style ranching in North America.

survive on green grass or brown. Although meager, churro wool was well suited to New World hand-processing and weaving, and its meat was of good quality.

Since tropical climates and hot, wet lowlands are ecologically far removed from the natural habitat of *Ovis aries*, upon their arrival in the Antilles in 1493 sheep did not undergo the population explosion exhibited by cattle and pigs. As chronicler Bernabé Cobo noted, lands not good for men were also unsuited for sheep. Yet some survived there and were available for shipment to the mainland during the Encounter period. Cortés imported Caribbean sheep to the dry, hilly parts of central Mexico, and in the 1520s Antonio de Mendoza used his influence to import Castilian merinos for breeding, the first to arrive in the Western Hemisphere.

Peru, even more than highland Mexico, was a land made for sheep. One Captain Salamanca imported them to Peru sometime between 1525 and 1527, and soon sheep were breeding and grazing in the high meadows alongside llamas and cattle. By 1571, the viceroyalty of Peru possessed approximately seventy wool mills; thirty years later, they were producing surplus woolens for trade. From Peru, following

A flock of 20th-century sheep engulfs a street in the town of Ushuaia, Tierra del Fuego (left), testimony to the vigor of *Ovis aries*, once it found a niche in the Western Hemisphere. Sheep are not adapted to the hot lowland climate that prevails in the Antilles but can survive on meager forage in areas too arid or too cold to support other kinds of livestock.

the same transmontane routes as cattle and horses, sheep spread south to Chile and southeast to Argentina. Predictably, the flocks did exceedingly well in dry, mountainous Chile; in 1614 the district of Santiago alone contained 623,825 sheep, which produced 223,944 lambs annually. Sheep ranching also became established in Tucumán in northern Argentina, where many sheep existed by 1600; eventually, after southern Argentine natives took up herding, the dry plains of Patagonia also became a major sheep-raising center.

In North America, Juan de Oñate brought more than four thousand head of shaggy sheep into New Mexico, the foundation of the modern Navajo-churro breed. In the nineteenth century, the Spanish government finally began to permit the exportation of merino sheep to non-Spanish territories. The first successful importation of merinos from Spain directly to the United States occurred in 1801. Bred in Pennsylvania and Ohio, the Delaine merino produced prodigious amounts of excellent wool. After the coming of the transcontinental railroad, ranchers began to ship merino rams west to improve the fleece of the churro. This crossbreeding began a dramatic shift in the nature of sheep culture in the western United States from mutton to wool production. Recently, the University of New Mexico in cooperation with the Navajo Tribal Council has begun a program to reestablish a purebred line of Navajo-churro sheep on New Mexico reservations, thus ensuring the future availability of its unique long-staple wool for Navajo weavers and preserving an ancient and genetically unique breed of sheep.

Goats are often called the poor man's cow, because nannies of *Capra hircus* produce large amounts of rich milk, which can be drunk, fermented into koumiss, or made into yogurt, butter, or cheese. While a few goat breeds have been developed to produce hair (mohair and angora) or fine leather (chamois), the species does not compare with the sheep in production of either meat or wool.

The physique, physiology, and habitat preferences of goats also differ from those of sheep. Goats prefer rugged mountain country and graze in meadows below the snow line. The dietary eclecticism of goats is legendary: while they graze on grasses, they also eat flowers, herbs, sedges, lichens, mosses, the shoots of young pine trees, the branches and leaves of shrubs, and the bark and leaves of trees. They seek refuge by climbing steep crags and will climb trees or farm buildings to reach food.

Goats came to the New World with the conquistadores and by 1600 could be found in large numbers wherever other grazing livestock were plentiful. In rocky terrain under cool climatic conditions, they often became feral. One Spanish colonist in Puerto Rico observed, "Goates live . . . securely, because they love cliffes of Rocks, or the tops of Hils, and therefore they are out of the ordinarie haunt of the murderous [feral] dogs." Goats also became feral on offshore Chilean islands.

Over the centuries goats have been too much of a good thing in certain areas of the tropical New World. For example, in the hill country surrounding the Venezuelan llanos, incessant and close grazing by goats has destroyed ground cover and speeded up erosion of fragile tropical soil.

Hogs

The hog (*Sus scrofa*) is the one species of hoofed Eurasian mammal imported to the New World during the Encounter period that is not associated in the American mind with ranching. In medieval Iberia, however, and elsewhere, hogs were kept as dietary delicacies and marks of wealth and social rank, as the legends and heraldry of the British Isles amply illustrate. The Romans concurred with the Celts of Gaul in honoring the hog, for it was included in that most solemn of all Roman sacrificial offerings, the *suovetaurilia,* whose very name is a compound that defines the hoofed mammals essential to a Roman villa or Spanish ranch: hog, sheep, and bull.

The Eurasian hog is adaptable, omnivorous, and fecund—in short, a perfect colonist. Less picky than its human masters about diet, immediately upon introduction to the Caribbean in 1493, hogs settled down to the business of helping to strip the islands of their native biota. Some pigs soon escaped and in the Antillean forests they exhibited near-logarithmic population growth. In 1514, Diego Velázquez de Cuéllar reported to the Spanish king that the two dozen pigs he had brought to Cuba in 1498 had increased to thirty thousand. This is understandable in view of the reproductive capabilities of *Sus scrofa,* whose sows can produce three litters of

Merino rams (opposite, top) belong to an ancient breed of sheep developed by the Romans and brought to Spain by the Moors in the 12th century. They were so prized for their wool in Renaissance Spain that for centuries their export was banned. At the urging of Spanish colonial administrator Antonio de Mendoza, the first Merinos were brought to the New World in the 1520s. Not until 1801 did Spain grant the importation of Merino sheep to the United States. For negotiating the agreement, David Humphreys garnered a citation from the Massachusetts Society for Promoting Agriculture (above).

three to twelve young per year, resulting in a reproductive rate about six times that of cattle or sheep and twelve times that of horses.

The flora of every island anywhere on which swine have ever been feral has been fundamentally altered by their presence. In the early decades of Spanish colonization, hogs were taken on ships with the idea that pairs were to be deposited on uninhabited islands to provide a source of familiar food for future European visitors. "If the horse was of real significance in the Conquest," Spanish historian Carlos Pereyra has judged, "the hog was of greater importance and contributed to a degree that defies exaggeration." Although their saddlebags were packed with cakes of Caribbean cassava, which Cortés's men substituted for bread in wheatless tropical territories, they still longed for their familiar diet, whose staples were wheat bread, wine, olive oil, and beef or pork. History may beguile us with a vision of the bold conquistador riding into the unknown forest in burnished morion and breastplate, but behind him always followed a motley commissariat on the hoof. Herded along by slaves came droves of swine, cattle, or goats, all of which had been bred in the Antilles.

The narrow dietary preferences shown by European immigrants of all nationalities and their slowness to learn from American natives are difficult to understand. Yet in some cases—notably the near-total starvation in the year 1535–36 of Pedro de Mendoza's first colony at Buenos Aires—the prejudicial preference of Europeans for cattle and hogs also saved the herds. Although some historians interpret the record otherwise, it appears that Mendoza (who was later brought to trial for this decision) kept back at least a few pigs, cattle, and horses in continuance of the Spanish policy of island and range stocking, even when, as Francisco de Villalta reported: "Such was the necessity and such the hunger they endured that it was a horror to tell. Some kept their dead companion around for three or four days, that they themselves might take his food ration and so survive; it happened that others, seeing themselves so hungry, ate human flesh. . . . Two men, hanged for their crimes, were eaten from the waist down."

The crime for which the two men were hanged, it should be noted, was eating a cow. Other expeditions endured less severe hunger but followed the same policies.

Because the hog was never sanctified by Hollywood, most Americans do not appreciate its importance in the New World. On the one hand, feral swine had devastating effects on native flora and fauna; on the other, they provided abundant, familiar food for Old World immigrants.

In 1531, Gonzalo Pizarro brought pigs to Peru, and after the conquest, pork became the first European meat to be sold in appreciable quantities in Lima.

While the Spaniards kept careful track of individual horses, rarely letting them stray, this was not the case with pigs, and it is not at all unlikely that the herd of pigs brought from Florida to Arkansas by Soto in 1539 provided the foundation for feral populations of hogs in North America. Later importations, notably by the Franciscan friars who founded missions in Texas, probably added to the gene pool in the wild. It did not take many generations for the fat, docile Spanish porker to revert to the wild hog hunted in Europe by brave men and dogs from Roman times onward. Fast, tough, lean, and self-sufficient, the American razorback still inhabits brush country in the wetter parts of the southern United States from Florida through the Carolinas to Arkansas and parts of Texas and is listed as a game animal in all of those states.

Asses

While swine, cattle, sheep, and goats all belong to the order Artiodactyla, the so-called cloven-hoofed mammals, asses *(Equus asinus)* and horses *(Equus caballus)* belong to the order Perissodactyla and bear but a single, solid hoof at the end of each leg. Asses and horses possess both upper and lower incisors; they crop grass coarsely and digest it relatively inefficiently, as they do not ruminate.

Humankind's association with the ass species is ancient, spanning some five thousand years. Wild asses *(Equus asinus africanus)* once roamed throughout the flat, rocky, and dry areas of East Africa and the Arabian Peninsula. It is not known for certain whether asses were first domesticated in Africa or in Arabia. By Roman times, wild asses captured in Arabia were frequently shipped west, where they had already become associated with the Iberian ranch life-style. With the fall of the empire and the rise of Christianity, they also acquired another association, with the ecclesiastical segment of a Catholic society.

To sit upon an ass is not the same as to sit upon a horse. Because a donkey's back is at once narrower, bonier, and proportionally longer than that of a horse, and because the animal as a whole is smaller, people ride asses not by sitting astride their backs but by balancing upon the much more solid croup. Of particular interest are Egyptian, Babylonian, and Assyrian artworks from the early eighth century B.C. that show warriors sitting donkey-style upon horses, a transitional technique.

After people learned how to ride and shoot from astride the back of a galloping horse, and after the invention of the light, spoke-wheeled chariot, horses came to be preferred over asses for chariotry and for riding. Then the status of the donkey declined, and it came to be used chiefly by the lower classes for packing loads, drawing carts, and pushing or pulling primitive machinery such as grindstones and pumps. The Romans continued the tradition of using both mules and donkeys for pack animals. No instance of cultural continuity more vividly unites the pastoral life of the Old and New Worlds than the use of the ass in the olive mill. In the Roman Empire, as later in Iberia and in the Americas, this was the donkey's most common task. Among the items of equipment needed for a Roman olive yard, Cato specifies manure hampers and baskets, three packsaddles, three back pads, and a donkey mill, while the farm is to be powered by three pack asses to carry manure and one ass to turn the mill. More than a thousand years after the learned Roman wrote, the olive orchards of Spain were still similarly equipped and powered. When,

seven hundred years later, in the 1760s, Franciscan friars founded missions along the camino real of southern California, they produced olive oil in exactly the same manner.

In ancient times, asses were valued chiefly as a means to beget mules—by mating a jack (the male of the ass species) to a mare (the female of the horse species). Genetically the horse and ass are similar enough that their matings produce live offspring, but sufficiently dissimilar that the offspring are themselves sterile. The "compatible dissimilarity" of each mule's genetic complement produces a biochemical serendipity called hybrid vigor, through which mules are stronger, smarter, and more enduring than either parent species. In ancient times mules wore fancy harness and pulled the solid-wheeled war chariots. They were also regarded—in preference not only to the ass but also to the horse—as the proper mount for noblemen.

Two thousand years later, the conquistadores brought donkeys to the New World. There too, many large mule ranches sprang up, usually in subtropical zones where the strong and disease-resistant mules were valued as relatively speedy alternatives to oxen for the deep plowing necessary in the production of cash crops such as corn, sorghum, cotton, and tobacco.

An 1879 photograph of Zuni Indians loading burros represents a tableau that was widespread in the Americas by the 19th century. *Equus asinus,* known variously in the New World as donkey, burro, and ass, was used here as it had been in the Old World—for transportation, milling, packing, and producing mules.

Horses

Again and again in European chronicles of the Encounter period echoes the sentiment "after God, we owe the victory to the horses." Of all the livestock brought to the New World in that era, only the horse had no surviving North American relatives; yet of all the hoofed domesticates, only the horse species itself, ten thousand years before, had actually existed here. With the coming of Paleo-Indian hunters and with the changes in climate and flora associated with the terminal Pleistocene megafaunal extinction, endemic American horses also became extinct. The horse *(Equus caballus)* survived, however, on the Siberian side of the Bering Strait, and ranged through all the steppe and grassland regions of Asia and Europe.

From the wild horse population of the Volga basin in eastern Europe were captured, some six thousand years ago, the first ancestors of the domestic horse. During the twenty-five hundred years following its domestication, *Equus caballus* came to have an important role in human culture in that region and in the Anatolian, Near Eastern, and African civilizations to the south. While the earliest use of horses was for draft and charioteering, by the eighth century B.C. steppe nomads had invented horseback riding and with it mounted bowmanship and light cavalry. From migration and interaction with the Celts to the west, the Mongols to the east, and the Persians to the south, the knowledge of lance horsemanship (invented in the steppe but later characteristic of medieval and Renaissance Europe) developed and passed westward to Iberia.

Iberian Horses

It is upon the sturdy, shaggy, full-bodied mares native to Iberia that all Iberian and American breeds of horses are founded. The single most important event in the history of Iberian horse breeding was the invasion by Roman legions and their allies in the late second century B.C. The Romans brought their stallions—all of Oriental strains native to areas far to the east and south—to a territory where such horses had never before set hoof.

Within a century of their arrival, legionnaires were settling in coastal Iberian towns and building amenities to their taste, including stadia where, as in Rome, races and games could be held. To breed horses for sport and warfare, the Romans used their Oriental stallions on the indigenous Iberian mares. The results of this, the world's first experiment in crossbreeding domestic horses, were notably successful. The cross unexpectedly resulted in the release of four new traits that today are regarded as typical of American horses: short speed, large size, strongly contrasting coat patterns, and gaitedness.

Spanish horses became known as the finest in the world for combat and noble display. Selective breeding soon produced three main Iberian types. The first of these was the proto-Andalusian, variously termed the Villano or Garraño. These substantial trotting and galloping horses were used for war, mounted games, and racing. Close-coupled and round-bodied, the best specimens possessed a high-arched neck. They typically possessed a short, broad head with a straight, undulating, or arched profile, topped by wide-based, rounded ears. They came in all colors and patterns. The second was a gaited type, the Jinete, Ginete, or Jennet, which was small but substantial, with a short back, rounded croup, and arched neck typically garnished with a full, wavy mane. The third Iberian breed was the Gallego ("Gallic horse"), a smaller, coarser type, more or less gaited, and affordable by the peasantry.

During the second century B.C., Roman allies, the *cataphractarii* or heavy-armored lance horsemen, brought cavalry to Spain. By A.D. 711, when most of Europe had been Christianized, this knightly form of mounted horsemanship had become the established mode for nobles in what had once been Roman Gaul. The date marks the invasion of Spain by the Islamic Moors, who crossed the Strait of Gibraltar in boats and, mounting their attack from beachheads in Granada, swept swiftly northward to occupy Zaragoza and Barcelona, then crossed the Pyrenees to Narbonne and Arles in southern France, where they were finally stopped by the (stirrupless) armored lancers of Charles Martel at Poitiers in A.D. 732. Southward thrusts by Charles's son Pépin III and his grandson Charlemagne established a Christian-Moorish frontier that was to persist, with near-constant skirmishing, for most of the next millennium. Nor did the Christian-Moorish conflict end in Iberia until the eve of Columbus's voyage; Ferdinand and Isabella triumphantly entered the city of Granada, lost to the Moors 781 years earlier, on 2 January 1492.

Thus for nearly eight hundred years the Iberian Peninsula served as testing ground for advancements in military technology and its horse-powered armamentarium. Christian knights passed from armor largely of mail to armor largely of plate, while Christian breeders of Garraño-type chargers in Galicia and Aragon strove to produce larger mounts. About the year 1100, Christian monks of the Carthusian order began to breed horses and after 1450 became the first to keep written pedigree records. After 1492, Andalusians were also bred at the royal stud at Córdoba in Granada. At the same time, Spanish Moors continued to value their near-purebred Barbs, which became the foundation of the Iberian population of feral Sorraia horses, a swift, agile breed suited to the charge-and-wheel tactics of the Moorish light-armored bowmen and saboteurs.

Spanish Horsemanship Comes to the New World

Soldier and historian Bernal Díaz del Castillo, a conquistador who served under Cortés, recorded the name, pedigree, color, sex, and qualities of every one of the horses who came to Mexico in 1519. Such recognition was not misplaced. The first of their species to set hoof on the North American continent in ten thousand years, all had been bred in the Caribbean from stock originally brought by Columbus on his second voyage. Later, Cortés imported more horses from the islands to aid in his military exploits, and other conquistadores followed his example. Yet despite the early dates of these expeditions, none of them appear to have seeded any part of the Americas with the bloodstock that would later populate the North American plains, the Venezuelan llanos, and the Argentine pampas with thousands of head of feral mustangs, *llaneros,* and *baguales.*

America's wild horse populations descend, first, from the Caribbean herds of Andalusian ancestry already mentioned, which were exported from there to Mexico, Nicaragua, and Panama beginning in the second decade of the sixteenth century. By 1532, when Francisco Pizarro fitted his expedition to Peru, horses in his train came from each of these areas. Between 1532 and 1538, despite governmental red tape, Pizarro also imported a few horses directly to Peru from Spain. From this bloodstock in the lush mountainous valleys of Peru, tough, hardy, fleet horses were quickly produced in great numbers. Juan de Arjolas imported horses to Paraguay in 1537, while Pedro de Valdivia first imported horses to Chile in 1541, the stock in both cases having been obtained in the Charcas region of southern Peru. The

For centuries before Spain's conquest of the New World, Iberians had been breeding superior horses and honing horse-powered military techniques. Spanish cavalrymen were formidable adversaries in the New World. The soldiers, however, recognized the source of their invincibility. "After God, we owe the victory to the horses" was a standard refrain in European accounts of the conquest.

herds of Bolivia, Chile, Paraguay, Argentina, and much of Brazil and Uruguay largely descend from Peruvian stock.

In the same year that the Spaniard Pizarro set out for Peru, the Portuguese captain Martim Afonso de Sousa brought horses to the coastal reaches of the São Francisco River of Brazil, but due to the ecological conditions of that region, the spread of horses from there was slow. Fifty years passed before Jesuit missionaries could bring Brazilian horses with them down the coast to Uruguay.

While in the tropical zones of the Caribbean, Central America, Venezuela, and Brazil the horse was somewhat slow to propagate, in the pampas of the Río de la Plata the horse found an ideal habitat. The species was brought to the Tucumán region of Argentina in 1542 by Diego de Rojas. The tale of the founding of the feral *baguales* of the Argentine pampas from stock abandoned by Pedro de Mendoza in 1541 is thus not the full story, but it is certainly the most colorful one. Mendoza is said to have preserved five mares and seven stallions alive despite the starvation of his colonists and then to have set these horses free to propagate in the pampas. They were soon joined by feral stock from Tucumán and within fifteen years by horses escaping through Andean passes from Chile. When the first permanent European population settled Buenos Aires in 1580, they found that enormous herds of horses had preceded them onto the grasslands. At the beginning of the seventeenth century, Vazquez de Espinosa wrote with awe of the pampas "covered with escaped mares and horses in such numbers that when they go anywhere they look like woods from a distance."

While the heartland of the South American horse lies in Peru, that of the mustang of the North American West lies in Mexico. Horses were first brought to Mexico for purposes of breeding by Antonio de Mendoza in 1535, and due to this importation and to the northward expansion of the colony into the grasslands of Sonora, by 1550 mounts were plentiful. Fifty years later, countless herds of mustangs were running 250 miles to the northwest, in Durango. In succeeding decades, horses continued to expand northward into the Great Plains, stopping only where habitat

was grossly unsuitable or physical barriers intervened. The colonization of New Mexico brought more horses north, beginning with the expedition of Agustín Rodríguez in 1581, followed by the larger one of Juan de Oñate in 1598. During the next three centuries, Santa Fe became the point from which most horses were disseminated by Spanish settlement, by trade, by Indians escaping from slavery, and by capture by unconquered tribes. It appears likely that captive Utes had already obtained knowledge of horses before 1641 and that Utes escaping from Spanish peonage first brought horses north of the Colorado River. By the 1650s Utes were using packhorses, although they did not yet ride them. Utes acquired more horses in the Pueblo Revolt of 1680, and this gain resulted in the rapid dispersion of horses to their neighbors to the north and east. To the west, between 1683 and 1698 Eusebio Kino established extensive stock ranching throughout the Papago and Pima country south of the Gila River. By 1690, herds of feral horses already roamed the Llano Estacado of New Mexico and Texas. They had reached the central Great Plains by 1720, the Great Basin and the upper reaches of the Missouri by 1730, and the northern Great Plains in the United States and Canada by 1750. By 1777, Antonio Morfi reported that the Rio Grande area in what is now Texas contained so many horses that "their trails make the country, utterly uninhabited by people, look as if it were the most populated in the world."

Horses reached California somewhat later, primarily through the Jesuit and Franciscan missions. By the time of the Revolution in the American colonies on the opposite coast of the continent, Franciscan missions along the camino real of California had brought horses as far north as Oregon.

While most importations of horses to the New World brought them from Iberia to regions south and west of the Mississippi River, Spanish horses also came to

Florida and the Carolinas at a very early date. The first came with Ponce de León in 1521, followed soon by other expeditions, including that of Hernando de Soto, who may have brought as many as two hundred to Florida in 1539, some of which certainly accompanied him on his fatal expedition to the Mississippi in 1542. However, it was Pedro Menéndez de Avilés, the founder of Saint Augustine, who brought the first breeding herds of horses to Florida in 1565 and to the Carolinas the following year. From that stable base, over the next half century Franciscan missionaries brought horses as far north as Georgia and Virginia, though by that time English thoroughbreds had also already been imported to the Old Dominion and to New England. The fierce Natchez, Chickasaw, and Choctaw tribes slowed Spanish penetration into the regions of modern Alabama and Mississippi. William Bartram, writing in 1789, reported that the Choctaws, who had earlier migrated from New Mexico across the Mississippi, "long since the Spanish invasion and conquest of Mexico . . . brought with them across the river those fine horses called the Chickasaw and Choctaw breeds . . . [while] the Seminole horses, or those beautiful creatures bred amongst the Lower Creeks, which are of the Andalusian breed, were introduced by the Spaniards at St. Augustine."

Only in the seventeenth century were the English, French, and Dutch able to import breeding herds of horses to the New World. Beginning in 1629, Dutch colonists began importing horses to their holdings in Brazil, while English importations to the thirteen colonies had begun earlier in the same decade. Dutch and Flemish drafters did not arrive in New England and the northern Shenandoah and Ohio valleys for another forty years, nor French saddlers and drafters to Canadian settlements. During the latter half of the seventeenth century and throughout the

The cowboy traditions of the New World were remarkably similar, from Tierra del Fuego to California.

eighteenth, by far the most popular riding horse east of the Mississippi was the English-Irish Hobby, now an extinct breed. These animals are the stock from which derive such familiar and important breeds as the Morgan, American Standardbred, Tennessee Walking Horse, Quarter Horse, and American Saddlebred, but the majority of the horses of the New World—North, Central, and South America, as well as the Caribbean—owe their ancestry to the horses of Spain.

Conclusion

The importation to the Western Hemisphere of these six species of hoofed mammals—cattle, sheep, goats, hogs, asses, and horses—fundamentally changed the ecology of the hemisphere. Because of their relatively large body sizes and herding habits, their mere physical presence had an immediate, visible effect upon areas where they were introduced. The ability of even the least fecund and most fragile hoofed domesticate to adapt to New World conditions of diet and climate is remarkable and somewhat surprising in view of the long isolation of North America from Eurasian biotic elements. The adaptation of these six species was, however, facilitated by the coimportation and rapid, wide spread of European and Asian forage plants and the vigilant elimination over the centuries of "varmint" species—that is, competitors and predators belonging to the native fauna—by European colonists. The only imported form that was able to out-compete similar New World species without human help was the hog. Goats and sheep, as well as asses, coexisted with mountain sheep *(Ovis* spp), mountain goats *(Oreamnos americanus),* antelopes *(Antilocapra americana),* and peccaries *(Tayassu* spp) in North America and with domesticated native llamas *(Lama glama)* and alpacas *(Lama pacos)* in South America, but imported species did not eliminate the natives. Feral cattle in Mexico and Texas existed on the fringes of the range of the buffalo *(Bison bison),* but the buffalo were exterminated only by hide-hunters two centuries after the introduction of cattle.

Horses, which had existed in the Americas during the Pleistocene, were evidently able to reassume their old ecological niche without much disturbance of either the native flora or fauna. Interestingly, many ranchers eventually came to regard feral horses and burros as pests, since like the native viscacha *(Lagostomus maximus)* of the Argentine pampas and prairie dog *(Cynomys* spp) of the Great Plains, horses eat grass and thus compete with cattle. Nor was the success of the cloven-hoofed imports without cost to the settled native peoples, whose plantations and seed stocks they rooted up, overran, and ate, and whose cultures and traditions were forever altered through the necessity imposed upon them to learn about and adapt to the presence of these new animals. Of all the imported species discussed in this essay, the horse—itself a native American—best suited and best served the Indians and was culturally assimilated and greatly appreciated by many tribes from Patagonia to Canada.

Of all the European livestock transplanted to the New World, the horse, itself a former native of the Americas, proved the most compatible with the environment and the native peoples.

110

Pleasure, Profit, and Satiation

Sidney W. Mintz

The conquest of the New World, beginning in 1492, set in motion complex processes of cultural interpenetration and population mixture. The seizure and control of the Americas became so important to Europe economically and politically that it had the long-term consequence of altering European interests worldwide. Before 1492, Europe's center was the Mediterranean Sea—its orientation was *thalassic*. After 1492, Europe's orientation shifted radically; it became centered around the Atlantic Ocean and, much later, around the Pacific Ocean as well. Its orientation had become *oceanic*.

During this global alteration in the European focus of energy and interest, and for the first time in human history, *planetary* empires, spanning whole oceans, were created (Konetzke 1946). As part of the transformation, the production and consumption of new foods, both animal and vegetable, were greatly stimulated on both sides of the Atlantic. Hundreds of useful domesticated plants and animals still unknown to the Europeans existed in the outside world at the time. Even before 1492, European plants and animals consisted largely of borrowings from Eurasia and Africa. This was the dawning era of collecting—the first museums of natural history, botanical gardens, and catalogs of flora and fauna—as conquerors and explorers discovered the world and sent or brought back what was new to them.

As part of the shift of the commercial center of gravity from the Mediterranean to the Atlantic, the locales of production of many commodities of increasing interest to European consumers were moved from the Old World to the Americas. The New World was defined over time as a frontier—a fluid (and often violent) sphere of expanding European power and interest, as well as a locus of rivalry among different European groups. As such, the Americas became an immense arena of conflict and enterprise.

The transatlantic production of commodities desired in Europe required great quantities of human effort, of labor. Except in highland Mexico and the Andean

mid-highlands, where efficient pre-Columbian horticulture and animal husbandry sustained vast populations, the indigenous Americans could never satisfy the insatiable demands for labor created by pioneering conquerors and colonists. This shortage fits with the idea of the frontier. Where population is sparse, rivalry involves control over space. If labor is absent or can flee, then space must be controlled, and controllable labor must be brought from somewhere else. Hence the saga of postconquest production in the Americas meant work, workers, and worker control. Much of the technology needed by European enterprise, such as that for processing agricultural commodities, had been invented elsewhere. Much of the labor would also come from elsewhere. Labor and technology, partly imported,

also changed form to meet new conditions; many features were improvised and added.

The movement and redeployment of domesticated plants and animals between New World and Old was one of the most important consequences of conquest and cultural interpenetration. Some items won a place in the evolving system of world trade and production. Many were native to the New World, such as potatoes and maize. Others, of Old World origin, acquired additional meanings, once they reached the New.

Among the commodities whose production was launched upon new paths after the discovery was what we call sugar, or sucrose ($C_{12}H_{22}O_{11}$). This sweet substance can be extracted from several plants, including the sugar maple tree, sugar beet, sugar palm, sweet sorghum, and—for our purposes here, most importantly—from

The *Ceres*, sailing for Liverpool with a cargo of sugar and coffee in 1804, was part of the new economic order set in motion by Columbus. Before 1492, European economic interests were centered around the Mediterranean. After 1492, markets and empires unfurled across the Atlantic and Pacific until they spanned the globe.

the sugarcane (*Saccharum officinarum* and other species). Here we are concerned with the sugarcane and cane sugar—its production, its consumption, and its meanings—as it became part of the Columbian saga in the New World. Over time sugar has become so commonplace, necessary, and inexpensive that we can hardly imagine living without it. Yet because of its very ordinariness, today we pay hardly any attention to it. To tell its story, we must glance at the past of this strange, at one time even exotic, food.

The Human Liking for Sweetness

Without the human liking for the taste of sweetness, sugar never could have acquired its past and present importance. If not universal, that liking is at least extremely widespread. Science has not succeeded entirely in explaining the seemingly universal human liking for the sweet taste. Human beings also like sour, bitter, salty, and other tastes. They can even learn to like such unusual tastes as that of hot peppers; of rotting food, such as cheese; or even of highly hazardous foods, such as mushrooms or the Japanese blowfish, fugu. Yet sweetness occupies a privileged place in the spectrum of human tastes. We know of no people who, once having eaten sweet foods, rejected them entirely. When such rejections have occurred, they have been linked to dieting or religious beliefs, to moral or self-improvement impulses of some kind—to a rejection of something *already* considered desirable.

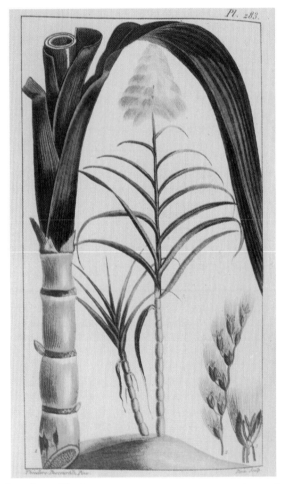

Most authorities believe that, during the history of the primates, the taste of sweetness served as a signal that certain foods were edible. Perhaps sweetness played a part in hominid evolution, because the sweet taste typified foods our primate ancestors could safely eat. Whatever the case, human beings certainly appear to have a predisposition toward the sweet taste—to favor it above other tastes.

Before the processing of sucrose from plants into granular sugars had been developed, honey was the commonest of all sweeteners. A Stone Age cave painting in Bicorp, Spain, showing people stealing honey from a remote hive, surrounded by angry bees, attests to this ancient liking. In the West, only after the appearance of partly crystallized sugar did honey begin to be supplanted as the sweetest of sweet foods.

No people who have partaken of sugar have been known to forego it, a factor that was integral to the dispersion of sugarcane from New Guinea, where it was first domesticated ten or twelve thousand years ago, to all parts of the world.

Most of the sugar in honey is not sucrose but invert sugar, that is, levulose (fruit sugar) and dextrose (grape sugar). Though proportions are now changing, most sweet foods eaten in the world today are sweetened by sucrose, not other sugars. Sucrose is produced in green plants by photosynthesis in a complex series of reactions in which the energy of sunlight is absorbed by the chlorophyll of the leaves to convert carbon dioxide from the air and water from the soil into organic compounds, liberating oxygen in the process. Manufacture of sucrose and other carbohydrates by green plants is a vital part of the architecture of life on earth. Since these plants are food for much of the animal world, plants and animals stand in a strikingly interdependent relationship. The remarkable capacity of green plants to produce sugars and liberate oxygen is the obverse of human chemistry. In effect, we produce carbon dioxide and consume sugars; while green plants give off oxygen and produce sugars, and consume carbon dioxide.

Sugarcane and the technology of sucrose extraction were brought to Europe by the Moors, and the Mediterranean and Atlantic islands were important sugar-producing areas until they were eclipsed by the Americas. Sicilian processing is illustrated about 1600 (top right). Over the years, cane sugar has had its rivals: British colonists learned how to make maple sugar from the Indians (left); after 1830 the sugar beet (bottom right) became a competitive source of sucrose.

Hence it cannot really be said that we humans *manufacture* sugar; we *extract* sucrose. While concentrating it and removing impurities, we change it to other states by a series of steps: separating from the plant fibers the juice containing the sucrose; cleaning the juice by adding substances to which foreign matter will adhere, then removing them; heating the liquid to reduce its volume and increase its density; and finally refining the syrup to produce a liquid or a solid sugar. Familiar granular white sugar is as pure chemically as anything we eat.

Sugarcane

Before about 1830, sugarcane was the most important sucrose-carrying plant used by human beings. It had been used to make partially crystallized sugar for at least fifteen hundred years. It still rules the world market for sucrose, though it has experienced periods of decline and has powerful rivals. The sugar beet is the other commercially important, worldwide source of sucrose. Sugar was extracted experimentally from the beet by the mid-eighteenth century, but beet sugar did not become commercially and economically practical until around 1830. Its importance in the New World is quite recent.

The story of sugarcane—and of cane sugar—is different. The sugarcane was first domesticated ten or twelve thousand years ago in New Guinea, only then diffusing to mainland Asia. Cane juice was probably not used to produce a solid substance until near the beginning of the Christian era. Between about 350 B.C. and A.D. 350, people succeeded in using controlled heat to turn the juice of the sugarcane into a taffy-like, partly crystalline solid—the first "sugar." This probably happened in Indo-Persian Khūzestān. From there, sugar and technical knowledge about its fabrication began to spread in every direction. It was known in China at a very early time. Though not mentioned in the Bible, sugar may have been known to ancient Greece and Rome (Forbes 1966). From the Middle East, it also spread westward, probably reaching the Levant and Egypt before the end of the seventh century A.D., then Cyprus (ca. 700), Morocco (ca. 709), Crete (ca. 818), and Sicily (ca. 827).

Sugar in Europe

The history of sugar production in the West can be divided into three stages or phases: the Mediterranean industry, from about 700 to about 1600; the Atlantic industry, from about 1450 until 1680; and the American industry, beginning in the sixteenth century (Galloway 1989).

The first period—the Mediterranean industry—concerns us little here. The second, Atlantic, period began under the Moorish stimulus. The sugarcane and the technology of sucrose extraction and elaboration were part of the Islamic expansion, carried across North Africa by the Moors. They brought cane with them into Spain (in the late ninth or early tenth century) and grew it there, as far north as Valencia. The Moors also brought with them knowledge of sugar making. Sugar was made from cane juice in Spain no later than the early tenth century. Cane sugar is produced in the Málaga-Motril region of Spain to this day.

Though small amounts of sugar reached western Europe before the Moorish invasion, we know only that it was used as a medicine and spice, rather than as a food or sweetener. Northern Europe's awakening appetite for sugar, beginning with the crusades around A.D. 1000, was fed at first by the Mediterranean plantations. But Spain and Portugal were fated to play a critical role in the spread of sugarcane and sugar technology.

In the fifteenth century, Spain and Portugal extended sugar production to the Atlantic islands, which included Portuguese São Tomé and Madeira and the Spanish Canary Islands. These islands had benign climates and fresh soils, better suited than the Iberian Peninsula to cane growing. But they were small and mountainous, and they never completely supplanted those older sugar-producing areas that had begun to supply Europe. Large-scale replacement of both the Mediterranean and the Atlantic island producers occurred after the Americas began to produce sugar.

New World Sugar: The First Centuries

The sugarcane was brought to the New World on Columbus's second voyage; it may have been planted in Santo Domingo as early as December 1493. It is thought that the first sugar made in Santo Domingo—the first in the whole New World—was shipped to Spain around 1516. Everything connected with the production of sugar was imported to the New World from the Old, as the cane itself had been; the Old World center from which plants, technicians, and technology all came was the Spanish Canary Islands. The path of diffusion, then, was from North Africa to Spain and Portugal with the Moors; from Portugal to Madeira with the Portuguese; from Madeira to the Canary Islands with the Spaniards; and from the Canary Islands to Santo Domingo with Columbus.

Honey was the most common sweetener before humans learned to process sucrose from plants. A Stone Age rock painting of a honey gatherer braving an attack of bees documents our longstanding fondness for the sweet taste.

Though some Native Americans may have been forced to work on the first Caribbean plantations, most workers for the American industry were probably enslaved Africans. Thus the cane, the mills, the technology of production, the plantation system, and the slaves themselves all came to the Caribbean islands from elsewhere. These were the first New World colonies; it was almost inevitable that the first New World sugar would be produced there.

Soon after the initial production in Santo Domingo, the sugarcane was carried to the remaining Greater Antilles—Cuba, Puerto Rico, and Jamaica—and in each colony plantations were established and sugar produced. But the industry in these four islands received meager support from the Spanish crown, which feared local developments in the colonies that might weaken or challenge royal control overseas. Hence the sugar industry pioneered by Spanish settlers declined after about 1580.

In contrast, the official Portuguese commitment to Brazilian sugar production was both early and strong. Duties were paid on sugar shipped from Pernambuco to Portugal as early as 1526; and a sturdy industry was in full swing by the time the Spanish Caribbean industry was stagnating, around 1580. Brazil's sugars always competed strongly with other New World producing areas thereafter.

For Spain and the countries of southern Europe, sugar was not so great a novelty as it became for northern Europe. Consumption of sugar in England and the Low Countries rose continuously from the late seventeenth century onward, and it has remained high ever since. Perhaps it was the novelty of such an intense sweet taste that helped to push up its consumption. One authority thinks the lack of "succulent fruit" in northern Europe enhanced the liking there for processed sugar (Nef 1950). Others have stressed the importance of sugar in making the bitter stimulant drinks, tea, coffee, and chocolate, popular (Mintz 1985). Whatever the case, by the mid-seventeenth century Europe's sugar came increasingly from the New World; that remained true until the 1850s. Big changes followed, when the Europeans launched sugar industries in Africa, on the Indian Ocean islands, in Australia, and elsewhere and when commercial sucrose extraction from the sugar beet became practical in Europe, beginning around 1830.

"Sharing them with swarms of flies, we can almost taste the sweets of the confectioner," a British historian wrote of this rendering of a 19th-century Hindu shop (below). India's long infatuation with sugar is demonstrated in the illustration, ca. 1495–1505, titled *Preparation of Sweets for the Sultan of Mandu* (right).

Once primarily a medicinal in the medieval European pharmacy (left), sugar became a common yet indispensible ingredient in pastries and confections (right).

The growth and spread of the cane-based sugar industry in the New World has to be seen partly in terms of these later changes. By the middle of the seventeenth century, and assisted technically and financially by the Dutch, who had pioneered sugar production in the Guianas, the British colonists in Barbados and the French colonists in Martinique established plantations. The Danes, the Swedes, and the Dutch also founded sugar plantation colonies in the Antilles in ensuing decades, though not all were successful.

A century later, the Caribbean colonies of French Saint-Domingue (now Haiti) and British Jamaica had become immensely lucrative sugar, molasses, and rum producers. Indeed, from 1650 until the dawn of the twentieth century, the Caribbean region was the world epicenter of cane sugar. But different colonies led the pack in different epochs. At one point the biggest producers were French Saint-Domingue and British Jamaica; at another, Spanish Cuba. Brazil remained important throughout. Such shifts were caused by changes in markets and international politics, as well as by the changing technology of the industry. Other cane plantations were founded in Mexico, in Peru, and elsewhere in the hemisphere. In Louisiana there was no successful cane sugar industry until the dawn of the nineteenth century. Much of the sugar produced in these locales was intended primarily for local use and was often of poor quality.

Yet the nature of the cane imposed certain preconditions upon potential producers anywhere. Cane production would be undertaken primarily in subtropical areas; the enterprises themselves would be predominantly large-scale; the cane would be grown mainly on coastal alluvial flatlands and in interior valleys; the production schedule would be seasonal. Because of the milling and processing phases, the plantation would be industrial, even though based on agriculture. Cane must be cut when it is ripe, ground when it is cut. Hence field and factory phases are tightly linked, and timing is vital; a tightly controlled labor force is needed.

There are important exceptions to these generalizations. The cane industry in Colombia is not seasonal; smallholders can produce cane and even make sugar in some locales; some estates lie in tropical, rather than subtropical zones. Yet as general statements these serve for most of the New World.

During the eighteenth century, the British and French West Indies, and particularly Jamaica and Saint-Domingue, came to rule the international market. They produced

primarily for their European masters, but considerable sugar, rum, and molasses went to foreign markets as well, sometimes as smuggled goods. In many ways the eighteenth century was the apogee of both cane sugar and New World slavery. In that century, especially the British and French but also the Dutch, the Danes, the Swedes, the Spanish, and the Portuguese had plantation colonies and imported enslaved Africans to the New World to man them in unprecedented numbers. All of this was possible because of the steady growth of the markets for sugar. Once a novelty and luxury, sugar was rapidly becoming an everyday necessity for masses of consumers who, a half century earlier, might never have tasted it.

Technology

The history of the sugar industry in the New World has been marked by important technical changes over the centuries, but these cannot be dealt with at length. At first and for long after the cane species was "creole"—*Saccharum barberi*—grown from cuttings brought from the Atlantic islands and the Mediterranean. But in the late eighteenth century, so-called Bourbon (Otaheite) cane—*Saccharum officinarum*—was introduced from Oceania. It had numerous advantages over creole cane and eventually supplanted it entirely. Efforts were made to improve production by irrigation, fertilizer use, and experiments in cultivation. Though cane breeding did not begin until late in the nineteenth century, such breeding would one day also increase greatly the local adaptiveness and optimum yields of particular zones and regions.

To release the liquid sucrose from sugarcane, the cane must be ground. Grinding power can come from human effort, draft animals, wind, water, or steam. In the New World, all such sources were employed, though steam did not become important until well into the nineteenth century. The earliest New World mills are supposed to have been edge-rollers: circular millstones, standing vertically, and pushed around a platform or in a track by human or animal power. Water-driven, horizontal two-roller mills are thought to have appeared in Hispaniola around 1520. A vertical three-roller mill, much more efficient than any sugar mills that preceded it, appears to have been invented in the New World, in Peru or in Mexico, around 1600 (Daniels and Daniels 1988). Apparently it was unrelated to earlier two-roller mills in the Old World. The importance of milling has to do with the efficiency and rapidity of juice extraction; the precise timing of harvests makes optimal extraction efficiency extremely important, and the lively concern with the improvement of milling arose from this fact.

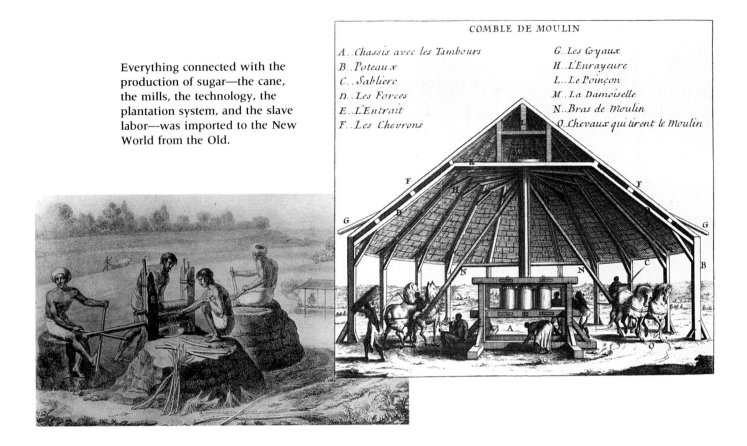

Everything connected with the production of sugar—the cane, the mills, the technology, the plantation system, and the slave labor—was imported to the New World from the Old.

COMBLE DE MOULIN

A...Chassis avec les Tambours
B...Poteaux
C...Sablière
D...Les Forces
E...L'Entrait
F...Les Chevrons

G...Les Coyaux
H...L'Enrayeure
L...Le Poinçon
M...La Damoiselle
N...Bras de Moulin
O...Chevaux qui tirent le Moulin

Other technical advances concerned the efficiency with which the juice could be heated and cleaned and the techniques for producing an ever-purer final product. Sugar refineries were established in Europe in the sixteenth century, the Netherlands leading the way and Britain and France soon following. Final refining was rarely done in the tropical regions where cane was grown and raw sugar produced. In the North American colonies refineries were established in the eighteenth century; there, coarse brown West Indian sugars were processed into finer grades. Nicolas Bayard, for instance, established a refinery in New York City in 1730, and was soon followed by others, such as the Havemeyers (Browne 1933).

A tremendous change occurred near the end of the nineteenth century, when giant mills were first created—mills that could grind the canes formerly ground by a dozen or more of the older mills. These "factory centrals" have supplanted older mills nearly everywhere, even though coarse brown sugar made by archaic methods is still important in several regions of the New World, such as Colombia, Mexico, and Haiti.

Sugar and Slavery

Between 1505, when the first enslaved Africans probably reached the New World, and 1888, when slavery was finally abolished in Brazil, at least 9.5 million Africans were enslaved, transported, and thrown into the European economic system in the Americas (Curtin 1969). Of this number about 2.5 million, or 25 percent, were deployed in the Caribbean islands. Since we are speaking of transatlantic travel in the seventeenth, eighteenth, and nineteenth centuries, these figures are astonishingly large.

Slaves were used for many different purposes in the Western Hemisphere, none as important as the sugar industry. Sugar and slavery traveled together for nearly four centuries in the New World. The demography of peoples of African origin in the New World was, until the twentieth century, largely isomorphic with the geography of the plantation system.

Of the nearly ten million slaves debarked in the New World, the majority were brought to this hemisphere during the eighteenth century. The volume of the trade varied according to many factors. But the growth in the scale of the sugar industry and the markets for its products, together with the improvement in naval transport,

For almost four centuries the sugar industry in the New World was run by a hostage work force. During that time almost ten million African slaves were transported from their homelands to unfamiliar surroundings in the Americas. The 1820s vessel (top) carried slaves to Brazil. Owners of slaves rationalized the enterprise in part by claiming that Africans were submissive by nature. This theory was clearly refuted by insurrections, depicted here in an illustration published in 1851 (center), although few were successful. In the late 19th century, giant sugar mills began to replace older mills powered by slaves and livestock (bottom).

did much to expand the commerce in human beings, even after international accords against it had been signed. Sugar had become an international commodity of first importance.

The rebirth of the sugar industry in the Hispanic Caribbean in the late eighteenth century, particularly after the Haitian Revolution, gave a new lease on life to slavery. Even though its days were by then clearly numbered, slavery would continue to destroy African American populations in Cuba and in Brazil for nearly another century. For at least 360 years slavery was the key labor form in the New World sugar industry. To explain its persistence, some have argued that American Indians were too frail to endure the labor—yet enslaved Indians long composed the bulk of the sugar labor force in early colonial Brazil and elsewhere. Others have stressed the tendency of free laborers to strike out on their own when land could be had as a gift, so that, in the open, frontier setting of the New World, planters might have had no labor at all, had their workers not been kept in chains. Yet other writers have called attention to features of New World slavery that have affected its success, even if they do not explain its origins. Enslaved Africans differed in language and

Working conditions on sugar plantations were appalling. Some historians have ruefully observed that in the frontier setting of the New World, planters might have had no laborers at all had they not kept their workers in chains.

culture, as well as in appearance, from those who enslaved them. Hence they were easily differentiated in every way from those who became their masters. Carried great distances to the New World, where they had to deal with unfamiliar environments and conditions, enslaved Africans were also at a serious disadvantage if they sought to regain their freedom by flight or violent resistance. Most of the slaves came from complex civilizations and were familiar with disciplined agricultural labor—unlike many of the Native American groups with whom the colonists in the New World were in contact. These facts do not explain the origins of the links between sugar and slavery, but they may have something to do with its lengthy history.

The plantation, an agricultural estate for the production of a single commodity for foreign markets, usually built on European capital and powered by slave labor, typified the agricultural expansion of European interest in subtropical America.

During the 15-year Haitian Revolution, 450,000 slaves struggled to overthrow their French rulers. They ultimately won the independence of Haiti, which became the second sovereign nation in the New World. The revolt was led by Toussaint L'Ouverture (left).

Such estates varied greatly in size; the sugar plantations of eighteenth-century Jamaica, for instance, were larger and had more slaves than the cotton plantations of the southern United States at that time. The sugar plantations were infamous for their factory-like pace, their massed labor, and their ghastly working conditions.

Planter society rationalized slavery by claiming both that Europeans were civilizing Africans by enslaving them and that Africans were temperamentally predisposed toward submission to others. Yet the successes of slavery in exacting labor always rested on the threat and use of deadly physical violence. Any belief planters may have had in the inherent submissiveness of Africans surely received frequent testing in practice. The most crucial such test was the Haitian Revolution, when some 450,000 slaves in Saint-Domingue overthrew their French rulers in a bloody fifteen-year war to declare the independence of Haiti, the hemisphere's second sovereign nation. Runaway slaves repeatedly formed independent communities beyond the reach of the planters; in several such cases, they signed treaties with representatives of colonial governments; and in thousands of instances slaves resisted their condition by both overt and covert acts.

Only gradually and painfully did the European and American slaveholding nations terminate the slave trade and then slavery itself. After emancipation, the sugar planters claimed to be in dire need of more labor. The freed people usually sought work off the plantations when they could, and the slightly more humane labor conditions occasioned by emancipation were also blamed for the need for additional labor. In many colonies the planters searched for migrant laborers, often with metropolitan assistance. For instance, at least 500,000 Indians were brought to Antillean sugar colonies such as British Trinidad and British Guiana, French Martinique and Guadeloupe, and Dutch Guiana (Suriname) to cut sugarcane and make sugar; more than 135,000 Chinese were brought to Cuba; and nearly 40,000 Javanese were imported to Suriname. Sugar continued to operate as a powerful demographic lever, even after emancipation, contributing importantly to the ethnic complexity of the New World. Because manual labor in sugar has always been underpaid, it continues to be done in most instances by migrant laborers—Jamaicans in Florida (Wilkinson 1989), Haitians in the Dominican Republic (Plant 1987). Such migrant workers continue to be maltreated and exploited, almost as if the past history of sugar can never be set aside.

Sugar in North American History

Not all cultures value sweetness equally; but in this century the United States became one of the world's largest consumers of processed sugar. The built-in human liking for sweetness does not explain why the figures for average consumption vary so widely around the world or why North American figures are so high. Since cane sugar is only one of several different sweeteners in American history and is now losing some of its importance, a backward glance may be useful before looking at the present.

The thirteen British colonies on the North American mainland were settled mainly by people of English, Scottish, and Irish origin. Their liking for sweetness predated their settlement of the Americas. As early as 1603, foreign visitors to England had commented on the immoderate English liking for sweet things (Rye 1865). In the mid-seventeenth century, British working people began to become accustomed to drinking tea, sweetened with molasses or sugar. Though the first English colonists were not people who could have afforded much sugar or tea in England, they were to become important users in the New World:

> What was to become a characteristic of the American diet—an addiction to sweet dishes—also appeared in the seventeenth century and was nourished by an ever-expanding supply of low-priced sweeteners. In their first years, New Englanders bought cane sugar from Holland and Madeira, but then the rapid expansion of sugar planting in Barbados and throughout the West Indies gave the mainland colonists a cheaper supply than Europeans had. . . . Far less expensive than sugar was West Indian molasses. This became the common sweetener of the poor everywhere in [North] America and found its way into the cooking of all classes. Not only would it sweeten cookies, cakes and puddings, but it would be used to flavor milk dishes, vegetables, and meats, especially pork. (Hooker 1981)

The East India Company eventually perceived the mercantile advantages of aligning with the antislavery movement and began to sell sugar bowls touting that their sugar was not made by slaves (right). Sugar production still required a large work force, and, after emancipation, slaves were replaced by poorly paid migrant laborers, exemplified by the Chinese workers on a 19th-century Louisiana plantation (left). In this way, the sugar industry remained a force in forming the ethnic complexity of the New World.

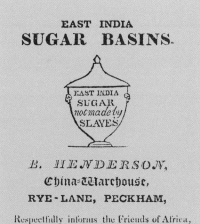

EAST INDIA
SUGAR BASINS.

EAST INDIA
SUGAR
not made by
SLAVES

B. HENDERSON,
China-Warehouse,
RYE-LANE, PECKHAM,

Respectfully informs the Friends of Africa, that she has on Sale an Assortment of *Sugar Basins*, handsomely labelled in Gold Letters: "*East India Sugar not made by Slaves.*"

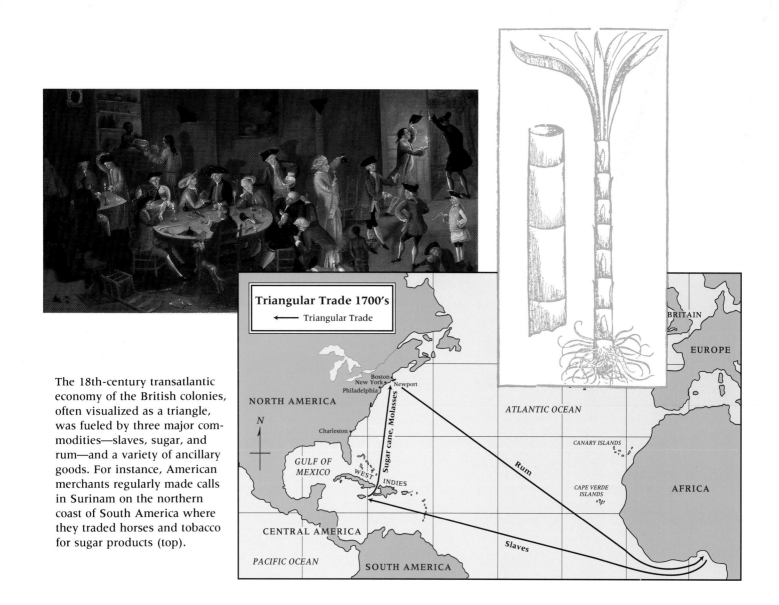

The 18th-century transatlantic economy of the British colonies, often visualized as a triangle, was fueled by three major commodities—slaves, sugar, and rum—and a variety of ancillary goods. For instance, American merchants regularly made calls in Surinam on the northern coast of South America where they traded horses and tobacco for sugar products (top).

In eighteenth-century North America, though most molasses was imported to distill rum rather than to sweeten food, molasses was a cheaper source of sweetness than sugar. The imperial decision to tax its importation was an important cause of revolutionary feelings in the colonies. "I know not why we should blush to confess that molasses was an essential ingredient in American independence," wrote John Adams in 1775. "Many great events have proceeded from much smaller causes" (Mintz 1985).

The early colonists had also learned about maple sugar from the Native Americans and had become big producers of it (Barbeau 1946). The European honeybee, imported to the New World by the Dutch and the English in the 1630s, supplied a familiar Old World sweetener. In the mid-nineteenth century, yet another source of sweetness, a sorghum *(Sorghum saccharatum)*, was introduced into the United States. Though no longer important commercially, sorghum syrup once provided a noticeable fraction of the sweetener consumed in this country (Winberry 1980).

The United States would also have its own cane sugar industry. Cane was brought to Louisiana in 1751. Two ships carrying troops from France to Louisiana touched at Saint-Domingue; the Jesuits there arranged for the transshipment of cane to members of their order in Louisiana. It was not until around 1794, however, that Jean Etienne Boré successfully produced commercial-quality sugar there. By mid-century, Otaheite canes had been imported and serious production undertaken. The

Civil War brought the Louisiana industry to a standstill, but cane sugar is still produced in Louisiana. It yields annually about 850,000 short tons of sugar, roughly 10 percent of the total United States cane and beet sugar production. Florida, Texas, Hawaii, and Puerto Rico also produce cane sugar within the United States system, while substantial quantities are also imported under specific quotas.

The Spanish-American War was by no means the consequence of North American interest in sugar. Yet North American access to sugar was vastly enhanced by those conquests, and the "new lands" were fertile fields for investment. Cuba, Puerto Rico, and the Philippines (and Hawaii, seized earlier, and the Danish Virgin Islands, purchased later) either already were important sugar producers or had enormous potentialities for sugar. Despite efforts to increase sucrose production in the continental United States—by encouraging the Louisiana cane industry, giving premiums for sorghum syrup production, and stimulating beet sugar—the sweetener supply was not equal to the demand. But the creation of plantations in the newly acquired territories (Cuba, though soon declared independent, remained a North American dependency until Castro) transformed the North American sugar situation and the world sugar economy. From 1859 until 1875, the annual per capita consumption of raw sugar in the United States had varied from a low of 18.6 pounds (during the Civil War) to a high of 42.6 pounds. By 1898, the year of the Spanish-American War, it had risen to 65.4 pounds per person per year. But ten years later, the figure was over 86 pounds, or nearly four ounces daily. The consumption of *sucrose*—processed sugar from cane and beet—reached around 115 pounds in the 1920s; but the present-day consumption of *all* processed sugars in the United States is higher than that. In the last three decades, and due as much to political changes as anything else, a corn sweetener called high-fructose corn syrup has captured an important portion of the sweetener market. (In addition to these various processed sugars, we should also mention in passing such things as saccharine, aspartame, and the cyclamates, noncaloric sweeteners that have become important as an aspect of dietetic and weight reduction regimens in the United States).

It should not be thought, however, that the high consumption of processed sugars is explained when we observe that human beings like sweetness. While the taste of sweetness may be attractive to nearly everyone, the actual consumption of sweet things varies greatly nationally and also by region, class, and other social features.

Until recent inflationary times, penny candy was a virtual birthright of American children.

127

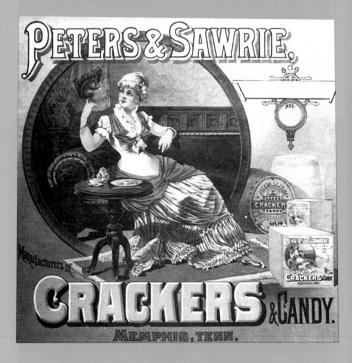

In the United States, new eating habits help to explain sugar consumption, particularly for the last half century. Among the changes in American life that affect consumption are the increased number of meals taken outside the home, the increased consumption of meals in the home that are already prepared, and the increased consumption of processed foods used in the preparation of meals in the home. All of these changes reduce the consumer's control over ingredients, delegating to the producers and technologists the composition of the food or meal. TV dinners, packaged foods to be heated in microwave devices, prepared salad dressings, so-called munchies, and all other ready-to-eat foods automatically increase sucrose consumption, for sucrose is an extremely useful ingredient. It lengthens shelf life in bread, improves the "mouth feel" of soft drinks, reduces caking in salt, smoothes the crumb quality in baked goods, slows decay by absorbing moisture in many packaged foods, counteracts acidity in catsup, and so on. Though sucrose—"sugar"— is the main sweetener, some of the same advantages to the technologist can also be provided by other sweeteners, such as high-fructose corn syrup, dextrose, maltose, fructose, and yet additional sugars. It is not uncommon to find three or even more different sweeteners used in the same packaged product; some products such as flours for breading and breakfast cereals contain up to half their weight in sugars. Hence, while it may not be possible to explain why North Americans consume as much sugar as they do, it surely is not enough to say that they like sugar.

Conclusions

The taste of sweetness is apparently so unusual that it has become linked to all agreeable things, including love. Terms of affection commonly refer to sweetness. Flowers smell sweetly, birds sing sweetly, and cars and athletes perform sweetly. In this sense, sugar is somewhat "magical"—its availability and its consumption are not simple economic facts but also complex cultural and psychological facts. Wedding cakes, sweets for festive occasions such as birthdays and Christmas, and candy for presents and treats suggest the immense power of this taste and, accordingly, of sugar.

Today the place of sugar and the sugar industry is vastly different from the roles they have played in the past. That Americans now drink more soft drinks than water, to take one example, is an outcome that could never have been imagined by the Hispanic Caribbean pioneers of the sugar industry in the early sixteenth century. Equally unimaginable is the importance of sweetened chocolate in modern American life.

Yet there remain some provocative continuities in the history of sugar. For instance, the manual laborers involved in its production, though no longer enslaved, are still poorly paid and badly treated. The political history of sugar—often bloody, corrupt, and mismanaged—is still messy and sensitive. The symbolic importance of sugar, though it is no longer a luxury of royalty, continues to affect people. Its economic importance, now challenged on all sides, has declined, but its proponents are fighting back. Would the history of the New World have been different without sugar? That seems certain. Would our lives be different without it? That seems even more certain.

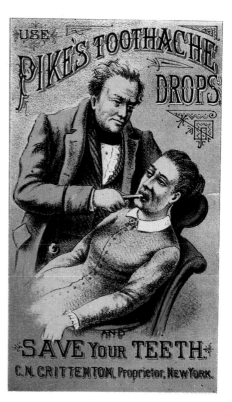

The consumption of sweetened foods in the United States has risen steadily over the years. Packaged snacks, soft drinks, and processed foods automatically increase sucrose consumption. Such products are conspicuous markers of American eating habits in the late 20th century.

Antigua Slaves
and Their Struggle
to Survive

David Barry Gaspar

In documenting the brutality of slavery in the Americas, scholars have long denounced the institution that created profits for slaveowners while inflicting suffering on slaves. More recently, anthropologists and historians have shown that in spite of the destructive tendencies of enslavement, the slaves were able to cope, to create viable communities, to develop autonomy in family and social relations, and to adapt resourcefully to their situation (Wayne 1983). This view of slavery is not meant to downplay its wrongs but rather to approach them from a different direction, from the vantage point of the slave. How slaves coped with slavery, survived it, and built from it and within it, is a remarkable achievement worth recognizing and celebrating as a triumph of the human spirit.

By the mid-eighteenth century, several European powers owned plantation colonies in the Caribbean where large numbers of slaves of African descent produced sugar for export. These slaves lived under such oppressive conditions that their numbers could not increase by natural means, only by frequent import of more from Africa. Clement Caines (1801), a planter in Saint Christopher, calculated in 1798 that 25 percent of newly arrived Africans died during the seasoning. Many more were lost to disease, hard labor, poor diet, and accidents, and none thrived under the harsh laws and customs of slavery. In the context of such demographic disaster and suffering, the survival strategies of Caribbean slaves assume major significance.

At the core of relations between masters and slaves was the subtle and complex interaction of slave resistance and the masters' quest for control. Slaves, individually or collectively, persistently pressed to open up the cracks in the system of slavery to achieve greater autonomy; slaveowners discovered that measured compromise and selective concession could be less counterproductive

than vengeful punishment, although in extreme cases, such as slave revolt, conspiracy to revolt, or physical assaults on whites, slaves were punished to the fullest extent of the law. Slaveowners, recognizing the possibility of revolt, were persuaded to rely on methods other than brute force to win the cooperation of the slaves. The resistance of the slaves therefore contributed to their survival.

Slave resistance must be broadly understood to include forms of slave behavior other than insurrection. Suicide, theft, lying, infanticide, insolence, insubordination, laziness, feigned illness—these were weapons that slaves possessed and used. Such day-to-day resistance, largely individual and nonconfrontational, was essential to survival. In fact, every willed response of the slaves to bend the system in their favor, to secure space for themselves within it, could be interpreted as resistance, even though such responses can also be interpreted as adaptation. Paradoxically, slave resistance involved some accommodation with slavery.

The subtle ways in which slaves resisted their masters is the obscured story within the brutal history of slavery in the New World. Examining their stratagems reveals how enslaved men, women, and families coped with their bondage, managed to survive it, and even improved their life through their own initiative.

Antigua in the British Leeward Islands was typical of Caribbean sugar colonies and offers an interesting case study of the slaves' struggle to survive. First colonized in 1632 by the English who drove out the native Indians, Antigua developed into a full-fledged sugar colony only in the late seventeenth century when the small island was rapidly deforested, large plantations were established, and sizable cargoes of African slaves were imported by independent traders and the Royal African Company. By 1720 the society and economy were so firmly based on sugar and slavery that slaves made up 84 percent of the population.

One way Antigua slaves pressed their claim to greater autonomy was to transform privileges that masters had allowed them into rights, which they then defended against the intrusion of masters and the colonial authorities. One such customary right was the field slaves' use of Sunday to work for themselves. "If any Master was so mad as to command his Slaves to work in the Field on the Lord's Day, they would disobey him, and run away with one consent," wrote the Reverend Robert Robertson, a slaveowner of Nevis, in 1730. "Slaves have (or, which is the same, think they have) some Rights and Privileges, of which they are as tenacious as any Freeman upon Earth can be of theirs,

Slaves lived under such harsh conditions on Caribbean sugar plantations that their own natural population growth could not keep up with losses to disease, hard labor, and malnutrition. Their ranks had to be constantly replenished with frequent importations from Africa.

and which no Master of common Sense will once attempt to violate."

In fact, open conflict occurred between masters and slaves in Antigua when the slaves' Christmas privileges or rights were abused. "Great Disorders have happened, and Murders have been committed by Slaves, because their Masters have not allowed them the same Number of Days for their Recreation at Christmas, as several of their Neighbours have done." To remove these grounds for rebelliousness the slave act of 1723 allowed slaves Christmas Day and the two following days "as Play-Days for their Recreation, and no more, or other Days, during the twelve Christmas Holidays." In other words, slaves before 1723 had steadily transformed Christmas privileges into customary rights, and slave resistance against arbitrary infringement of their rights convinced legislators it was in their best interest to guarantee in law the slaves' claim to the holidays.

Evidence from plantation papers shows that, on a more private level, slaveowners, out of a combination of self-interest and humanity, tried to minimize the potential for complaint and resistance among their slaves through better management of the plantations. The economic ravages of day-to-day slave resistance were never far from slaveowners' minds. Two concerns stand out in communications to overseers: that slaves should not be overworked, and that they should be adequately fed.

The prevalence of theft on plantations, particularly of stored supplies or from provision grounds, indicates how important a deterrent to resistance adequate feeding of the slaves might be in tiny, drought-prone Antigua, which relied greatly on imported food. Access to a sufficient, suitably varied diet was an important prerequisite to the comfort and survival of Antigua slaves, who therefore quickly became attached to their provision grounds and to opportunities to support themselves beyond mere subsistence levels.

An African named Cinque (top) led a revolt of fellow captives on the slave ship *Amistad* in 1839. Armed with cane knives, the mutineers overthrew the ship's crew, killing in the process the captain and cook (bottom). Insurrection was the exception, however, not the rule. Instead, slaves drew upon an arsenal of more oblique behavior, which included theft, lying, infanticide, insolence, insubordination, laziness, and feigned illness. This day-to-day resistance had economic consequences not lost on the slaveowners.

An early entitlement that masters extended to slaves was the use of Sunday to work or relax. By defying attempts to change this custom, slaves transformed a privilege into a right.

The slaves' struggle to cope with slavery, to overcome adversity, to survive, and to make slavery work for them rather than against them was obviously complicated. While they certainly hoped for emancipation some day, in the meantime they had to live, and they exploited every possibility that slavery offered to ease their burden. One of the most interesting and successful strategies was their deep involvement as producers and consumers in the internal economy of the colony. Although the element of accommodation in subsistence cultivation and marketing appears strong, the ultimate result, whether the slaves meant it or not, was to improve slave life largely through the slaves' own initiative.

The development of activities through which Antigua slaves carved out their place in the internal economy of the island can be traced back perhaps to the beginnings of the provision grounds on the plantations and to the slaves' claim to Sunday as their own free day. Slaves most often used their free time—on Sundays especially, but also on holidays and even during the rest periods of the regular day—to work in their provision grounds.

Early patterns of slave resistance in the Leeward Islands affected the origins of provision grounds and associated economic activities. Believing that many slaves resorted to theft because their masters did not feed them adequately, the legislatures of Nevis and Montserrat in the late seventeenth century enacted regulations requiring owners and supervisors of slaves to plant sufficient acreage in provisions. Antigua legislatures did not pass similar laws, but custom may have had the same effect. In any case, in all of the sugar islands both planters and slaves benefited from the private garden plots. Planters were freed from some of the cost of feeding slaves who supplemented their rations not only by cultivating their assigned grounds but also by trading their surplus for other food and goods.

The scarcity of surplus land on the tiny sugar islands limited the allocation and size of provision grounds. In Antigua, some plantations assigned provision grounds and some did not. The basic rationale that determined who received provision grounds when available was that the slave, male or female, should be able to attend to the plot. Sometimes grounds were given to heads of families in relation to the size of the family. Before 1798 there was no established minimum size, but the Leeward Islands Amelioration Act of that year ruled that every plantation owner or director should "allot and give to every slave . . . who is capable of working the same, a piece or spot of good well-laying land of forty feet square at least, immediately round or close to his house." If this could not be done "without pulling down or injuring any other Negro house," the proprietor was free to allocate other outlying lands. The act was the first to establish provision grounds at Antigua, but obviously it was meant only to impose greater uniformity and minimum standards on a differentiated system that had already evolved. After 1798 there was, of course, still variation. Some plantations, according to the act, could "allot portions of land to their Slaves more than sufficient for their support and maintenance, and from which such slaves grow rich." At the other extreme were plantations where the slaves were fed mostly from rations of imported or locally produced food.

The sugar revolution had established the island's reliance on imported provisions quite early. By the late eighteenth century Antigua imported large supplies of "dry provisions" including corn, beans, peas, wheat or rye flour, Indian corn meal, oatmeal, rice, cassava flour or farina, and biscuits; imported "salted provisions" including herring, shad, mackerel, beef, and pork. On their provision grounds the Antigua slaves cultivated various food crops, mostly yams, guinea corn, potatoes, and eddoes. Conditions on the dry and riverless island did not favor much cultivation of plantains or bananas.

Division of labor on the provision grounds, as to gender and age, is unclear, but, as Pulsipher indicates in her discussion of slavery in Montserrat, women dominated the distribution of goods, which took place at the weekly market in the towns, at the slaves' Sunday market, or through hawking and peddling. The Sunday markets and peddling derived from the productive use slaves made of their provision grounds and from other opportunities to acquire saleable goods. Caines (1804) noted that many field slaves increased "their scanty fare by picking grass, cutting wood, or collecting a variety of articles, that the country furnishes and the demand of the town renders saleable." By the early nineteenth century slaves were involved in gainful economic pursuits all over the island, thereby displacing whites from many occupations. Several factors encouraged this trend: the proportion of resident whites dwindled as Antigua became a mature sugar colony; slaveowners were acquisitive, as were non-slaveowners and free people of color who, as hucksters, employed slaves to hawk their wares or purchased goods from the

A 1902 photograph of the market-place in St. Johns, where in previous centuries slaves came to barter goods they had made or raised on their provision grounds. Such gatherings, on Antigua and other Caribbean islands, provided the slaves with important moments of social and economic autonomy in a world otherwise bereft of freedom.

slaves, especially at the Sunday markets, to resell later; most important, slaves themselves seized initiatives to improve their lives.

The significance of the slaves' Sunday markets and their strong attachment to them cannot be overemphasized. When the markets first appeared in Antigua is uncertain, but their existence was acknowledged in the 1697 slave act. They were held at various places on the island, especially in the towns. Several visitors to Antigua recorded vivid impressions of the "Great Market" in Saint Johns, the capital, on the northwest coast. "Slaves of every description assembled," wrote T. Wentworth in the 1830s, "where the gratification of their vanity in the display of their finery was no inconsiderable incentive to their congregating, as well as the more ostensible motive of traffic."

To the Sunday markets, the slaves brought whatever they had to barter or exchange from their provision grounds and from other opportunities they had taken to work for themselves. Wentworth noted the large number of pigs, goats, turkeys, geese, ducks, and guinea fowl. "What with the jabbering of their voices, the noise of pigs, goats, and poultry, and the compound animal and vegetable odours, the whole thing was enough to confound the senses of any man that had not become familiar with such an ordeal." The vitality of the scene is clear, even through Wentworth's lens of European culture and sensibility: "their jeers and jokes . . . semi-civilized proverbs and quaint sententious remarks, accompanied by gesticulations . . . all [are] so exquisitely ludicrous."

Most of the market sellers were women. But sellers and buyers and observers, men and women and children, black and white and brown, visitors and residents, all participated at the marketplace in an institution of great social, economic, and symbolic significance to the slaves, on the one day they could call their own.

The authorities wisely did not interfere too frequently or too forcefully with the Sunday "Marketings and Merry-makings" or with other customary activities. The markets were not supported by positive law, but this made little difference to the slaves for whom long-standing custom had the force of law. In March 1831, however, the Antigua legislature abolished the markets—ironically, as part of a program to ameliorate slavery—without fixing a substitute market day. For the slaves this spelled an arbitrary invasion of their rights and a brutal subversion of their autonomy. According to John Felvus, a Methodist missionary who worked among the island's slaves at the time, they interpreted their situation as "oppression upon oppression, degradation upon degradation and the greatest aggravation of their present sufferings." The slaves vented their protests in two important ways. During the initial phase of their protests they set fire to 22 of the perhaps 153 plantations on the island. The slaves also demanded that the legislature establish a new market day, and eventually Saturday emerged as the choice of most slaveowners.

On the very eve of general emancipation in the British colonies (which would come in 1834), the Antigua slaves secured their market privileges or rights that had been a fundamental component of their complex strategies of coping with slavery. In their struggle to survive the slaves tried to carve out livable space for themselves, and these survival strategies necessitated some accommodation with slavery. But accommodation in order to survive was also integrally related to the slaves' will to resist the worst tendencies within slavery, which were to dehumanize and completely subordinate them. Slaves fought back as best they could, and their resistance did not result only in brutal punishments, but also in concessions from slaveowners who understood that there were less costly ways to win the cooperation of their troublesome and expensive human property. That the slaves of Antigua exploited these concessions to the fullest is amply demonstrated in the expanded role they came to play in the internal economic life of the sugar island. In spite of the harsh realities of life under slavery, the Antigua slaves, like their counterparts elsewhere in the Americas, found ways to determine the paths their lives might take.

From the toehold of their Sunday markets, African slaves took on expanded roles in the economies of the Caribbean sugar islands and by so doing managed to improve their lives against formidable odds. Their heirs, during the civil rights movement of the 1960s, began to secure basic rights long denied to blacks in the New World.

Galways Plantation, Montserrat

Lydia M. Pulsipher

Of the thousands of plantations established in the New World after the voyages of Columbus, Galways estate on the tiny eastern Carribean island of Montserrat was not remarkable in any way. It was not owned by an important family; it was not particularly large or productive; and in its three-hundred-year history, it has been home to no more than two thousand people. Galways was just one of many American places that suddenly became connected to the wider world, giving its human and natural resources to the cause of European development while assimilating a bewildering array of people, plants, animals, and ideas from far away. While today the Galways ruins and the mountains that surround the site seem unusually beautiful and mysterious, even these perceptions are primarily the result of our modern need for connections to the past and may not reflect at all what the place meant to those who lived out their lives there.

Indians settled on Montserrat more than 2000 years ago, and in its well-watered uplands (previous pages) cultivated maize, peanuts, cassava, pineapple, sweet potatoes, papaya, avocados, and other New World fruits and vegetables. While European sugar planters would try to impose a rigid agricultural order on Montserrat, their slaves adopted the garden style of their Indian predecessors.

It is because Galways plantation and the island of Montserrat are quite ordinary that they serve so well as a case study of the role that sugar and all the many other seeds of change played in transforming the world after Columbus. By simply looking at the daily lives of enslaved Africans who were brought to a common plantation on an undistinguished Caribbean island to grow and process sugar, we can view the human results of Columbus's voyages of exploration. We can come to appreciate the resilience and creativity of people throughout the Americas and beyond who chose or were forced to create a new life for themselves either in new and alien environments, or, in the case of Native Americans, in situations radically changed by the abrupt contact between the Eastern and Western Hemispheres.

French cartographer Jacque Bellin, in this sketch of 1758, emphasized the craggy topography of Montserrat. The tiny island contains a complex array of tropical environments: coastal drylands, scrub woodlands, and dense rain forests. European settlers did not successfully adapt their clothing, architecture, land use, or diet to fit these climatic conditions.

Montserrat before Columbus

Montserrat is a small mountainous island in the volcanic archipelago of the eastern Caribbean and lies 17 degrees north of the equator. In just thirty-nine square miles it contains a wide variety of tropical environments. Coastal drylands, mangrove wetlands, grasslands, and scrub woodlands line the coast and grade into dense tropical forests in the uplands and high mountains. On the very highest cloud-covered peaks are elfin woodlands adapted to wind, high moisture, and low sunlight. Several active volcanic fumaroles and vents dot the rugged landscape.

In the thousands of years prior to settlement by Europeans and Africans, Montserrat underwent slow evolutionary changes, influenced only rarely by natural or human introductions of plants, animals, and other organisms from the surrounding hemisphere. The island was settled perhaps as early as twenty-three hundred years ago by successive small groups of Indians who moved up the island chain from the Orinoco River basin in South America. Some think the island was known by these early inhabitants as Alliouigana, perhaps meaning island of the Arawaks.

When, in 1493 on his second voyage to the New World, Columbus passed by on a northerly route to the Greater Antilles and gave the island its European name, Montserrat was occupied by people who did not trade widely and who sustained themselves with fishing, hunting and gathering, and the produce of tropical gardens.

There are no firsthand reports of where the original inhabitants were living on the island in 1493, but archaeological evidence indicates that at or before the time of Columbus there were at least two large villages located on broad alluvial fans, one on the leeward (west) side in what is now the capital of Plymouth, near the mouth of Fort Ghaut, and one on the windward (east) side near the present airport on the lower reaches of Farm River. Other occupation sites have been found in a wide range of locations. These people had a rich tradition of pottery making, and they tended horticultural plots that contained a profusion of plants domesticated primarily in South America and improved over thousands of years of careful genetic selection. Early European sojourners in the eastern Caribbean reported that typically these gardens were large and complex, including maize, peanuts, cassava, an edible canna lily, pineapple, sweet potatoes, papaya, peppers, squash, guavas, avocados, various New World beans, and medicinal plants. In some cases they were fortified with earthen banks planted with tall trees arranged in a sort of stockade (Jesse 1966). Strangely, two Old World domesticates, plantains and sugarcane, were mentioned repeatedly by early seventeenth century European travelers as being cultivated by the Indians. Apparently these Old World crops fit easily into Indian foodways and were so suited to the New World environment that they quickly diffused and soon were assumed to be indigenous to the New World.

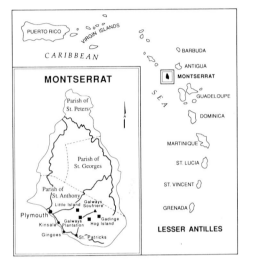

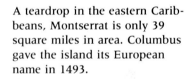

A teardrop in the eastern Caribbeans, Montserrat is only 39 square miles in area. Columbus gave the island its European name in 1493.

An early reference to a "Great Indian Garden" in Montserrat suggests that it was in a well-watered upland region, perhaps in the saddle between the Centre Hills and the Soufriere Hills to the south. It is interesting to note that every one of the New World domesticates listed as being in Indian gardens was later adopted by the African slaves in Montserrat, who cultivated similar complex horticultural plots around their houses and on the high mountain fringes of the plantations. In addition slave gardens contained domesticates from Africa, Asia, the Middle East, and Europe.

For more than 130 years after Columbus passed by, the pace of outside influence in Montserrat remained slow, principally because the island was too small to attract the interest of early European colonizers. The Indians continued their occupancy more or less undisturbed, though the possibility of the occasional intrusion during this time of influences from Europe, Africa, and Asia as well as the American mainland in the form of diseases, insects, rats, weeds, and domesticated animals and plants should not be dismissed. Beginning in 1632, when the island was settled by English and Irish colonists from the neighboring island of Saint Kitts (perhaps accompanied by a few African slaves), Montserrat entered a period of rapid environmental and cultural change that continues apace to this very day.

The Period of European Settlement

Had the European settlers come to the New World with the idea of learning to live in these pleasant new surroundings in amicable coexistence with the native inhabitants, history would have taken quite a different turn. Instead they came with the vision that there was money to be made by taming these alien tropical environments into efficient production units supplying Old World markets. Within just fifty years, the colonists imposed a new European order on Montserrat's tropical landscape. More than two-thirds of the island was deforested; and the land, once held in common by the Indians, was divided into rectangular plots and registered to specific European owners. Scores of plantations were established in the countryside; towns, fortifications, harbors, and roads were laid out. European sawed wood and masonry structures replaced the more transitory woven and thatched shelters of the Indians. Alien species of domesticated plants and weeds displaced indigenous vegetation, and Old World rodents and domesticated species like sheep, goats, cats, dogs, cattle, horses, donkeys, mules, oxen, and fowl, began to compete for resources. The original occupants were reduced to wandering hostile bands who conducted sporadic raids on the new settlers (Pulsipher 1986).

All of this effort to adjust Montserrat to European occupancy required labor well beyond the settlers' capacity to supply. In addition to clearing and building, workers were needed to perform the many tasks connected with sugar production: preparing the soil, planting cane, weeding fields, cutting the mature crop, extracting the cane juice, boiling it down, preparing the sugar and by-products for market. People were required to tend food crops, to care for grazing and draft animals and for fowl and pigs, and to cater to the personal needs of the upper class.

In the early years of settlement, hundreds of Irish and a few Scottish indentured servants performed these duties; their numbers were regularly augmented by new shipments of prisoners and refugees from the British subjugation of Ireland under Oliver Cromwell. But in Montserrat things did not go well between the English planters and the Irish servants. The Irish, who outnumbered the English six to one, proved as unwilling to accept Anglo dominance in Montserrat as they had in Ireland, nor were they content to remain passively on the small rocky plots allotted to them upon completion of their indentures. They were openly contentious and insolent to the English, and they took every chance to leave Montserrat for other islands or North America. The possibility of substituting African slaves for the troublesome Irish servants had been recognized for some time; but by 1660 there were at most five hundred to one thousand Africans on Montserrat. Then the conditions in Ireland that had encouraged indentures to the West Indies changed. Labor grew especially scarce and Montserrat planters began to import Africans in ever greater numbers. By the 1730s blacks outnumbered whites by five to one and by the late eighteenth century by nearly ten to one.

The overwhelming majority of these slaves were settled in the countryside on plantations varying from a few acres to more than one thousand. On the larger plantations like Galways there might be from fifty to two hundred slaves, while on smaller holdings there might be five or fewer. Some slaves, reputedly the most abused, were owned by jobbers, who leased out their slaves to work as field laborers during times of high labor demand or to work on the roads and construction projects.

Galways Plantation

Galways plantation was established sometime in the 1660s by David Galway, an Irishman who seems to have had strong English rather than Irish sympathies. He was a major in the island militia and by the late 1670s was serving on the Montserrat Council, an appointed position usually given only to prominent landowners.

David Galway's estate lay on the southwest slopes of the Soufriere Hills and consisted of some thirteen hundred acres stretching from the sea to the top of the mountains between Germans Ghaut and the White River. The limited seventeenth-century documentary evidence, when combined with archaeological and geographic field data, places the early plantation buildings on the dry lower reaches of Galways Mountain just above Germans Bay, near the modern village of Saint Patricks. Archaeological evidence that came to light in 1989 indicates that the seventy-four slaves mentioned in the 1677 census may have lived in a village near the estate house. The 1673 map of Montserrat suggests that the 311 Irish who lived at this time in fifty-nine households on or near Galway's land were settled on the barren windswept slopes to the south of the sugar works on small plots where they kept

The ruins of Galways plantation on Montserrat provide a window on the everyday world of the European sugar planter and his community of laborers, Irish indentured servants and African slaves.

goats, sheep, and pigs and probably provided seasonal labor to the plantation. Interestingly, the map also indicates that Galway's sugarcane fields were in wetter zones high above the sugar-processing facilities. According to the 1677 census, population density was quite high throughout the southwest region: more than 40 percent of the total island population lived there. Most were white and nearly all were Irish. This large proportion of the island population lived on less than 10 percent of the total island territory—and it was poor dry land at that (Pulsipher 1987). In 1669 David Galway was placed in charge of enforcing the island laws in this southwest district—laws that frequently focused specifically on the need to control the Irish underclass.

It appears that this spatial organization of sugar production on Galways Mountain remained well into the eighteenth century; but between the 1670s and the 1720s the plantation declined as an economic enterprise. It is probable that the dry stony lower slopes proved a difficult venue for human habitation. Certainly water and soil resources were meager; and the high cane fields were too remote from the lowland sugar works. According to a 1729 census, by then the Galway family had no white servants and just sixty-two slaves. And whereas many planters had added windmills for cane crushing, and used the older technology of animal mills only as a backup, Galways still had only a cattle mill.

Then sometime after 1730 new owners relocated and modernized Galways plantation. A new sugar works, warehouse, and great house, all in an elegant Georgian style, were built in a high, cooler, and wetter zone at 1100 feet above the sea. The complex included an extensive water management system and a slave village located just below and in view of the new installation. That these measures to upgrade Galways plantation were taken at this particular time is significant, for the mid-eighteenth century was a time of major change in the West Indies. Due to the enormous success of sugar in the markets of Europe, many investors were coming out to cash in on the sugar boom. The older planter families like the Galways were happy to divest themselves of marginal, unproductive holdings; and the new owners were so optimistic that they not only invested in a more salubrious location and modern technology but also spent considerable money on architectural aesthetics and on what they perceived to be rational water management. This eighteenth-century plantation complex, which has been the subject of a ten-year interdisciplinary study, will provide the stage for understanding human adaptation and hence the course of the daily life of slaves on Galways Mountain in the plantation era.

Human Adaptation on Galways Mountain

The primary factors that influenced life on the eighteenth-century highland site of Galways plantation were varied but can be grouped under three topics: the structure of the plantation system, the characteristics of the physical environment, and the cultural characteristics of those, enslaved and free, who lived at Galways.

The *plantation system* can be summarized as a method of exploiting the resources of colonial territories based on the production of a cash crop, a market for which was actively developed in the mother country and in the wider world. Reciprocally, the colonial territories provided an outlet for surplus population and a market for manufactured goods from Europe.

The plantation system produced a remarkably standard type of rural settlement throughout the New World. Although the size of plantation landholdings varied greatly, they were generally recognized as large, when compared to other types of holdings in a given territory; but only a fraction of the holding was used for the prime cash crop, with some of the land lying fallow and some used for pasture and

The plantation system put a European stamp on the New World landscape. This 19th-century illustration of a sugar plantation on Antigua is so Old World in aspect that only the palm trees give a clue to the scene's New World location.

144

British and Irish colonists from nearby Saint Kitts first settled Montserrat in 1632, after which the environment and culture of the island experienced rapid change. This 1673 profile of the leeward side of Montserrat graphically illustrates European influence inching up the slopes.

food crops. There was almost always a central processing and storage complex on the plantation and near it a settlement, the spatial organization of which reflected centralized control of the laborers by an elite owner-manager class. Also, each plantation included ancillary activities related to the overall production of the cash crop and to sustaining the laborers and managers in daily life: blacksmithing, barrel making, equipment and building maintenance, animal tending, provision gardening, food preparation, health care, child care, and pottery making.

The *physical environment* of Galways Mountain is the result of many interacting factors, both natural and human. Galways Mountain is actually a long volcanic finger on the southwest slope of the Soufriere Hills, bounded by Germans Ghaut on the northwest and the White River on the southeast. The steep slope rises from the sea to 3000 feet in just over two miles; and at about 2000 feet, in a partial crater, is Galways Soufriere, an active volcanic fumarole. The landforms of the entire mountain are so convoluted by patterns of volcanic deposition and subsequent erosion that angle and orientation of slope, wind patterns, and variable rainfall conspire to create a complex mosaic of ecological zones.

The availability of moisture on Galways Mountain is directly reflected in the vegetation patterns and has particular implications for understanding the human history of Galways plantation. Rain almost always comes from the east where the high mountains intercept the warm moist northeast tradewinds, forcing them up into cooler elevations so that they drop their moisture on the peaks and on the leeward (western) slopes. Showers move from east to west across the higher slopes several times a day, and here much of the land is covered with a dense mantle of rain forest. Today, small shifting horticultural plots occasionally interrupt the forest canopy, as they probably did since pre-Columbian times and throughout the plantation era.

The intensity of the rainfall decreases as the air masses move down into warmer elevations. The zone between 2000 and 1000 feet receives enough to support tall trees, but grasses and scrub vegetation tend to take over for an extended time if the land is cleared of trees. It was this zone that was favored for sugarcane fields. At 1000 feet the winds shift to the north carrying any rain clouds with them and so the lower elevations of the mountain receive very little moisture. The natural

Although arduous to reach, high mountáin retreats were prized garden spots for slaves because they offered rich soil, ample water, and seclusion from their overseers.

vegetation is a low xerophytic thicket, though in deep ravines that receive runoff from above, fingers of lush vegetation and tall trees stretch down toward the sea. In the seventeenth century this dry territory was cleared and settled by Irish tenants and smallholders. Their goats and sheep kept down the regrowth, giving the advantage to hardy grasses, to plants that hug the ground, and to tough, thorny shrubs like acacia, many of which were introduced from Europe.

Occasionally, when large tropical high-pressure systems bring prolonged dry conditions to the whole island, the land and even the air take on a dry, dusty yellowish look, and the vegetation in all zones dies back significantly. At other times, low-pressure systems can dump huge amounts of rain on the entire mountain slope in a very short time—twelve inches in just four hours during a tropical storm in the early 1980s. Where the vegetation is thick, the environment can handle this amount of water; but where vegetation is sparse, due to natural or man-made conditions, the surface runoff is excessive and erosion is severe. Gullies can quickly become ravines, and fast-running watercourses become mud flows carrying huge boulders hundreds of feet. After such a storm a fan of sediment eroded from the slopes stretches far out to sea.

In spite of the high rates of rainfall in upland zones, nearly all watercourses on Galways Mountain carry water only immediately after a rainfall. The exception is the White River, a sulfurized stream that flows through Galways Soufriere, down over the Great Apse waterfall, and eventually to the sea. A few small springs emit fairly consistent trickles, while others are often dry. Some experts think that the springs and streams may have run more consistently in the past before plantation clearing of the forest canopies; but shifts in the volcanic substructure may have caused some streams to move below the surface.

Mrs. Annie Reid, a descendant of African slaves and Irish indentured servants, still occupied this house on the eve of the Quincentenary. It is located near the first site of the Galways plantation and is typical of houses built already in the 1670s by the Irish in this arid lowland region of Montserrat.

Other environmental features to which the Galways settlers had to adjust were the year-round moderate temperatures and the occasional violent weather. For the cultivation of sugar, the climate was advantageous in that it provided an uninterrupted growing season for the twelve- to fourteen-month cycle of cane growth. But, the consistently warm temperatures and high humidity provided a fertile breeding zone for insects, diseases, and fungi, which attacked crops and shortened human life or made it unpleasant. Episodic tropical hurricanes dealt severe blows, destroying the buildings, killing people, and devastating both crops and the natural vegetation.

The different *cultural characteristics* of the European and African settlers greatly affected the ways in which they adapted to the New World island tropics. In part because Europeans came intending to stay only a short time while they extracted wealth from the resources of the West Indies before returning to Europe, and to some extent because they were unfamiliar with tropical environments and hence had no long-standing coping strategies, Europeans seem to have been particularly

147

conservative culturally and exploitative in their adjustments to the Caribbean. They found the climate debilitating, in part because they made few concessions in clothing, shelter, and food. Concerns with status kept them wearing clothing designed for mid-latitude climes; they often eschewed a tropical diet in favor of a nutritionally poor, imported one; and they only slowly learned to construct sturdy, yet well-ventilated structures oriented to shut out the rain and the heat of the sun, yet to admit the breezes. Richard Ligon, who visited Barbados in the 1650s observed: "They should have made all the openings they could to the East, thereby to let in the cool breezes, to refresh them when the heat of the day came. But they . . . closed up all their houses to the East, and opened all to the West; so that in the afternoones,

In the 17th century, draft animals powered the mills used to extract the juice from the sugarcane (top). By 1700, however, sugar planters began to rely on more efficient windmills.

148

when the Sun came to the West, those little low roofed rooms were like Stoves or heated Ovens . . . not considering at all that there was such a thing as shutters for windowes to keep out the rain . . . and let in the winde to refresh them.''

The plantation system the Europeans created, and the large numbers of people they settled on the land, led to over-exploited resources and environmental problems that demanded expensive compensatory adjustments. Dalby Thomas reported that already in 1672 many planters were migrating to fresh holdings in Jamaica, only recently taken by the British from the Spanish, because their original plantations in the eastern Caribbean were "worn out and their woods wasted." Some planters tried to improve the rapidly depleted soil by importing cattle solely for the manure

Cultural extremes developed in close proximity on the New World sugar plantations. The sugar works at Galways, elegantly Georgian but massive, looms over the more indigenous but flimsy homes of the slaves. This painting is a modern Montserratian artist's interpretation, based on the archaeological record, of 18th-century Galways.

they would produce, others resorted to complex and expensive engineering schemes to make the industrial processing of the crop more efficient or to better manage water resources.

The relocation of Galways in the mid-eighteenth century to a higher elevation was undoubtedly to secure better access to fertile upland soils and to more consistent supplies of water; at this higher elevation rainfall would be sufficient to grow cane as well as the provision crops necessary to sustain life on the plantation. But the move was only one more episode in a difficult European relationship with the

Art supplements the sparse written record of the domestic life of slaves. This 1820s sketch, by a visitor to Saint Kitts, shows a row of slave houses in the village of Cayon, surrounded by gardens, coconut and banana trees, and flocks of chickens and pigs. By tending livestock and cultivating gardens, slaves raised food to consume or to sell at the Sunday markets.

hydrology of Galways Mountain. The archaeological evidence tells us that elaborate structures were necessary to control the rapid surface runoff generated by forest clearing in this zone of heavier rainfall. Buildings and fields on the steep slopes had to be protected from the ravages of erosion by complex drainage systems. Furthermore, streams and springs, which had slowly released accumulating groundwater for thousands of years, now ran very rapidly just after a storm and then quickly went dry, so structures were needed to capture water for human use. As was the case with the plantation system as a whole, the water problems encountered and the strategies devised to handle them reflected the prevailing European attitude toward resources: they should be controlled by humans and managed to enhance profits.

Just as the attitudes of the European planter class towards the New World island tropics may be learned from their written records and from the economic and social systems they devised, as well as from the landscapes they left behind, we also can discern how the enslaved Africans viewed the new land. The sources of this information include historical records and accounts, analyses of historical and modern landscapes, archaeological evidence, and ethnographic data from the present and recent past.

The written record of African occupancy in Montserrat is distinctly incomplete; and, with the notable exception of the slave-mariner Olaudah Equiano, who wrote eloquently of his life in eighteenth-century Montserrat, this record was kept by whites, who were rarely objective observers. Nonetheless, in the laws, correspondence, and travelers' accounts there is much indirect evidence of how, within the constraints of slavery, the enslaved Africans assessed and then put to use the New World tropical islands. From the laws passed to control slave activities, we learn that slaves grew gardens and regularly met at Sunday markets to sell their surplus produce to other slaves, to the planter class, and also to itinerant traders who plied the Caribbean. From artists' depictions of slave domestic scenes, we learn that they kept pigs and chickens and goats and grew trees and gardens around their houses. Laws passed to control thievery by slaves let us know the surprising fact that slaves could legitimately own cattle and other livestock. Laws seeking to control fires in cane fields state that slaves commonly hunted for land crabs at night with lighted torches. That laws to control slave entrepreneurial activity were passed repeatedly throughout the seventeenth and eighteenth centuries shows not that the activities were successfully repressed but rather that the authorities were unsuccessful in stamping out what were common practices. Other sources of evidence, like those discussed next, both enhance this written record and supply additional information specifically about Montserrat.

The parameters of the physical world within which Galways people had to operate was established by geographic analysis of Galways Mountain, which included field reconnaissance and the interpretation of historical and modern maps and aerial photos. This inquiry combined with ethnographic study revealed the ways in which the slaves and their descendants used the various environments over time, such as where they cultivated and how they procured water.

The archaeological investigation of the slave village and burying ground at Galways both corroborated written accounts of slave life in the Caribbean and supplied new information about these particular people: the spatial patterns of their domestic life, their material culture and house types, their diet and food processing, their economic plants and animals, their perception and management of resources such as water and building materials, and the state of their health and well-being.

Ethnographic study with the descendants of Galways slaves provided insights on their connections to the past and filled in details on their environmental knowledge, resource management strategies, gardening practices, their use of wild plants, their plant-based (and hence biodegradable) material culture, and their customs regarding food processing and recipes. Concepts of proper gender roles and family relationships were clarified by studies of the arrangement and use of modern domestic spaces;

The stereotyped scene of disporting slaves notwithstanding, evidence suggests that they reserved their free time for productive activities. They grew vegetables and herbs, fished, raised goats and geese, collected eggs, baked cassava bread, gathered materials to weave baskets. Food and crafts could be bartered or sold at the slave markets. Clay tobacco pipes and ceramic artifacts found at the Galways slave village document the material culture of enslaved people.

Slaves had to squeeze into their free time the full range of household and familial obligations, from caring for children and aged relatives to laundering clothes and mending tools. Hoes, essential in the cane fields and also in home gardens, were particularly prized by slaves who could afford to own them.

and analyses of historical records revealed continuities between these present concepts of family life and responsibilities and those of the past.

"Sunday at Galways in the Early Ninteenth Century" portrays the texture of the daily life of slaves to the extent that it can be reconstructed from a distance of more than 150 years. The setting is the Galways village and the surrounding mountainside; and each detail of the environment and of lifeways, relationships, and material culture is substantiated by one or more of the four sources of information I have described: the archaeological record, ethnographic studies, historical documents, and landscape analysis. The names and general characteristics of each person were taken from the Galways slave list of 1817. The personalities and physical features are those of modern individuals who reside on Galways Mountain and who have helped us with our study. The illustrations and quotations throughout this section serve to document the overall history of Galways Mountain or specific details from the scene.

Daily Life

Sunday was not a typical day in the lives of slaves, but it was perhaps the most important to them because it was a day of relative freedom—freedom to organize their own time, freedom to engage or not to engage in a variety of entrepreneurial activities that brought an improved standard of living and contacts with people from outside the plantation. Monday through Saturday noon slaves had to be in the fields working before dawn, or at their other posts as craftsmen, animal tenders, or domestic servants. They got a half hour off at nine o'clock for breakfast and as much as one and one-half hours off for the midday meal—a simple repast of boiled vegetables, served in the field. Then they worked again until dark at six-thirty or

Sunday morning in town.

Sunday at Galways in the Early Nineteenth Century

It is five o'clock on a Sunday morning in June 1817. The wind sighs through the crowns of the tall palms and dips down to rustle the leaves of the banana, pawpaw, and cedar trees. Finally, it stirs the cane leaf thatched roofs of the small wood houses and animal pens nestled in informal terraces on the mountain slope. The sails of the windmill just above in the plantation yard can be heard straining against the tethers that tie them down on Sundays when, for a day, the processing of sugarcane is suspended. In the east the sky behind the mountains begins to turn pink, and far below to the west the ocean glints silver.

Garrick struggles up off his mat and stretches, filling the doorframe of the tiny house with his shoulders. His head, covered with tight greying curls, juts out above the opening and brushes the cane-trash roof. He notices the calm sea and wishes briefly that some of his precious time today could be spent fishing. The structure shudders a bit as he sits down heavily on the doorsill and rests his feet on the boulder just outside. He checks furtively over his right shoulder to see if Fagan, the estate manager, might be idly monitoring the early morning activity of the slaves from the boiling house windows. He sees no one and relaxes a bit, pleased that the thick foliage around the house shields them so effectively from observa-

tion. Rummaging on a ledge inside the door for his white clay pipe, Garrick asks the boy Quacou to interrupt his "Chiney Money" game with Granderson from the next house and hand him an ember from the cooking fire so he can light the tobacco. The first draft of the homegrown stuff is a raw one and he suggests to his companion, Margaret, that she should buy him a bit of imported tobacco while she is in town today at market.

Garrick suddenly leans over and peers under the house. There, beside one of the wooden nogs that supports the structure above ground level, he finds the broken stone ax and stone ring he picked up yesterday evening by the mouth of the White River. No one uses things like these now, and he wonders what they could be and who made them. Stories of the "old time people," short, with long straight black hair, who used to live past Palmetto Point on the south coast come to mind. When he first saw the ax, he could see that it was not just an ordinary stream-worn rock; and now that he is looking closer, he can see where it was lashed to a handle and where the blade cracked off with a heavy blow. But the ring, about the size of his fist, completely puzzles Garrick, unless . . . could it have been used to weigh down a lobster trap?

Margaret has just finished heating up last night's peppery stew of pigeon peas and plantains in the heavy black clay cooking pot. As Garrick replaces the mysterious items back under the house, she hands him a calabash bowl full of the stew and offers the same to Quacou and Granderson. Margaret does not join them. She has eaten earlier. While they eat, she tugs at a handful of loose fibers on the banana tree, rips them down the length of the tree and ties together a large cloth bundle containing flat disks of cassava bread and other items to sell in town. Leaving the bundle, she walks along the irregular terrace and past several other small houses, giving a quiet greeting to the residents. At the water stone she stops to rinse the soil off her hands. When she reaches the line of red cedar trees just past the cassava press, Margaret takes her cutlass and first cuts a huge leaf from the philodendron plant growing in the crotch of one tree. Then, from the same plant she cuts a six-foot tendril, a "chaney string." Walking back to the house, she twists the string into a round "cotta" pad for her head; the leaf she ties around a bunch of thyme, which she adds to the bundle. She smooths her white cotton osnaburg dress and red striped apron, straightens and reties her blue head tie, places the cotta on top of it and hoists up the bundle.

Women on their way to market, "heading up" bundles of their wares.

In a moment, Margaret will join Beneba, Lettice, Cumba, and Jenny Ebo for the hour's walk to market; but first she reminds Garrick to bring some dasheen down from her mountain ground at Gadinge and shallots and thyme from his garden at Hog Island. She tells him she hopes to find gar fish at market to make the savory fish stew Mas' Fagan has requested for Sunday night supper, and, if the price is right, she will buy a little extra fish to make Garrick and Quacou some as well.

Quacou, child of her dead sister, Venus, will spend this Sunday with Garrick, first helping him put a new handle on the hoe and then accompanying him to harvest the dasheen in the high plot at Gadinge and to weed the patch of groundnuts and peppers at Hog Island. The fertile dasheen plot was first worked by Judy Congo, an African woman who was grandmother to Margaret and Venus. The use of the steep plot at Hog Island comes to them through Garrick's family, having been passed from uncle to nephew for several generations. Lying in a steep ravine within ten minutes of the plantation, it is prized for its covert convenience. A third plot lies with many others on a strange tabletop land formation completely surrounded and shielded from view by deep forested ravines. This secret garden also can be quickly reached from the slave village but only via a steep treacherous track. The plantation manager knows of the existence of these gardens, but he has never taken the trouble to look for them since they cannot be easily reached on horseback. Almost daily his own kitchen is furnished with slave-grown produce, some of which is given to him and some of which he buys at reasonable rates.

The waiting women call as Margaret turns carefully under the heavy load and swings across the terrace and onto the tree-lined winding cobbled road. The women "heading up" bundles of garden produce, baked goods, guava cheese, cocoa rolls, handmade pottery, woven palm and colita mats, and other crafts for market are joined by assorted children swinging calabash bottles in which they will fetch water at Spring Ghaut on the trip home. With the young girls walking demurely beside the older women and the boys scampering about boisterously shouting at each other, the group makes rapid progress down the steep slope through the tall trees surrounding the plantation complex. At Black Mango the children look longingly at the ripening mangoes hanging on long slender stems. As an extra cash crop of the plantation, they are far from free for the taking. Mas' Fagan has them harvested and sold in Antigua every week during the summer. Last week a twelve-year-old slave girl was taken to court and lost her life's savings in fines for just picking up five overripe fruit. At that she felt fortunate because she had been spared the usual lashes. Mangoes, only recently brought to Montserrat from the Pacific via Jamaica, are in fact not very common; and the only ones slaves can have legitimately are from their own trees. There is one small tree in the slave village, and several planted five years ago on various mountain grounds are just reaching fruit-bearing age.

Below Black Mango, the group emerges into the early morning sunlight of the cane fields stretching down toward the sea along Milaun Ghaut. Just as they begin to breathe easier at being out of sight of Mas' Fagan and of "Fat Boy," as they call Cassius, the black driver who enforces Fagan's orders, they hear a shout. It is Joe Portagee, a midsize boy recently added to the slave community. His origins are a mystery as he is quite light skinned and speaks English with a distinct accent. Since 1809 when slaves could no longer be brought legally from Africa, the plantation has gotten few new slaves; and Galways is, if anything, over-staffed. Joe calls that Mas' Fagan's wife needs Lettice because one of the children is sick. And so, Lettice, who has just finished an order of palm mats for a white lady in town, and who was so looking forward to this trip to market, has to stay behind. Her daughter will carry the mats to the lady and collect the payment.

At Church Yard Gate, they pass Miss Eliza, a free colored woman, who lives along the road to

154

the burying ground. She greets them cheerfully but walks more slowly since these are not people with whom she associates openly.

There is nervous laughter as Jenny Ebo repeats an off-color bit of gossip about the plantation manager's wife. Jenny, the leader of the group, is sixty years old; she was born in Africa and as a woman of twenty was forcibly taken from her Ibo village and brought eventually to Galways. She often speaks of her early life as the daughter of a market woman living near a seaport town. She copes with the lingering horror of her capture, separation from her mother, and trip across the Atlantic by always maintaining a comical attitude. Her witticisms, combining African expressions with an Irish inflection learned in Montserrat, never fail to delight her audience; and her clever commentary on the passing scene seldom stops even when she is quite alone. Now, "heading up" a stem of reddish "Hy-tee" bananas on this Sunday market morning, her dark face is lit up by gold hoop earrings, mischievous eyes laughing under a deep brow, and a sparkling smile that shows up dimples and high round cheeks. Her beautiful teeth are maintained by daily cleaning with cane fiber.

The overall sensuous effect that Jenny Ebo creates is unexpected in a person of her age. Though she never took a husband and never bore a child, Jenny is careful to explain to her women friends that she is not barren. Rather, as Miss Ellen, the obeah woman at Cork Hill, explained, the seed of her various lovers just never matched up with her seed. But, never mind! She still enjoys the status of a mother because she raised Estherbrawn, who was orphaned at three; and now, because this "daughter" is so often sick with the big leg, Jenny is raising Estherbrawn's ten-year-old son, Ned Ryley.

Ned's father, Dan Ryley, a free mulatto cultivator and baker who lives with his sisters and mother in Morris Village at the bottom of Galways Mountain, brings food and clothes for the child and recently gave him a baby goat to raise. Dan, whose own mother's freedom was bought by his Irish father while she was pregnant with Dan, hopes to be able to buy Ned's freedom before he gets much bigger and his value to the plantation increases.

Margaret, always a little wary of Jenny's popularity, is nonetheless glad to be in her company, because around Jenny there is an aura of good humor and high adventure. Jenny's cheerful entourage invariably has a good day at market, helping each other to sell all their wares and make the right contacts for needed items like Garrick's to-bacco or the knife blade Margaret bought last week from that slight swarthy traveling trader who every so often buys and sells out of the thatched hut in Wapping—the fellow with the strange turn of phrase.

Near the foot of the mountain they take a short-cut past the ruins of the old plantation, greeting Joe Piper, a wizened poor buckra (poor white) in a greasy knit cap, who herds goats and sheep for Mas' Fagan on these dry lowlands. Joe, always ready with an outrageously ribald remark for the women, gets the usual hooting, derisive reply from several and slinks back into the smelly shanty he inhabits in the ruins of the old great house.

Heading over the hill into Germans Ghaut, they check the flow at the spring. Water is coming out at a fast trickle and the line of children waiting to fill vessels is short. Several girls are plaiting each other's hair as they wait; and two older women are washing clothes in the overflow. Jenny Ebo announces that they will stop back to fetch water on the way home. She leads them down the ghaut and onto the dusty main road running along the sea cliffs north toward Plymouth. Just then, before they can dodge out of view, a horseman thunders around the bend. It is Major Johnson, a member of the militia who checks the passes that slaves must carry whenever they are away from their home estates. Old Beneba has forgotten her pass. She pleads for leniency, but he replies that he has to enforce the regulations. She sits down heavily on a boulder just inside the plantation bounds and waits while her grandson runs all the way up the mountain to find her pass in the bowl under the floor boards. Because she now stands to lose the best hour at market, she agrees when Jenny and Margaret offer to take her six eggs, her bottle of goat's milk, and the most perishable produce to sell for her. The cooks shopping for the big kitchens of the white people in town pay the best prices, but they are finished with their shopping by seven o'clock.

Reconstructing the life at Galways plantation has helped strengthen the notion that slaves became intimately acquainted with the details of their New World surroundings—the flora, soil types, and weather patterns—and that they had a vital stake in conserving the environment that provided them with a profusion of resources and places of privacy.

seven. Although the work was very hard, the breaks were not used only to rest. Often slaves used this time to tend to their family's well-being—to cultivate house-yard gardens and nearby small subsistence plots. In 1824 Thomas Cooper reported that in Jamaica small plots near the slaves' dwellings were called "shell blow grounds" because slaves would often hurry to these grounds to get in an hour of gardening when the conch shell blew to signal the beginning of the noonday dinner break. During this same period slaves also produced specialty foods like guava preserves, pottery, baskets, or other handcrafts; and women would sew or tend to the needs of their children or aged relatives. When in the mid-eighteenth century slaves got the right to Saturday afternoons off, this time also was put most often to productive, rather than leisure, use. The extra half day meant it was possible to cultivate more remote mountain grounds that offered ecological advantages not available at lower elevations. In some cases, slaves constructed shelters and spent the night in these distant gardens, thus gaining a bit more autonomy.

The sources of information on how Galways slaves used and viewed the environment indicate that they held attitudes quite different from the Europeans. They developed a wealth of knowledge about the mountain and forest resources around them: the subtle variability of the soils, moisture, and angle of sunlight at different elevations and on different slopes; the attributes of wild plants that made them useful for food, fiber, construction, craft, and medicinal purposes; the location of water resources and clay deposits for pottery. They had a stake in preserving the woods and natural areas of the land not only because of the resources they provided but also because of the protection and privacy they afforded. Whether this more elaborate yet conserving use of local resources was due to their station as relatively powerless slaves who had to make do with what was at hand or to an environmental ethic more conserving and sustainable than the Europeans' is open to discussion; but reconstructing the daily lives of slaves in this particular place called Galways reinforces an idea developed by historian David Barry Gaspar, that ultimately everything slaves did in a day was related to their resistance to dominance. They were either pushing the limits to garner a little extra time and space within which to exert their own initiative to improve their lives, or, after they had pushed too far, they were accommodating in order to strike a necessary balance with the authorities.

Whatever their conscious environmental ethic, the slaves seem less inclined to treat the environment as something to be used up and discarded in the march toward personal wealth; rather, being intimately dependent upon the environment, they accommodated to its bounties and scarcities, improving their standard of living in good times and retracting to minimum subsistence in times of drought, hurricane damage, decline in the plantation's prosperity, or when the management became more restrictive and oppressive.

As participants in the Columbian exchange, slaves are particularly interesting. They themselves, of course, were unwilling migrants; and the millions that survived the horror of the capture and passage from Africa substantially modified New World demography. But it is the cultural attributes of resilience and resourcefulness they brought with them that are the most significant. Early African settlers in Montserrat must have been particularly inventive in adjusting to the new environment because they not only adapted many African plants and customs to the Caribbean setting, they also borrowed many ideas from the remnant of Native Americans who survived into the early eighteenth century. The gardens of slaves were a mixture full of African, Indian, and European domesticates, and the same is true for their descendants today. Even more indicative of their cultural exchange with the original inhabitants of Montserrat is the adoption of indigenous methods of plant processing

Monday through Saturday slaves were in the fields by dawn. They got a half-hour off for breakfast and an hour or so for a midday meal, served in the field. They worked again until dark at six-thirty or seven.

and cooking, only slightly modified to accommodate to a different African-European tool complex. Cassava, a staple in Indian diets, became the same for the slaves. In the Galways slave village archaeological evidence shows that the slaves there may have mass-produced cassava as an entrepreneurial activity. They used metal graters, fabric meal sacks, the fulcrum press, and metal griddles rather than the stone-shard board graters, basket presses and sieves, and clay griddles of the native tool complex.

The slaves also amalgamated New and Old World foods into their cuisine. Goatwater, a ceremonial Montserratian stew that in its preparation and consumption carries Yoruba sacrificial connotations, contains a number of ingredients that were exclusive to the New World prior to Columbus. And duchno, a dish considered throughout the Caribbean to be quintessentially African, is in fact made up of items from all over the world: grated sweet potatoes from northern South America, peppers from Mesoamerica, sugar and coconut, both ultimately from Asia, and wheat flour from the Near East. The duchno dough is wrapped in banana leaves and boiled or baked. Bananas, although originally from Asia, were brought to the New World in the early 1500s from Africa.

What happened at Galways plantation on the island of Montserrat is only one tiny fragment of the story of "Seeds of Change," and the debate over how the African experience in the New World should be interpreted will continue for many years. Certainly the brutality of the system must be constantly reexamined and confronted; but the research at Galways has shown that the story that best credits those who perished and those who survived is the life-affirming saga of resilience, resistance, and creative adaptation.

The heirs of Montserrat's slaves who are striving to preserve the details of their culture and the pride of their race have a rich legacy upon which to draw.

Savoring Africa in the New World

Robert L. Hall

Like religion, oral traditions, music, dance, and material culture, cuisine and culinary practices not only survived Africans' capture, the middle passage, and hard servitude but also enriched the cultures of the Americas. Fried chicken, among other southern dishes, reflects this African influence; even the seasoning of southern dishes, often far heavier than in northern recipes, constitutes another African influence. When Americans of any hue sit down to a meal of gumbo, spicy chicken garnished with peanuts (goobers), black-eyed peas or pigeon peas and rice, cola, and dessert of banana pudding or yam pie sweetened with sorghum molasses, we are savoring a taste of Africa. The vitality of these culinary traditions in the Americas is a testament to the richness of African cultures and to those Africans who shared that richness with their host societies. Of all the

Diners at Bob the Chef's soul food restaurant in Boston enjoy a cuisine with strong if sorrowful links to Africa (previous pages). Many wild plants were first domesticated in Africa and with other important foods came to the New World with slaves. The women in the rock painting, ca. 4000–1500 B.C., are thought to be gathering wild grain.

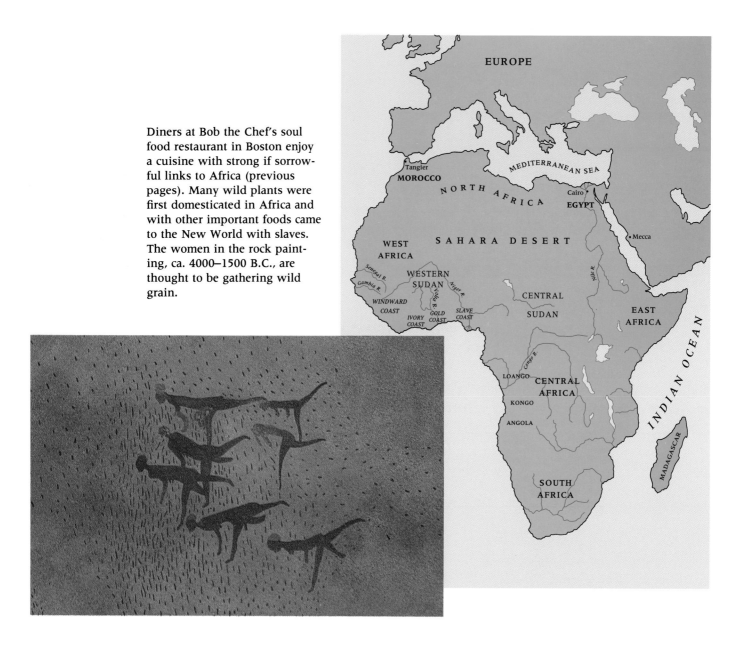

plants it would be possible to mention, this chapter discusses the links between the Atlantic slave trade and the dispersal of yams, millet and sorghum, rice, bananas, citrus fruits, corn, cassava, and melegueta pepper.

African Agriculture and Indigenous Crops

The domestication of plants and animals in Africa is of great antiquity. Evidence of grain cultivation at Al Fayyūm dates to at least 4000 B.C. African groups began to experiment with wild grasses from which they eventually domesticated the millets—sorghum, pennisetum, and eleusine—around the third millennium B.C. Sesame was also developed on the southern *sahel,* or shore, of the Sahara desert and had diffused to Sumer before 2350 B.C.

Vegeculture based on the domestication of wild yams native to sub-Saharan Africa may have begun as early as 5000–4000 B.C. About twenty-five hundred years ago the introduction of iron working into West Africa advanced yam-based agriculture further into the forest zone with the result that "yams were increasingly favored ecologically at the expense of grain crops. The yam-using ethnic groups were thus able to evolve a higher cultural level as they had a more adequate, reliable, and generally superior nutritional base" (Coursey 1976).

During the late eighteenth and early nineteenth centuries, yam plantations employing slave labor dominated the economy of the Fouta Djallon region of Senegambia. René Caillié, who visited the area in 1820, found near Gneretemile "an ouronde, or slave village, surrounded by good plantations of bananas, cotton, cassavas and yams." At the plantation of Popoco, located about two days' travel from the capital of Timbo, Caillié saw "between one hundred and fifty and two hundred slaves, who are employed in agriculture." They cultivated cassava, yams, peanuts, rice, and millet.

The incidence of yam cultivation and consumption within Africa was not without far-reaching political and religious ramifications. The yam's reliable yield "led to high population densities and the necessity for both a political superstructure to coordinate [indigenous] activities and a religious superstructure to ensure its successful continuity" (Posnansky 1969). Among the Ewe of Aloi, Togo, the yam was the focus of a harvest festival in which, before partaking of any of the yield, the Ewe prayed to Mawu (God) for another plentiful harvest in the coming year.

Foods of the Middle Passage

Slave traders, interested in ensuring that as much as possible of their lucrative cargo survived the middle passage, may have been inadvertently responsible for the transportation of yams, as well as other indigenous African crops, to the Americas. By at least the early 1700s, slavers had learned that, although some English foods were acceptable, slaves fared better when fed their customary food. An Englishman who made a number of slaving voyages as ship's surgeon during the late 1770s and early 1780s, Alexander Falconbridge, attested, "Yams are the favourite food of the Eboe, or Bight Negroes, and rice or corn, of those from the Gold and Windward Coasts; each preferring the produce of their native soil." Falconbridge also noted that at least once a day slaves were fed their own foods. In 1705 the Royal African Company's factors at Ouidah recommended corn, yams, melegueta pepper, and palm oil as items suitable for the slaves' diet.

Yams

Whether of Asian or the indigenous African varieties, yams were frequently put on slave ships as provisions for slaves, particularly when the involuntary African passengers came from yam-eating societies. In 1678 the British slave ship *Arthur*, which had put on a considerable load of yams as provisions, faced the problem of their rotting before they could be consumed. The large quantities of yams the slavers provisioned are demonstrated by John Barbot's assertion that "a ship that takes in five hundred slaves, must provide above a hundred thousand yams," or about two hundred yams per person. The accounts of the *Othello* (1768–69) reveal that hundreds of baskets of yams were taken on board as provisions along with lesser quantities of "gobbagobs" (goobers or peanuts), plantains, limes, pepper, and palm oil (Donnan 1930–35).

Once in the Americas, one variety of yam, *Dioscorea alata* (the water yam), became a central item in the diet of Haitian slaves and eventually spread throughout the tropical New World where it became standard fare for black peasants.

Two hundred yams per person was the rule of thumb among slavers provisioning their ships for the Atlantic crossing. One variety, the water yam (below), became a principal food first for Haitian slaves and eventually for blacks throughout the tropical Americas.

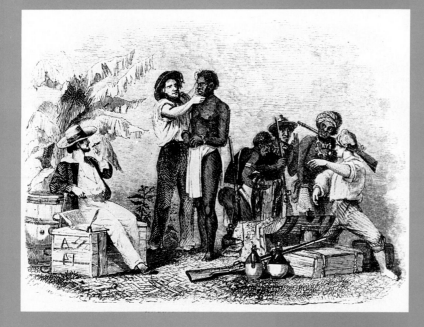

164

Not only did the yam cross the Atlantic, but even the word we use to refer to the yam is derived indirectly from African languages. This derivation reflects the probable path of the vegetable's diffusion. Likely sources of the English word *yam* are the Portuguese *inhame* or the Spanish *(i)ñame*. These words in turn probably derived from one or more West African languages. They are akin to the Wolof terms *nyam* or *nyami*, the latter a verb meaning "to eat." In Mende, *yambi* refers to the wild yam.

Millet and Sorghum

Although it now seems that yam cultivation predates millet and sorghum domestication, the millets remain among the oldest cereal crops grown in sub-Saharan Africa. Millets and sorghums were dominant staple crops in Africa at least one thousand years ago. There is some confusion of names, as "millet" and "sorghum" are sometimes used synonymously. One translation of early Arabic sources of West African history arbitrarily renders the Arabic *dukhn* as millet and *dhura* as sorghum. In the *Mukhtasar Kitab al-Buldan*, published in anno Hegirae 290 (or about A.D. 903), Ibn al-Faqih described the food of the country of Ghana, referring to the medieval Sudanic kingdom: "The food of the people there consists of sorghum (*dhura*), which they call *dukhn* 'millet' and of cowpeas (*lubiya*)" (Levtzion and Hopkins 1981). When introduced into the New World this grain-yielding plant, widely grown for food in North and West Africa, was known as guinea corn. Most of the peoples of central Africa, too, were peasant farmers who raised small livestock and cultivated millet and bananas, for instance, in 1482 when the first contacts with the Portuguese began.

It seems that not only did a significant percentage of the African slaves originate in millet-raising societies, but an equally significant percentage may have been involved in millet farming immediately before embarking. For instance, among the slaves the British traded to Spanish America between 1700 and 1739, African agricultural cycles determined the availability of captives for export. "African traders were least likely to sell their slaves during planting and harvesting periods. The captives were evidently being employed in agrarian tasks and were only parted with when their labor was no longer required." The same circumstances pertained at Gajaaga, Senegambia, "where slave owners used their slaves to plant millet prior to selling them to the French" (Palmer 1981).

Rice

Like millet domestication, rice cultivation in Africa dates to at least the first millennium of the Christian era. Wet rice (*Oryza glaberrima*) was first domesticated on the middle Niger about 1500 B.C. with a secondary *berceau*, or cradle, between the Sine-Saloum and the Casamance rivers. It was cultivated by A.D. 50 at Jenne-Jeno, the oldest known Iron Age city in sub-Saharan Africa. The bones, grain fragments, and utensils unearthed at the site reveal a mixed diet that included rice as well as fish and beef.

Both in Africa and in Carolina, slave buyers preferred captives from those African groups that had millennia of rice-farming experience. A notice in the 11 July 1785 *Evening Gazette* (Charleston) announced the arrival of a Danish ship bearing "a choice cargo of Windward and Gold Coast Negroes, who have been accustomed to the planting of rice." As Peter H. Wood has pointed out, "literally hundreds of black immigrants were more familiar with the planting, hoeing, processing, and

To protect their assets, some slave traders gave slaves familiar foods to eat during the middle passage. In this way, the slavers were the unwitting conveyers of yams and other indigenous African food crops to the Americas. The recommended diet for slaves included yams, peanuts, plantains, corn, and palm oil. Some agents also consulted with black healers about which plants, herbs, and spices were useful in treating illnesses. Africans especially extolled the medicinal properties of cayenne and melegueta pepper. A healthy-looking slave would bring more money on the auction block (below). Palm oil served more than a dietary function; it imparted a sleek, youthful appearance when rubbed on the skin.

cooking of rice than were the European settlers who purchased them." Although the type of rice that became a staple crop in colonial South Carolina was probably the Asian variety *Oryza sativa* rather than the African domesticate *O. glaberrima*, the know-how was contributed by the Africans, many of whom had probably cultivated both species of rice before their arrival in North America. Scholars have argued not only that "much of the initial success of South Carolina owed to its black population" but also that "subsequent agricultural advances depended in no small measure upon African contributions" (Vlach 1978). The fanner and storage baskets and rice mortars that survive and continue to be made in coastal South Carolina by the lineal descendants of Africans imported into South Carolina are symbols of the African-derived technology and know-how that enabled rice to flourish in the United States.

Plantains and Bananas

Several plants of Asian origin, among them plantains (*Musa sapientum* var. *paradisiaca*) and bananas (*Musa sapientum*), were established in Africa well before the Portuguese landed there in the fifteenth century. Indeed, when al-Mas'ūdī visited Madagascar during the tenth century A.D. he found the peoples of eastern Africa eating bananas and coconuts.

The Portuguese found bananas in West Africa when they began their voyages of exploration in the fifteenth century and took this fruit to the Canary Islands. There is little credible evidence of bananas in the New World before Columbus; therefore, the introduction of bananas from the Canary Islands to Haiti in 1516 was their entrée into the Western Hemisphere.

Melegueta Pepper

The red pepper that flavors our spicy chicken with peanuts reminds us that a significant part of African culinary practice consists of the condiments and seasonings used to prepare foods. Many African traditional dishes achieve their hot taste with either red pepper (cayenne) or melegueta pepper. The Windward Coast of Africa between Cape Mount and Assini (roughly present-day Liberia and Ivory Coast) was

Slaves brought okra (top), ackee (bottom), and many other foods that over time have enriched New World cuisine. But it was the Africans' long acquaintance with the cultivation of grains that enhanced their appeal to European slave traders, who were quick to perceive the value of workers already equipped with agrarian skills that would prove indispensable on the American plantations. The granary in an ancient Congo village (below, right) and a modern rice harvest in Haiti (opposite) attest to the contribution of Africans to New World agriculture.

particularly noteworthy for its melegueta pepper, derived from the small, spicy berry of the wild tree called by many names including African pepper, British pepper, Jamaican pepper, paradise grain, and guinea pepper. It was used to prepare both food and beverages and was thought to prevent dysentery and stomach disorders, the major scourges of the middle passage.

Records of the Royal African Company indicate that some agents in the trade tried to discern what treatments for illnesses the Africans themselves used, especially for disorders prevalent during the middle passage. In 1699, for example, the Royal African Company factors at River Sherbro were instructed to "keep friendship with some natives that understand the best remedies for their distempers." William Bosman said of the Gold Coast area that the "chief medicaments" were lime, melegueta pepper, cardamon (an East Indian spice), several varieties of herb, and roots, branches, and gums of trees.

Foods from the Americas

Besides the export of plants and foods from Africa, another long-term result of the Columbian discovery was the import of plants into Africa. From the New World came peanuts, papayas, guavas, avocados, maize, pineapples, and manioc (cassava). The Portuguese also planted lemon, lime, and orange groves along the Atlantic coast. Resourceful captains then provisioned these citrus fruits to inhibit scurvy among their human cargo. Besides oranges and limes, pawpaws and groundnuts were introduced into the Gambia by the Portuguese. E. J. Alagoa believed that "cassava was apparently introduced to the Niger Delta by the Portuguese through Warri and Benin." According to him, the plant name was recorded at Warri by John Barbot in the late 1600s: "Magnoc bushes, which they call *Mandi-hoka* in their language; of which they make *cassaba*, or *Farinha de Pao*, that is in Portuguese, wood-meal, which is the bread they commonly feed on." Once the American crops the Portuguese introduced became African staples, a land-use revolution resulted that facilitated denser settlement of the forests.

Linguistic evidence corroborates the working hypothesis that the Portuguese introduced these foodstuffs to Africa. In the Niger Delta of southern Nigeria the names by which cassava, rice, oranges, limes, and coconuts are known are all derived from Portuguese. These derivatives suggest that Portuguese naval squadrons, with their far-flung contacts, were among the chief agents of importation.

Maize is first documented in the African regions of most direct interest to the Portuguese during the late fifteenth and early sixteenth centuries. Although Roland Portères thought that the Spanish introduced maize from the Caribbean to the Mediterranean basin and Egypt, he still concluded that the Portuguese brought maize from Brazil to the Guinea coast.

Local folklore reflects the first contact of the Portuguese with the Congo-Angola coastline in the 1480s: "The white men arrived in ships with wings which shone in the sun like knives; they brought maize and cassava and groundnuts and tobacco" (Birmingham 1967). According to the oral traditions of the Bushongo peoples of south-central Congo, maize was first introduced to them in the 1600s. In the same century, the European visitor Olfert Dapper noted an abundance of maize on the Gold Coast.

The American crops promoted the growth of West African populations; however, the slave trade siphoned off these increased numbers. Elaborating the cruel irony, Alfred Crosby speculated that increased production of maize, manioc, and other American plants "enabled the slave trade to go on as long as it did without pumping the black well of Africa dry. The Atlantic slave traders drew many, perhaps most, of their cargoes from the rain forest areas, precisely those areas where American crops enabled heavier settlements than before."

African Culinary Survival and Acculturation

One inescapable implication of the Columbian Quincentenary for African-derived New World populations is that all of the food products we have discussed, as well as some we have not treated, were inextricably linked to slavery. These foods either served to increase the African population and thus support the overseas slave trade, or were used cosmetically to make slaves look young and sleek for sale (rubbing with palm oil), or were fed to slaves as provisions during the middle passage (yams, peanuts, corn, and rice), or were provided to keep slaves healthy during that voyage (citrus fruits and melegueta pepper), or became plantation products that required or utilized slave labor in the New World (rice and sugarcane).

Our hypothetical dinner does not merely reflect centuries of hardship and endurance. The extent to which that dinner is stereotypically American, the frequency with which it appears in advertising, fiction, and films as the quintessence of the American family meal, is an indicator of the extent to which African cuisine has been assimilated into and enriched American culture. Indeed, Sidney Mintz has observed, "How 'African' *all* Americans are is conventionally hidden by the assumption that, under conditions of oppression, acculturation is a one-way street." To the extent that it reflects mutual acculturation, the African and American culinary exchange is representative of the cultural amalgamation that typifies the Columbian exchange.

Food and culinary practices cannot be easily disjoined from a people's music, dance, and oral traditions. At the Dooky Chase restaurant in New Orleans, diners can experience more than one facet of African culture in a meal that is stereotypically American.

169

Nature and Nurture among African Americans

Studies of diet and disease in Africa are important for persons of African descent in the Americas. On the one hand, such studies may reveal shared genetic traits that predispose certain persons of African descent to specific diseases, and if this predisposition exists, as it does in the case of sickle-cell anemia, careful voluntary genetic screening and counseling might be called for. On the other hand, comparative studies of disease patterns can help us guard against hasty attribution to genetic factors of various black-white differences in the incidence of particular diseases.

Nurture: African babies who receive almost constant tactile and social stimulation from their mothers thrive in their first year.

Nature: For individuals living in areas infested with malaria-carrying anopheles mosquitoes, sickle-shaped red blood cells have adaptive value.

Cancer

Prostate cancer has a higher incidence among American blacks than among American whites, and the hasty conclusion could be drawn that genetics cause the difference. We know, for instance, that common internal cancers are associated with a diet that is high in fat and low in fiber. Prostate cancer, which has a very low incidence among Africans in regions known to have contributed significantly to the United States' black population, has a very high incidence among black Americans. One study conducted jointly by Howard University and the University of Ibadan in Nigeria, while generally inconclusive, found that one of the most consistent differences between black American males and Nigerian males was the higher fat content and lower fiber content of the American diet (Scarupa 1986). Thus, what on the face of things appeared to be attributable to genetic differences between American blacks and whites proved, upon examination, to be attributable to dietary factors.

Neonatal Alertness and Infant Growth

Child development specialists long have been puzzled by the greater gains by African babies in their first year compared to their American counterparts (largely white), and given the American racial climate throughout much of the twentieth century when these questions were being explored, these specialists were tempted to suggest that genetic differences may have been involved. In an effort to explain the phenomenon, T. Berry Brazelton of the Harvard Medical School studied Zambian and American infants during the first ten days after birth. He found that by the tenth day, despite prematurity at birth, African newborns were more attentive to social stimuli than the white Americans. Brazelton believed that the rapid progress in health and social development of the Africans derived from child care practices which stressed maternal contact. A Zambian infant is carried on the mother's hip from as early as its second day and receives almost constant tactile and social stimulation.

Protracted breast-feeding is an essential of the extensive maternal contact in Zambia, as well as other African societies. Indeed, most African babies are nursed for two to three years, carried in prolonged body contact with their mothers, and nursed on demand. Mother-baby sensory contact among the Yorubas of Nigeria involves eighteen to twenty-two months of breast-feeding; "the baby will remain from birth until about the second year of life almost constantly in close physical contact with the mother who will feed it at irregular intervals usually determined by the onset of crying" (Matthews 1955). Children of the Hausa of northern Nigeria "are breast-fed for about two years, during which time the mother should avoid sexual relations." The Afikpo Ibo women "traditionally nursed their children for about two and a half to three years" and customarily abstained from intercourse until the child was weaned. When a Fulani child is born it is given undiluted cow's milk for a couple of days followed by nine months of exclusive breast-feeding. The suckling child is carried slung on its mother's back up to two years during which time mother's milk is gradually replaced by cow's milk and solids. Here again, it is the child's social inheritance—the child-raising practices of his culture—rather than the child's genetic inheritance that accounts for the child's phenomenal development.

Malaria

In the case of malaria there initially appears to be a correlation between nutrition and health in the apparent relationship between the geographical distribution of the sickle-cell trait and the incidence of yam cultivation. Indeed, Frank B. Livingstone has observed that "the frequency of the sickle cell trait coincides with this spread of yam cultivation." Further scrutiny has revealed that yams are grown in West Africa using slash-and-burn techniques. These farming methods also provide additional breeding locations for the malaria-carrying anopheles mosquito, and herein lies the connection between yams and sickle cell.

While potentially lethal when inherited from both parents, the sickle-cell trait has adaptive value for populations living in malaria-infested areas when the trait is inherited from only one parent. Sickling, which alters the shape of red blood cells, increases the chances that an individual will survive an attack by the malarial parasite that the anopheles mosquito carries. Sickle-cell trait is not, then, a result of a diet of yams; it is rather an adaptation to a malarial environment.

If it is true that "societies with the greatest dependence on agriculture have the highest frequencies of the sickle-cell trait" (Wiesenfeld 1967), it may also be true that differences in the incidence of hemoglobin S among black American populations suggest the differing degrees to which the African ancestors of subregional populations of black Americans came from societies with varying degrees of reliance on slash-and-burn agriculture for sustenance.

Conclusion

Examining prostate cancer, the growth of newborns, and the relationship between yams and sickle-cell trait has revealed the foolhardiness of hasty conclusions when analyzing complex situations in which both heredity and environment can be factors. We must bear in mind, whether discussing Africans, Asians, or Europeans, animals or plants, that we have barely begun to understand the intriguing intricacies of nature and nurture.

Hispanic American Heritage

Joseph P. Sánchez

Nineteen-ninety-two will be more than the five hundredth anniversary of Columbus's voyage of discovery to the New World. It will be a commemoration of half a millennium that began with an encounter between two worlds: Indian America and Europe. This encounter began a process of social interaction on a scale rarely equaled on earth, a process that continues today. Nineteen-ninety-two will offer an opportunity to reflect on the process, on the Pan-American experience that links all people in the Western Hemisphere. Pan-Americanism has been painfully clouded by war, genocide, and cultural misunderstanding, preventing citizens of North and South America from seeing clearly their commonalities in history, culture, and heritage. At first the view was blocked by European colonialism, then by nascent nationalism burdened with ethnocentrism; political majorities became blind to the Pan-American heritage they shared with minorities. The Columbus Quincentenary offers Americans, especially in the United States, an opportunity to reflect upon who they are as a people. Given the common Western European and colonial backgrounds, together with the Native American heritage, being an American in New England is not unlike being an American in the Southwest, although too often the differences are emphasized. Our national heritage mixes the Indian, Spanish, and English. This essay will address first some reasons the contribution of Hispanics to United States history has been obscured and undervalued and, second, some sources for the construction of a clearer, more complete picture. Hispanic America is a vital link to the recovery of the national and Pan-American heritages of the Western Hemisphere.

Colonial Rivalries and la Leyenda Negra

The contradictory perception of Hispanic America has its roots in the colonial rivalries of the sixteenth century. In 1604, during the golden age of Spain, the great Spanish intellectual, Francisco Gómez de Quevedo y Villegas wrote *España defendida*. In it, he presaged another sort of encounter: that between English America and Spanish America. He called attention to a malaise that had pervaded Spanish-English diplomatic relations. Quevedo pointed out that anti-Spanish propaganda and misconceptions were deeply rooted in the lore of Protestant Europe. More than three hundred years later, in 1912, another Spanish writer, Julian Juderías, observed that anti-Spanish—indeed, anti-Hispanic—distortions in both Europe and the Americas constituted a *Leyenda Negra*—a Black Legend. Sixty years after Juderías

La V. M.ᵃ Maria de Iesus de Agreda. Predicando à los Chichimecos del Nuebo-mexico. Antt.ᵈᵉ Cosᵗᵒoᶠ.

In this woodcut of 1631 Mother María de Jesús de Agreda is seen preaching to the Indians of the Southwest. Despite opposition from England and France, by the end of the 1700s Spain had cast the net of Hispanic culture across North America from San Francisco to Saint Augustine.

had coined the term "Black Legend," scholars in the United States responding to the civil rights movement and Chicano activism sought to understand historical anti-Hispanic attitudes that had continued to affect public policies at home and foreign relations with Spain and Latin America. They concluded that the Black Legend had resulted in beliefs that Hispanics were uniquely and inherently evil. The centuries-old anti-Spanish propaganda became folklore with far-reaching consequences and denigrating stereotypes of Hispanics.

The basis upon which the Black Legend rested was the fear, envy, and enmity for Spain of those nation-states that clashed with Spanish power shortly after the New World voyages of Columbus. Spain and Portugal, by dint of their discoveries and explorations, won exclusive approval of their claims to the Americas from Pope Alexander VI in 1493. Other western European nations did not agree. King Francis I of France quipped, "I fain to see Adam's will to see how he divided the earth." Despite belligerent efforts by England and France, the Spanish sphere of influence grew to an empire that stretched from North Africa across the Americas to the Philippines. By the end of the 1700s, Spain's New World claims were anchored in the north by settlements that began at San Francisco in the west and crossed the continent to Saint Augustine in the east. In the North American interior the claim was effectively held by outposts at Tucson in Arizona, Santa Fe in New Mexico, and San Antonio on the Texas frontier. East of them, Saint Louis and New Orleans along the Mississippi River began a series of Spanish towns that stretched to Florida's Atlantic coast by way of Mobile, Pensacola, and Tallahassee. From there the Spanish claim ran southward, inclusive of Caribbean islands, to the Strait of Magellan. Missions, presidios, and towns, as well as Indian villages, dotted the imperial Spanish map. This widespread colonial empire aggravated the propagandists who despised Spain's grip on the New World.

Neither Spain's powerful claim to the New World nor anti-Catholic attitudes among Protestant Europeans were enough to make Spain a scapegoat for European frustrations and jealousies of the period. Ironically, Spanish efforts to administer justice and to reform certain colonial practices in regard to Indians played into her rivals' hands.

Reform of the Encomienda

Far from European courts, missionary priests in the wilds of the New World worked to Christianize Indians and to establish a colonial presence among them. One of them, the Dominican friar Bartolomé de las Casas, argued that Indians had a legal status under Spanish law, but in practice Indian rights were not often observed. Although conquistadores had been brought to trial and imprisoned for abuses of such laws, Las Casas believed that not enough had been done to right the situation, especially in the area of Indian tribute and servitude. In 1540, after years of collecting information related to violations of Indian rights by Spaniards, Las Casas submitted a report entitled *Brevísima relación de la destrucción de las Indias*—A Brief Account of the Destruction of the Indies—to the Hapsburg Emperor Charles V.

Cadiz, a point of entry for the treasure-laden Spanish fleets returning from the New World, was a target of English raids. Colonial rivalries of the 1500s led Protestant Europeans—the contenders for global prestige as well as New World treasure—to paint a picture of the Spanish as being uniquely and inherently evil. This indictment constitutes *la Leyenda Negra,* the Black Legend, which lingers into the late 20th century as prejudice against people of Hispanic descent.

Charles was aware that Las Casas sought to reform the tribute-collecting system that had wreaked havoc on Indian populations and economies. The *encomienda,* the authority given to a conquistador to collect tribute, was often the guise for indentured servitude, if not outright slavery, of natives who could not pay the tribute. Aside from urging the abolition of the encomienda, Las Casas complained that the military conquest of the Americas had been much more traumatic than theretofore realized, and he recommended that the license to conquer be restricted. As the "Protector of Indians," he worked for reform and social experimentation that would show Indians and Spaniards coexisting in a modified colonial society. Charles read the report, listened to his council debate it, and decided that reform was in order. The result was the New Laws of 1542. When word of the abolition of the encomienda reached *encomenderos* and investors, rioting occurred in Peru and

175

Mexico. The king was petitioned and as a result of the outcry, the encomienda, which was as old as the Moorish wars, was given new life.

When Las Casas began his crusade for reform, he collected data to support his case that Spaniards abused Indians. The examples he gave in his report were intended to incite the king and his court to action. Las Casas did not discuss other relationships such as intermarriage between the two groups, actual friendships that had developed among them, religious affiliations that created spiritual bonds and obligations, or the many kinships that the inclusive Spanish colonial culture had wrought throughout the Americas.

Las Casas's plea for reform succeeded admirably. After 1542, more changes were instituted, and finally the laws of 1572 brought the period of conquest to an end. Slowly the evolutionary pattern of colonial-native relationships had been enhanced. If nothing else, Las Casas had achieved his goal of bringing the plight of Indians to the attention of his king.

Misuse of the Las Casas Relación

But Las Casas's intentions were subverted by anti-Spanish propagandists. Ten years after his bid to reform the Indies had run its course, the Dutch acquired a copy of his report and published it. The English and French followed suit. Within a few years, translations of the *Relación* circulated throughout the Protestant countries of Europe. The damning report, claimed Spain's foes, was proof that Catholic Spain was bigoted. Catholic Spaniards, they wrote, had exterminated and brutalized Indians. The sixteenth-century Dutch artist Theodore de Bry, who had never been to the Americas, sketched pictures depicting Spaniards randomly torturing and killing Indians. Unwittingly, Las Casas had given propagandists ammunition to describe Spaniards as depraved and cowardly people who had committed crimes against defenseless natives.

Intermarriage, friendship, religious affiliation, and other affirmative links bound Spanish colonials and native peoples. In accentuating the problems of colonial oppression, Las Casas did not enumerate the many examples of positive cultural interaction.

In this way, the Black Legend, in the ideological ferment of the Reformation, took on strong anti-Catholic implications. Anti-Spanish propaganda, predicated on simplistic and faulty analysis of historical information, was disseminated by Spain's rivals in the Dutch Lowlands, England, France, and the Germanies to promote the falsehood that Spaniards were *uniquely* cruel, bigoted, tyrannical, lazy, violent, treacherous, and depraved. The alleged depravity of Spaniards implied some unforgivable original sin that undermined the legitimacy of Hispanic culture throughout the world. Thus, the anti-Spanish propaganda of the past created the body of misconceptions known as the Black Legend and formed the basis of anti-Hispanic stereotypes.

Perpetuation of la Leyenda Negra

In the next four centuries, the Black Legend was kept alive, especially whenever conflict arose between English- and Spanish-speaking societies. In the 1800s, four events revived and perpetuated Black Legend stereotypes: the Texas Revolt (1836), the Mexican War (1846–48), the California gold rush with its attendant westward movement (1849–56), and the Spanish-American War (1898). Each was characterized by conflict and an anti-Hispanic campaign during which publishers of books and

news-papers exploited the misconceptions of la Leyenda Negra. During the Spanish-American War, a deluxe version of Bartolomé de las Casas's *Relación,* illustrated with Theodore de Bry's sketches, was published and circulated by a New York publisher.

In recent years, historians, popular writers, and textbook authors have unwittingly or intentionally lent their prestige to the legend. In today's popular media, elements of the legend are obvious in newsprint, television programs, and Hollywood depictions of Hispanics. In four centuries the Black Legend leapt from a few quill-written manuscripts, to mass-produced literature, to electronic media that project moving images in support of yesterday's propaganda.

The perception of Hispanic Americans by the dominant society has been biased throughout history. Published diaries and collections of letters as well as newspaper accounts by Anglo-Americans, especially in the nineteenth century, reinforced the Black Legend stereotypes of Hispanics. The accounts, written for an English-speaking audience, taken in their totality, were nothing short of name-calling. Moreover, the printed generalizations supported the oral tradition as if newspapers, diaries, and short stories were evidence of Hispanic depravity. In the perspective of the late twentieth century, the impact of the propaganda is abundantly clear. Between 1845 and 1947, Hispanic Americans in the Southwest were subjected to laws and practices similar to the Jim Crow laws that discriminated against free blacks after the Civil War. As in nineteenth-century Texas, law enforcers in other parts of the West, sometimes modeled after the Texas Rangers, justified murdering innocent Mexicans by relying on the long-held misconception that Mexicans were treacherous, cowardly, and diabolical. Historian Walter Prescott Webb best expresses the attitude that rationalizes these atrocities. In *The Texas Rangers,* Webb wrote that the Mexican has "a cruel streak," which in turn "must be dealt with cruelly." Such beliefs pervaded American thought in the nineteenth century and persisted in the twentieth.

The missionary priest Bartolomé de las Casas brought the plight of the New World Indians to the attention of the Spanish monarch, which ultimately led to reform in colonial dealings with natives. His report on the abuses of his fellow Spaniards also reached the attention of the Dutch, French, and English, who circulated translations of it throughout Protestant Europe and used its most incriminating portions to portray Spaniards as a diabolic race. Their distortions of Las Casas's work helped initiate *la Leyenda Negra.*

Americo Paredes, renowned folklorist, explored the consequences of misconceptions about Hispanics in his studies of American literature, published diaries, and everyday speech. He concluded that injustices had caused Hispanics in the Southwest to see themselves as "foreigners in a foreign land." In his study of "The Ballad of Gregorio Cortez," Paredes recognized that not only was there an Hispanic explanation for the injustice against Cortez, there was another story, an unwritten Hispanic history with deeper traditions and broader implications related to American history and culture. In 1958, Paredes published his study under the title *With His Pistol in His Hand: A Border Ballad and Its Hero.* In it he narrated the story of the false accusation, persecution, and imprisonment of Gregorio Cortez from a bicultural point of view, for he had discovered the ballad in the Hispanic oral tradition and compared it with newspaper accounts and court transcripts of Cortez's trial in Texas at the turn of the twentieth century. Paredes's analysis of the case against Cortez demonstrated the implications of historical stereotypes of Hispanic society. Not only were anti-Hispanic biases deeply rooted in Texas, they acted as a divisive force between two peoples, keeping one dominant and the other subservient.

Quincentenary Opportunities

The Columbus Quincentenary provides a chance to reassess the meaning of Hispanic history, culture, and heritage in relation to the greater American experience. One does not need to look far to make that reassessment. In *The Spanish Pioneers* Charles Lummis wrote: "When you know that the greatest of English textbooks has not even the name of the man who first sailed around the world (a Spaniard), nor of the man who discovered Brazil (a Spaniard), nor of him who discovered California (a Spaniard), nor of those Spaniards who first found and colonized what is now

Creating frightful images of scenes he had never witnessed, the 16th-century Dutch artist Theodore de Bry was particularly successful at warping the intent of the Las Casas report.

When nationalistic emotions run high, racial prejudice comes easy. In the 19th century, anti-Spanish sentiments boiled over during the Texas Revolt, Mexican War, California gold rush, and the Spanish-American War.

the United States, and that it has a hundred other omissions as glaring, and a hundred histories as untrue as the omissions are inexcusable, you will understand that it is high time we should do better justice than did our fathers to a subject which should be of the first interest to all real Americans.''

Almost a century has passed since Lummis's words were first printed. Yet, little has been done to include the Hispanic story in our textbooks. James Axtell criticized textbook writers and publishers of American history by exposing their disregard of the Hispanic role in our nation's development. Likewise, William H. McNeill wrote: ''Historians, by helping to define 'us' and 'them,' play a considerable part in focusing love and hate, the two principal cements of collective behavior known to humanity. But myth making for rival groups has become a dangerous game in the atomic age, and we may well ask whether there is any alternative open to us.'' While sixteenth-century anti-Spanish propagandists indulged their immediate nationalistic needs, they also influenced the intellectual and popular thought of the English-speaking world far beyond their generations and culture. In 1992, mythographers will get a second chance to set the record straight.

Documentary resources for a reassessment of a common American history are available in Spanish colonial archives throughout Europe and the Americas. The Archivo General de Indias in Seville contains an estimated forty-four million pages of documents that tell the story of 328 years of Spanish administration of the Americas. The Archivo General de Simancas near Valladolid holds another important multi-million-page collection of manuscripts, as do various Spanish colonial archives and libraries throughout Spain. Similarly, the Archivo General de la Nación in Mexico City and related colonial archives in all of the state archives contain historical materials that weave a fascinating story of North America. The colonial archives of

During the 19th and 20th centuries, anti-Hispanic bias took a virulent twist in the southwestern United States and became a means for keeping one culture subservient to another. "The Ballad of Gregorio Cortez" tells the story of a young Mexican who was falsely accused, persecuted, and imprisoned in South Texas at the turn of the century. The folk ballad laments the harms that result from Hispanic stereotyping. The folklorist Americo Paredes wrote a book about Gregorio Cortez, which in turn was made into a movie in 1982.

the various countries of Central America and South America, likewise, reveal a parallel frontier culture. The story of the Western Hemisphere, formed by European expansion, is based on the common thread of colonialism. European colonials administered, exploited, and competed for natural resources and cheap native labor forces. Their documents tell the story of colonial-native relationships that still affect the twentieth century, but they also reveal relationships between Spanish colonial frontiersmen and their English and French counterparts.

The documents in the various colonial archives demonstrate that within one lifetime after Columbus's landing, Spanish explorers had run the entire eastern coastline from Labrador to the Strait of Magellan, conquered the Aztec kingdom in Mexico and the Inca empire in Peru, explored vast regions of southern South America and Central America, and had made an important reconnaissance of the lands between Florida and California. Although exploration and conquest were essential elements of European expansion, settlement of the Caribbean Islands and the coastal and interior areas of the mainland began a common cultural heritage and exchange that continues today. That common heritage is manifest in the population of the Western Hemisphere and in its history.

In the Archivo General de Simancas is a map which tells that Spanish frontiersmen knew that the English were trespassing on the Spanish claim when they settled Jamestown in 1607. "The English are living in poverty," Spanish mariners reported a year later, and one of them sketched the first known map of the location of Jamestown. Actually, Spain had claimed the eastern seaboard much earlier and had by 1529 given the entire coastline in land grants to enterprising Spaniards. Between 1539 and 1543, three major expeditions revealed to the world the existence of numerous tribes and natural resources of the area that lay between Florida and California. These expeditions—by Hernando de Soto across Florida to the Mississippi River, by Francisco Vásquez de Coronado from Sonora to the Great Bend of the Arkansas River in central Kansas, and by João Rodrigues Cabrilho along the

California coast to Oregon—resulted in the first descriptions of North America and its immensity from coast to coast.

Between 1565 and 1821, the Spanish colonial map was filled with place-names that continue to grace America's cultural landscape. Colonial names of mountains, rivers, and topographical features reveal the Hispanic component of America's national story. Many familiar towns date from the Spanish colonial period: San Francisco (1776), San Diego (1769), Los Angeles (1781), Santa Fe (1610), El Paso (1680), Saint Augustine (1565), and others. They are more than vestiges of a forgotten colonial past, for at present almost one-fourth of the population of the United States is Hispanic. Not surprisingly, most Hispanics reside largely in an area between California and Florida, the region that formed the vast northern end of the Spanish empire. It is a truism that what was Spanish-speaking at the end of the Spanish colonial period in 1821 is still, to an extent, Spanish-speaking today.

New Perspectives on the American Revolution

Spanish colonial documents present an alternative view of English-Spanish frontier relationships. Contrary to perceptions presented in textbooks, Spanish and English colonials were not isolated from one another. A whole new world of interpretation concerning the American Revolution awaits the researcher in the Spanish colonial archives in Mexico and Spain. At least twenty-five hundred bundles of documents (a thousand pages each) related to the American Revolution have been located in the Archivo General de Indias in Seville. Most of the documents were gathered by Francisco Rendon and a team of agents who passed them to Madrid for Spain's ministers to use in evaluating the rebellion against England. They contain reports concerning American and British troop strengths, locations, and accoutrements; battle maps and communiqués; Spanish interviews with George Washington and other commanders, American and British alike; documents related to Benedict Arnold's betrayal of West Point; and much more.

The American Revolution is part of a common heritage that binds the Pan-American tradition in a profound way. For example, Spanish colonial frontiersmen in California, Arizona, New Mexico, Texas, Louisiana, and the Gulf Coast were also cognizant of the American Revolution. Indeed, Spain raised three million pesos in aid for the American patriots. One million came from Mexico where, in the out-of-the-way settlements at San Francisco, San Diego, Tucson, Santa Fe, San Antonio, and countless other villages, Hispanic settlers and soldiers passed the hat for the American cause. Eventually, some donations made their way to finance the American victory at Yorktown. Aside from support given by frontiersmen in Texas, New Mexico, Arizona, and California, other areas of the Hispanic world contributed their share as well. Spanish Cuba gave George Washington 1.2 million pesos to finance the battle of Yorktown that led to England's defeat. Earlier, in 1778, the patriot Arthur Lee received 285,500 pesos and thirty thousand blankets from Spanish sources; Oliver Pollock received 40,000 pesos from Spanish frontiersmen at New Orleans and Cuba; Alexander Gillon, admiral of the South Carolina forces, was given 50,000 pesos by Bernardo de Gálvez to continue the rebellion against England. Along the Mississippi River, Spanish soldiers supported battles in Illinois and kept the English from taking the area and cutting off provisions that Spain had sent Anglo-American rebels by way of Saint Louis from New Orleans. Spanish ships and troops captured British coastal forts in Alabama and Florida in behalf of the thirteen colonies in revolt. Among the fighters for American independence were Gálvez, for

Within a generation of Columbus's landing, Spanish explorers had traversed the eastern coast of the New World and scouted vast interior regions of both American continents. Juan Ponce de León (top) Hernando de Soto (center), and Vasco Núñez de Balboa (bottom) each led expeditions.

181

whom Galveston, Texas, is named; George Farragut Mesquida, father of David Glasgow Farragut of Civil War fame, the first Hispanic American admiral; and Francisco de Miranda, the great Venezuelan liberator, who fought alongside Gálvez at the battle of Pensacola against British forces in 1781.

Hispanics and Westward Movement

Later, in the 1790s, Hispanic frontiersmen stayed informed about the dynamic little country, the United States of America, that pushed against the Spanish claim along the Mississippi. In California, Governor Pedro Fages wrote his viceroy for permission to propose to George Washington a continental trail from Virginia to California that could be joined at the Spanish fort at Saint Louis. The idea came to naught then, but in 1869 the transcontinental railroad united east and west along the same line. Meanwhile, Spain ceded Louisiana to France, which in turn sold it to the United States. Needless to say, Spain watched the American westward movement with interest.

America's westward expansion is also intertwined with the Spanish colonial heritage. Aaron Burr, Daniel Boone, General James Wilkinson (who is buried in Mexico City), and others on the Spanish and American frontiers were friends of the Spanish. From time to time, they collaborated with Spanish frontiersmen along the Mississippi. Furthermore, Hispanic frontiersmen preceded Anglo-American explorers throughout North America. When Zebulon Montgomery Pike crossed the Missouri River on his march to the west, he was following a recent trail blazed by Captain Facundo Melgares of Santa Fe, who had been among the Pawnees trading and making peace. Likewise, when Lewis and Clark reached the Columbia River in 1805, they had been preceded by Captain Bruno de Hezeta who had explored and mapped the mouth of the river and its interior for twenty miles in 1775. In the

Francisco Vásquez de Coronado and his forces trekked across the deserts of Sonora to central Kansas.

The support of the Spanish-speaking world for the cause of the American Revolution is a little-known facet of the conflict. The governments of Spain, Mexico, and Cuba, as well as Spanish frontiersmen in Texas, New Mexico, Arizona, and California, lent significant financial aid and moral support to the patriots. Donations from Hispanic settlers across North America helped finance the American victory at Yorktown (above).

1790s, when English and American mariners reached the Pacific Northwest, they were two hundred years behind Juan de Fuca, who had been there in 1590 to explore the strait that today bears his name. Moreover, the Spanish claim to Alaska, dating from the middle 1760s, was intensified in the 1790s, resulting in written descriptions, maps, and sketches of the flora, fauna, and native peoples of the area. Spanish knowledge of Yellowstone, deep in the interior, had resulted in a map and descriptions in 1819 with a promise by the commander at Santa Fe to explore the Yellowstone River "as soon as the weather warmed." The Great Salt Lake Desert and Timpanogos Lake had been known to Hispanic frontiersmen of Santa Fe who had explored western Colorado and Utah since 1711. Today the Old Spanish Trail commemorates the colonial route from Santa Fe to Los Angeles via Utah. Meanwhile, when William Becknell, "Father of the Santa Fe Trail," crossed the Great Plains to the Great Bend of the Arkansas River thence to Santa Fe, he had been preceded by Hispanics from New Mexico by almost three hundred years. The complete story has yet to be told of the Hispanic side of the Santa Fe Trail.

Hispanics in North American History

Given the ignorance that surrounds the Hispanic contribution to the development of the Americas, it is small wonder that in 1970 the late John Francis Bannon, author of *The Spanish Borderlands Frontier, 1513–1821,* began his history with these words: "The farther the Anglo-American frontier edged toward the heart of the continent and the closer it came to the Mississippi River, the less true it became that the frontier was moving into a so-called virgin wilderness. . . . The story of the

183

American frontier began, it has often been asserted, when the first Englishman stepped ashore on the Jamestown site or when the pilgrims landed at Plymouth. If we properly qualify the statement by the addition of a national prefix, the statement is correct: The story of the Anglo-American frontier does open in those early years of the seventeenth century. However, if we wish to talk of the American frontier, even limiting consideration to the northern of the two continents, then we must go back to a full century, and more, to pick up the tale at its historically correct beginning, with the first Europeans who were, or at least represented, the Spaniards. Even the history of the American frontier, if confined only to lands that in time became part of the United States, must antedate 1607 and 1620 by many, many decades. There, too, the first hyphenated Americans were Spaniards, and the starting date was 1513."

The historical record is rich in evidence that supports the common heritage of the Americas and the role of Hispanics in the development of the United States. From the American Revolution to the wars of the twentieth century, Hispanics have participated in major historical events in defense of the United States. The trends and linkages have continued into the modern era. In recent times, Latin America has contributed enormously to the economy of the United States by supplying a variety of raw materials at low prices. Similarly, Hispanics in the United States currently represent a major economic consumer force with a purchasing power estimated at $120 billion per year. The heritage of the Western Hemisphere, forged by time, history, and culture, approaches its five hundredth year.

In 1792, Benjamin Franklin and the American Philosophical Society recognized the role of Spain and Hispanic America in the making of the New World by sending a representative to Spain to present a memorial on the occasion of the tricentennial of Columbus's discovery. Again, in 1892, the United States participated in the four hundredth anniversary of the occasion, and in 1930, the United States Congress declared Columbus Day a national holiday. With each passing century, the thread of Hispanic images is woven into the indelible tapestry of the historical record. The legacy runs deeper than a list of contributions and participation. More than three hundred years ago, Miguel de Cervantes recorded his thoughts regarding Hispanic images and identities. He simply wrote: "Rejoice, O Sancho, in the humility of your lineage, and don't be afraid to say that you came from laboring men, for when you are not ashamed of yourself, nobody will try to make you so, and always strive to be held thoughtful and virtuous, rather than proud and vicious. An infinite number from low beginnings have risen to high positions as bishops and kings, and to confirm this, I could bring you so many examples they would weary you. Note, Sancho, that if you follow virtue as a way of life and strive to do virtuous deeds, you need not envy those who are born of princes and great men, for blood is inherited, but virtue is achieved, virtue is of worth by itself alone, so is not birth."

Indeed, Cervantes expressed the universal search for identity. Perhaps 1992 will offer a reflective moment for those in the Americas to ponder the similarities, not the differences, that are so much a part of the historical identity shared by North and South Americans. Both were born from an encounter between two worlds: Indian America and Europe. Both developed from a European colonialism that forged the basis of present-day institutions, culture, and languages. From the wilderness, where Indian met European in 1492, emerged a frontier culture that is characteristically American. Within the continuity of that encounter lies the uniqueness of the Western Hemisphere.

An American Indian Perspective

George P. Horse Capture

The Landing

The association with the well-known historical image is easy for me: the prow of the boat cuts through the salty, choppy waves and grinds to a halt on the unfamiliar shore.

The occupants scramble ashore, aware of their long journey and the new world that their landing will usher in. Their determined first steps to the higher land and rocks will end the old order and ultimately change their world forever.

Sound familiar? Maybe so, however, these explorers were not Columbus and his crew, but fourteen American Indian college students, and their landing took place on the shores of Alcatraz Island in San Francisco Bay. Since then, it seems a lifetime has passed, but the action occurred only a few years ago, on 20 November 1969.

The landing of the students was a grand culmination of the civil rights decade for all American Indian people. It had been only seventy-nine years since the Wounded Knee Massacre in Sioux country, and only fifty-seven since the American Indian population had reached its post-Columbian nadir. Encouraged

by the black and Chicano civil rights movements of the 1960s, however, American Indian people across the country began earnestly to question their lowly status. Away from their restricting home reservations, Indian college students enjoyed firsthand the advantages experienced by non-Indian people, and they were determined to do whatever necessary to bring these advantages home to their people. Indian college students on campuses nationwide felt an urgent need to unite with students from other tribes, many for the first time, and to work toward common goals.

It was one of these newly united groups who sailed to the island in San Francisco Bay and helped create a new world for American Indian people everywhere. The word quickly spread across the waves and on the moccasin telegraph—"The Indians Have Landed." There was universal rejoicing from the Indian reservations in the country to the Indian centers in the cities. For the first time since the Little Bighorn, the Indian people, instead of passively withdrawing and accepting their fate, had stepped forward in the bright sunshine and let it be known that they were Indian and proud, and their present situation must and would change.

Upon landing, one of the students proclaimed, "On Alcatraz, we have no electricity, no fresh water, no food, no flush toilets and no money. We feel right at home because it reminds us so much of our reservations." The first Thanksgiving on the island drew international attention as journalists and media crews from around the world attended the Indian event. Empathetic citizens and organizations sent water and food, including scores of baked turkeys, on boats and barges as the Indian people told their story to the world.

In the following months, the movement continued to capture public attention, and non-Indians learned more than ever before about the hundreds of years of injustice to the Indian people. More important, the occupation by the young warriors forced the Indian people themselves to reexamine their acquiescence to the non-Indian world and seek to determine their own social and cultural responsibilities.

Though not members of the original landing party, other Indians from all tribes came to take part in this epic historical declaration, as I did myself. One night, an Indian arrived on the last boat from the mainland. When I asked what he thought of his island, he exclaimed in wonderment, "I don't believe it. It's incredible. I just hitchhiked from my home in New Mexico to see if the news was true. I have to return tomorrow. It is true. We did it!"

A New World

The occupation of Alcatraz Island eventually ended more than a year later. The horses were out of the corral, and the emerging Indian people began to change their world and their lives, which had been altered catastrophically because of Columbus's voyage. Some 477 years earlier in 1492, this proclaimed genius, seeking trade routes to the Far East and India, landed by mistake near San Salvador in the Caribbean, a whole hemisphere short of his stated goal. Thus arrived, he claimed the territory in the name of his sponsor, implying that the land occupied thousands of years by the native peoples, was, in fact, uninhabited by humans.

Although the total native population of the New World in 1492 remains controversial, Russell Thornton, in a demographic history of the Indian people since that time, estimated that there were more than seventy-two million people in the Western Hemisphere. Of this number, over five million Indian people lived in what is now the conterminous United States.

Indians claim Italy by right of discovery

**From Our Correspondent
Rome, Sept 24**

Italy, cradle of Western civilization, woke up today to the fact that it has never actually been discovered. The situation, however, was remedied at 11 o'clock in the morning when the chief of the Indian Chippawa tribe. Adam Nordwall, stepped off an Alitalia jumbo jet and claimed it for the Indian people.

The intrepid explorer, in full Indian dress, accompanied by his wife—in ordinary clothes because her suitcase had been lost in New York—stood on the tarmac of Fiumicino airport here and took possession of Italy "by right of discovery".

The fact that Italy has long been inhabited by people who consider themselves to be in full possession of the place was exactly the point that Mr Nordwall was trying to make. "What right had Columbus to discover America when it was already inhabited for thousands of years? The same right that I have to come now to Italy and claim to have discovered your country", he said.

The difference, however, was that Columbus "came to conquer a country by force where a peaceful people were living, while I am on a mission of peace and goodwill".

Mr Nordwall led a party of Indians which occupied the prison on Alcatraz in San Francisco Bay in 1969 to call attention to the conditions in which Indians were compelled to live in America.

The Alcatraz episode inspired other sardonic commentaries on Columbus's presumed discovery of America, as in 1973 when a Chippewa leader claimed Italy for the American Indians.

—

When the two races first met on the eastern coast of America, there was unlimited potential for harmony. The newcomers could have adapted to the hosts' customs and values or at least understood and respected them. The discovery could have been the start of a new and better age. But this did not happen. The vast differences in basic beliefs and values of the two groups continually proved that they could not live together in peace.

Inspired by the civil rights movement, a group of American Indian college students occupied Alcatraz Island during Thanksgiving week in 1969 and stayed for more than a year. Their landing—an ironic caricature of Columbus's arrival in the Caribbean and the celebration of the Pilgrims—was intended to call attention to the ongoing plight of American Indians. For many, including the author, the landing on Alcatraz marked the beginning of sweeping efforts among American Indians to reclaim their cultural heritage.

Being a typical product of fifteenth-century Europe, "The Admiral" viewed the native of America with ethnocentric arrogance and disdain. His correspondence tells the story (Jane 1988). Of the people he called "los Indios," which then meant people of a darker race, Columbus wrote:

> The people of this island, and of all the other islands which I have found and of which I have information, all go naked, men and women, as their mothers bore them; although some women cover a single place with the leaf of a plant or a net of cotton which they make for the purpose. They have no iron or steel or weapons, nor are they fitted to use them, not because they are not well-built men and of handsome stature, but because they are marvelously timorous. . . . They never refuse anything which they possess, if it be asked of them; on the contrary, they invite anyone to share it, and display as much love as they would give their hearts, and whether the thing be of value or whether it be of small price, at once with whatever trifle of whatever kind it may be that is given to them, with that they are content.

Upon determining their peaceful nature, Columbus responded: "And as soon as I arrived in the Indies, in the first island, which I found, I took by force some of them."

The Inhumane Beginning

Bartolomé de las Casas, a Spanish Dominican missionary and historian, argued in the sixteenth century that the forcible capturing of the people was "wholly unjustifiable." He was convinced that this incident set policy for the mistreatment of Indians in the New World.

In a report to his superiors concerning the riches from the New World, Columbus wrote of gold "as much as they [their highnesses] may need," and of spices, cotton, resin from a tree like the European mastic tree, aloe wood, "and slaves, as many as they shall order to be shipped and who will be from the idolaters."

"They are always assured that I come from Heaven." A 17th-century print depicting the arrival of Columbus in the Bahamas confirms the early confusion among Native Americans about his exact origins and station. Columbus and his successors would use this bewilderment to their advantage. While hindsight perceives much ground for accord between the convening races, they themselves found virtually none. For the most part, the newcomers demonstrated little patience for learning or appreciating the rituals, customs, and skills of their hosts.

Although none of his group could understand the unknown language, Columbus described his status among the Indian people:

> I still take them with me, and they are always assured that I come from Heaven, for all the intercourse which they have had with me; and they were the first to announce this wherever I went, and the others went running from house to house and to the neighboring towns, with the loud cries of "Come! Come to see the people from Heaven!"

On his return to Spain, Columbus took several of the native prisoners with him as evidence of his discovery and as interpreters on later voyages. However, only seven survived the trip.

And so the Europeans located a New World, met a beautiful people full of love on its shining beaches, claimed the land, and enslaved the people who had occupied it for centuries. When the peaceful Arawak-speaking people met Columbus, they numbered two to three million. Within a hundred years they became extinct in the Antilles. In fact, each subsequent encounter between the non-Indian and the Indian somehow became detrimental to the latter, and the full story of horrors fills many books. A brief historical look is necessary, however, to feel the full impact of the pain, cruelty, and loss.

Disease, the Specter Immigrant

One of the worst things brought by the Europeans to the natives of America was disease. When the first people migrated to this continent many thousands of years ago across the Bering Strait, they came in small groups and spent an enormous amount of time in the frigid zones before moving south to occupy eventually most of the land area. The extended time in the harsh temperatures of the north allowed only the hardy to survive and subjected their physiology to a "cold filter," locking up harmful germs and diseases in the icy environment. Living in small groups, they had little opportunity to get diseases from others, and by not domesticating animals, they did not catch diseases from them, such as measles, which may originate from canine distemper, or smallpox, closely related to cowpox.

The Old World diseases, especially smallpox, brought devastation to the Native American tribes. People who had never experienced epidemic diseases not only lacked immunity; they also could not comprehend the idea of contagion. One Indian summed up the confusion when he said that the spread of disease was incomprehensible since a warrior could not convey his battle wound to another.

These conditions combined to render the American Indian people relatively healthy. An early New England colonist observed:

> The Indians be of lusty and healthful bodies not experimentally knowing the Catalogue of those health-wasting diseases which are incident to other Countries, such as Feavers, Pleurisies, Callentusres, Agues, Obstructions, Consumptions, Subsumigations, Convulsions, Apoplexies, Dropsies, Gouts, Stones, Tooth-aches, Pox, Measles, or the like, but spinne out the threed of their days to a faire length, numbering three-score, four-score, some a hundred yeares, before the worlds universall summoner cite them to the craving Grave. (Thornton 1987)

But death did plague the American Indian people after a period of contact and it took many new forms, including removal and relocation, diseases, warfare and genocide, and alcoholism, all contributing to the destruction of the native way of life. Diseases caused the most fatalities, far more than the battlefields. Although there is continuing controversy about which diseases were brought by the outsiders, it is generally agreed that smallpox, cholera, measles, diphtheria, typhoid fever, some influenza, and the plague came from Europe and Africa. The deadliest killer was smallpox.

Smallpox was noted in the Caribbean as early as the winter of 1518–19; from there it moved north spreading and killing. In several Atlantic coast settlements from 1520 to 1584, according to recent studies, the disease reduced the Indian population by 25 to 30 percent. Another period of epidemic from 1584 to 1620 may have reduced the survivors by another 90 percent. While resettling that same area, the Pilgrims gave thanks to God for having cleared the lands of Indian people (Josephy 1982).

Such diseases had a more severe impact on the native peoples because the Europeans had experienced this affliction and others for a long period of time. Most had an immunity built up from these previous exposures and at least had knowledge of infection and contagion: the Indians had neither, and the disease returned again and again. When commenting about the contagious nature of the diseases, one warrior said they could not understand how one could pass this damaging ailment to another because one could not pass along a battle wound.

As the scourge moved westward, it continued its carnage into the northern Great Plains. When it hit the Blackfeet in 1781, more than 50 percent of the tribe died. When it returned in 1837, the survivors suffered a 66 percent loss: six thousand perished (Ewers 1958).

As the tribes were physically ravaged by diseases, their very culture and way of life were threatened. Unable to cure the sick, the medicine men suffered loss of prestige. The time-honored way of curing other ailments revolved around the sweat bath and a cold plunge in the creek: with smallpox this combination is fatal.

The educational method of the tribes suffered the most as the elder passes the accumulated tribal knowledge on to the young. In the epidemics the old and the young sustained the greater losses.

In many regions by the time the first white man actually appeared, his biological accoutrements had devastated the Indian populations by more than 75 percent. Entire tribes became extinct, and the surviving tribal remnants were critically weakened.

Fight or Flight

Columbus and most of his contemporaries believed he was the first discoverer of the new continent, but they were all wrong. It is now widely accepted that the Scandinavian Leif Eriksson briefly colonized what is now called Newfoundland in A.D. 1011. Other earlier arrivals may also have taken place. For example, the historian David Beers Quinn suggests that Englishmen arrived in 1481, a few years before Columbus. Other pre-Columbian ocean travelers surely discovered the American continents long before 1492, perhaps crossing the Pacific Ocean to do so.

Others came soon after Columbus, and their names fill the history books: in 1497 John Cabot sailed from England to Newfoundland; in 1497 Amerigo Vespucci sailed from Spain to the coasts of southern North America and Central America and

received credit for discovering other nearby places; in 1508 Sebastian Cabot sailed from England to Hudson's Bay. The Spaniard Ponce de León landed near Daytona Beach, Florida, in 1531 to enslave the local Indian people to work on the Caribbean plantations. When he returned eight years later to continue this loathsome but widespread practice initiated by Columbus in the New World, the Indians killed him.

As the knowledge and promise of the New World spread throughout the Old World, an increasing number of European groups settled on the eastern coast and began to change this ancient, balanced world. The alternatives for the American Indian people were assimilation or extermination. Military extermination was out of the question for several reasons. First, it would be too expensive to kill so many Indians, and besides, they might be needed as allies later. And last, blatant murder was unthinkable to settlers who considered themselves good Christians. The only other option—assimilation—failed in the short run as the settlers' land needs could not wait for the two groups to develop a common bond. Therefore, other actions prevailed.

Many Europeans believed that Indian people could change from hunters of the forest to civilized farmers of the fields if given enough time. However, the constant pressure from living next to each other took its toll in lives and bad feelings, and

Running Face, a member of the Mandan tribe, bears the marks of the disease that killed most of his people in the smallpox epidemic of 1837. Drawings on a cotton cloth record major historical events among the Sioux over a period from 1798 to 1902, not the least of which were smallpox epidemics in 1810, 1837, and 1844.

194

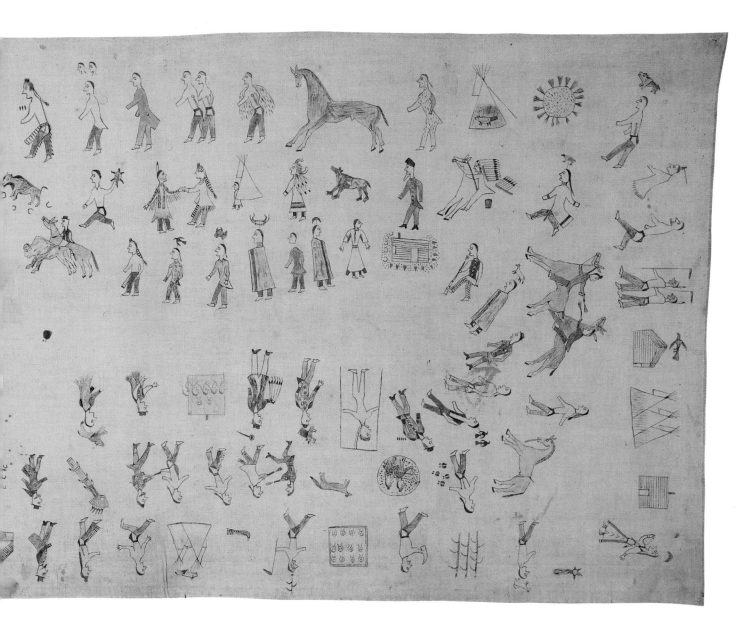

time was not available. The English government belatedly enacted restrictions to inhibit unfair practices to obtain Indian land, but to no avail, as these regulations were only marginally enforced (Tyler 1973). In 1754, conferences were held between the Indians and the Albany Congress where the Indian people made their resentment known in unmistakable terms. Again and again the Indian people bitterly complained about the illegal encroachment of the whites upon their lands, but it did no good. Their resentment was graphically demonstrated when they sided with France against England in the French and Indian War.

Boundaries, Imaginary and Real

An official Indian policy was finally issued by King George III. Among other things, this British Proclamation of 1763 established a boundary line between the unclaimed Indian lands and those already claimed by the Europeans. This official recognition of Indian landownership appeared to be beneficial to the native people, but subsequent events proved differently. This first dividing line was one of many that separated the two groups. It ran down the divide of the Appalachian Mountains from the Chaleur Bay in Canada to the tidewater limits of East Florida. The new Indian country west of the line had all the protection of European land, but it was

The Three Cherokees, came over from the head of the River Savanna to London. 1762
& their Interpreter that was Poisoned.

soon evident that the boundary was only temporary and was meant solely to appease the Indians and to forestall the formation of western colonies. White encroachments continued.

Subsequent actions had little effect on the situation. An Indian policy was set by the Continental Congress in 1775. A year later, the Articles of Confederation not only elaborated the plan in the general enumeration of powers to be granted the central government but also provided for "regulating the Trade, and managing all affairs with the Indian." It was the American colonies' turn to deal with the Indians.

New treaties with the tribes abounded, always seeking peace and more land. Congressional communication to the Indians indicated a desire to "keep the hatchet buried deep," but encroachments continued, and the treaties were broken (McNickle 1973). Other treaties fixed different, new boundaries, always located further to the west. The Northwest Ordinance of 1787 promised, "The utmost good faith shall always be observed toward the Indians." But the movement west continued unabated.

This Old Northwest area between the Great Lakes and the Mississippi River soon underwent the same encroachment that had occurred further east. First, the traders moved in with goods that the Indian people quickly became dependent upon. The settlers came next and were met by the natives who were now familiar with them and their materials. This sequence broke the initial barrier and encroachments became easier.

As in the East, the federal government's responsibility was to protect the land for Indians and whites alike, according to the agreements and treaties. But in practice, the two groups were not treated equally. When Indian people broke the law enforcement was swift, but when settlers committed crimes against Indians, justice did not prevail (Washburn 1975). Justice gave way to political pressures, and Indians did not have the right to vote.

New World visitors attracted curious attention in Europe, like an Inuit woman and her daughter put on exhibition in Antwerp in 1566 (right) and three Cherokees who accompanied an Englishman to his homeland in 1762 (left). On his return to Spain, Columbus brought along native prisoners (seven of whom died) as evidence of the wonders and wealth of the lands he had reached.

In 1787, statesmen gathered in Philadelphia to correct weaknesses in the federal compact. The Indian situation seemed to have been overlooked in the Constitution. James Madison proposed that Congress have power "to regulate the affairs with the Indians, as well within as without the limits of the United States." His proposal was sent to committee for action. Later, in the clause granting Congress the power "to regulate commerce with foreign nations, and among several states," the words "and with the Indian tribes" were added. Only five words were used to establish a federal Indian policy.

Congress soon enacted new laws designed to address the many aspects of the Indian issue. Because Indian extermination was considered too expensive and objectionable, the laws were designed to bring about peace (McNickle 1973). A series of ordinances to implement and enforce the treaties against the unruly settlers was supplied by Congress in 1790. Intercourse acts replaced the ordinances over the next twenty-five years, but they changed nothing. Encroachments continued.

In the meantime, the Louisiana Territory was acquired from France. A vast amount of new land was now available for expansion, but it was not without what was perceived as a drawback: the area contained an untold number of Indian tribes. This development called for a reassessment of Indian relations and led to the creation in the War Department of the Bureau of Indian Affairs, a basic component of federal Indian policy even today.

Removal and Reservations

Another program developed at this time to speed up the process of dealing with the Indians. Known as the policy of *removal,* it offered to protect the Indian from the evils of white society by taking his homeland and removing him west of the Mississippi River. There he could have additional time to adapt to civilization, as this land was relatively free of foreigners, although white settlement was already nearing the area. This concept had been first stated by Thomas Jefferson in 1803, when he obtained the Louisiana Territory (Spicer 1969).

The Indian Removal Act passed Congress in 1830, and a year later the first official victims were the Cherokee Indians of Georgia (Foreman 1953). Utilizing the white man's own tools, the Cherokees sued the state of Georgia to protect their land and government after gold was discovered there. The Supreme Court of the United States ultimately ruled in their favor, but President Jackson disagreed. Instead of benefiting from the court decision, the Cherokee people were removed.

The prominent anthropologist James Mooney described the tragedy:

> Men were seized in their fields or going along the road, women were taken from their wheels and children from their play. In many cases, on turning for one last look as they crossed the ridge, they saw their homes in flames, fired by the lawless rabble that followed on the heels of the soldiers to loot and pillage. Systematic hunts were made by the same men for Indian graves, to rob them of the silver pendants and other valuables deposited with the dead. A Georgia volunteer, afterward a colonel in the Confederate Service, said, "I fought through the Civil War and have seen men shot to pieces and slaughtered by thousands, but the Cherokee removal was the cruelest work I ever knew."

The six-month journey of thirteen thousand Cherokees began in October 1838 from Charleston, Tennessee. The exiles, guarded by soldiers, died by the score each day from hunger, sickness, and exposure. When they finally settled in Indian Territory, more than four thousand of them had perished.

As the frontier advanced in the 1840s, the settlers inevitably confronted the Indian tribes once again. The westward travelers needed protection from these natives and the government provided it. In addition, the Taylor administration initiated a more active Indian policy. The earlier idea of isolating and restricting the remaining Indian people to reservations, thus freeing new regions for settlers, was again considered. In the transition, a new, different, specific concept was stated: "There should also be a clear and definite understanding as to the general boundaries of the sections of the countries respectively claimed by them (the Indians), as their residence and hunting grounds and they should be required not to trespass upon those of each other without permission from the occupant tribes, or from the proper Agent of the government" (Trennert 1975). The adoption of these guidelines was the first step toward establishing the Indian reservations of today.

The tribes of the Southwest were still struggling against the settlers, while the groups of the far central Great Plains were undergoing a different fate. Liquor, disease, dispossession, and other foreign scourges continued to take their deadly toll of the once-proud Pawnees, Otos, Missouris, Omahas, and Sioux, as well as the transplanted tribes, such as the Potawatomis, Ottawas, Chippewas, Winnebagos, and Sac and Fox. They were few in number and in a severe state of destitution.

Further north the tribes were not as well known. Traders and trappers had returned with tales of the mighty tribes: Blackfeet, Assiniboins, Crows, Gros Ventres, and others. All were patriots like their eastern brethren, ready to fight and die to protect their country. These groups were never beaten in battle by the white man and were relatively free from encroachment, but pressure was building daily. Travelers were passing through their country and annihilating the Indians' food supply, the buffalo, without any regard for consequences.

As the tribes of the northern Great Plains signed the first important treaty in 1851, their way of life ended, but perhaps its demise allowed them to live undefeated. Although the treaty had no immediate effect, it foretold the direction of future policy.

While the British and Americans established various boundaries beyond which white settlers were not to advance, these bounds were invariably breached. The United States government then established a policy of outright removal of Indians. In the bitter winter of 1838–39 some 13,000 Cherokees from southeastern states were herded west to present-day Oklahoma. Along the way as many as 4,000 may have died. Their exodus came to be known as the Trail of Tears.

The Wounded Knee Massacre of 1890 marked the final subjugation of the Indians of the Great Plains. At the time, whites were fearful that a resurgent interest among Indians in the Ghost Dance religion would lead to an uprising. Several thousand troops were dispatched to South Dakota to quell the tensions. Instead, a series of disasters ensued, beginning with the murder of the charismatic Sioux leader Sitting Bull and culminating with the massacre at Wounded Knee Creek. As soldiers entered an Indian camp on the Pine Ridge Reservation to collect weapons, a random shot set off gunfire on both sides. The soldiers opened fire on the Sioux with rapid-firing Hotchkiss guns, killing in a matter of moments as many as 400 men, women, and children. Later medals of honor were awarded to a score of soldiers who participated.

Eagles Caged

The eagles were now caged. No more could they freely travel and hunt in their traditional patterns. Now they were boxed in by square houses rather than protected by the natural circular shapes of their *tipis*. Foods were doled out as disciplinary measures by corrupt agents, while the tribes starved. Basic values that had enabled the tribes to survive for thousands of years were questioned for the first time by the Indian people themselves. The native religion lost many believers, and the vitality ingrained into the people by their rigorous life-style faded still more. The example set by Columbus continued almost everywhere in Indian country.

Once-migratory people were suddenly forced to stay in one place. Men could no longer gain experience and respect as warriors in battle; now they had to show their strength by just surviving and protecting their families until life improved. Natural leaders could no longer prove themselves in the traditional manner, but they had to emerge by taking actions that protected whatever was left of Indian culture. The tribes adapted and changed once again.

The barbed wire of early reservations kept the Indian people inside and kept the settlers out—for a time, anyway. A reservation therefore was and is a hybrid of a prison camp and a sanctuary, with the cultural sterility more than offset by the warmth and love of its people for their own. Thus, while reservation boundaries restrict people from reaching their full potential in this world, they nevertheless give much in return. This Indian land keeps us Indian, and that is a tolerable trade in anyone's book.

The Indian Way of Life

Throughout the 19th century, many treaties were signed by Indians who had been assiduously wooed in the days prior to the signing, who misunderstood the terms of the compact, or who were not the legitimate spokesmen for their tribes. The goals of these treaties were always the same: the whites sought peace and more land. Sauk and Fox Indians, seen in the 1867 photograph (above), ceded their remaining lands in Kansas for $1 an acre in return for a reservation in Indian Territory. After scores of tribes were removed from their homelands and shuffled across the continent, it was then left to teachers at schools like the Port Gamble Indian School on Puget Sound (left) to acculturate children of a people whose values, religion, oral traditions, and means of imparting knowledge were at odds with prevailing white standards.

Non-Indians, however, were and still are blinded by the fallacies of the concept of Manifest Destiny and never attempted to understand the essence of the native people. Constant conflict remains today between the Indian and the white man, and the Indians still lack power, comprising only one half of one percent of the total United States population.

Taking Indian land was only another step as the assault on native peoples continued. Soon Indian religious beliefs came under attack as missionaries rushed in to save "heathen" souls from spiritual ways that had sustained people since the beginning. In addition to the ethnocentric ways of the invaders, one of the major problems was that these new people did not understand the structure of Indian beliefs.

It is not that they were incapable of understanding, but that they were raised in a different world. The natural concepts of native religion were totally foreign to their way of life and were never adequately explained to them, nor did they care to listen. The Europeans believed that their own religion was supreme over all others and that all actions they took, good and bad, were somehow justified by their beliefs.

Early accounts of foreign explorers and settlers described the Indian people as ignorant, even though Indians have always placed great value upon knowledge and education. The passing of accumulated knowledge is essential to the survival of a people, and, as a preliterate group, the American Indians utilized the oral tradition for this purpose. Passed from elder to youngster, the mysteries of life and death were often explained in stories of Coyote, Spider, and others. The system worked well and the children could see where the Big Race of the stories actually took place, or where Red Whip triumphed over evil. The lessons were well learned.

The Indian religion or philosophy is a way of life that has been with the people since they entered this country tens of thousands of years ago, and it is relatively easy to understand. Indians believe that there is "A One Above," "The Maker of All Things," "The Great Spirit." There is no doubt that a gentle spring breeze that whispers across one's cheeks is the breath of that power. It is He who makes the world turn, the leaves change colors, or the water flow to the sea. This power has no beard, nor face; there is no need for these things. He is the earth we walk upon and the air we breathe. He is everywhere and does everything.

This is not a rigid, fear-filled religion but a gentle, personal one that urges us to do the right thing for ourselves and others. The believer is expected to live a good life, to appreciate and protect the earth, and to do no harm to others. The Indian religion also allows us to seek divine assistance when necessary. These beliefs have persisted to this day, in spite of all the outside, destructive forces.

These destructive forces began arriving after 1492; like everything else, the educational process changed as the newcomers preached their own beliefs. In their evangelical frenzy, the missionaries dismissed the existing native religious practices and attempted to replace them with their Christian beliefs.

Harmful Zealotry

The Christianizing of the Indian people had many purposes. Theoretically, it made a believer more patient and forgiving, when, perhaps, his land was taken by others; it made him dependent upon human preachers rather than upon pure spiritual concepts; it made him docile when strength was needed; and it taught warriors the ways of the people of the eastern Mediterranean, people who were farmers and city dwellers. All of this Good Book exposure was to replace ancient native principles and make the Indians Europeans.

Christianizing was most aggressive from Columbus's time to the 1870s. Missions were often set up on or near Indian reservations, and the missionaries dealt harshly with the Indian people, often enslaving them for labor. After being pressed to attend the schools, the young Indian student was forced to give up his religious beliefs and traditional clothing and to cut his hair short. He was brutally punished when he was caught speaking his native language. By discarding this paraphernalia from his past, the student supposedly would be more receptive to his non-Indian lessons and could more easily become Christian, no matter what the cost. Indian elders of today still have bad feelings toward the missionaries for their harsh treatment, but they continue to attend the Sunday Mass.

This educational method may have been the most devastating element, because it struck at the heart of the people's essence—their basic belief in life and in themselves. By approaching the spiritual people in a spiritual way, the missionaries ensured their intimate access, and once in the proper position, often guaranteed by the federal government, they commenced upon their missions, attacking the Indian ways.

Ironically, however, even though the traditional beliefs had been devastated, there was no adequate substitute for the older values. Much of the new teaching was too cruel and unnatural for most Indians to believe in for long. By destroying many of the standards that strengthened social cohesion, the missionaries, who were striving to save the Indian people, almost destroyed them. Or perhaps they were only after the souls, not the persons.

Alcatraz Again

I remember hearing about the Alcatraz takeover by students much younger than I. I was shocked and exhilarated and my heart raced and my eyes watered. I felt anxiety as I never had before. I realized that this was a great moment in Indian history and that the motivating reasons for this monumental action by the students were mine as well as those of all other real Indian people.

For at the time, living in the Bay Area with my family, I considered myself quite a success. We had some money; I had a good position with the state government, and we even had a boat. Everything was progressing according to the white notion of achievement, and I could easily envision peaceful retirement on the far horizon. I had reached my goal of distancing myself from the turmoil and poverty of my youth, and I fitted, somewhat, within the larger society of non-Indians. It was a comfortable, albeit dull and monotonous, life, but I was content.

After the occupation of Alcatraz Island, however, many Indian people decided that they had been pursuing the white man's way instead of their own. The takeover forced us to rethink our values and to remember our past. For me, memories of childhood came flooding back.

Grandmother Singing Rock

It seems like several lifetimes ago that I lived with my grandmother. Her Christian name was Clementine, but her Indian name was Singing Rock. As in the older traditional Indian days, she took a firm hand in raising her grandchildren and other stray kids who often became part of our group.

We lived in a wooded area near the northern border of the Fort Belknap reservation in north central Montana, and life for her was difficult. Her husband, my grandfather Paul, had died from a heart attack at age fifty-one several years before, leaving her to raise their four younger children and others. Thinking back, I do not know how we lived, but somehow we did.

Time tends to ease the pain, and most of my childhood memories of living with my grandmother are filled with pleasure. I remember awakening one particular morning after a heavy snowfall that had covered the brush and trees with a heavy white blanket. Our uncle Charlie lived in a smaller house a hundred yards farther into the brush, and he was an early riser. In the dawn hours, he would let himself into our log house and make a roaring fire in the wood stove. Sipping a cup of hot tea, he would begin to sing Indian songs. These songs gently woke us up and, snuggled warmly in the bed quilts, we would savor the music and the comfortable family surroundings. It was a good moment.

Other times were not so good. On our part of the reservation there were no schools, so we had to be bused four miles into the nearest town. It was during these early years that I discovered Indian people were different. I often heard in town that we were a burden to society and not as good as the white folk. The school reinforced this view, for we never learned about Indian people, only white ones. The father of our country was white, as were other famous people, such as Thomas Jefferson, Benjamin Franklin—even Jesus was white. It was in these surroundings that many of us began to believe that we did not belong in this place and time: we were strangers and even interlopers. There was no real reason to excel in school because it was not our world, and many of us gave up.

I remember one later shame-filled day, when I was living with my mother in Butte, Montana. A number of white classmates relentlessly made fun of my last name, and that filled me with shame and guilt. I believed that being an Indian was no good and countered them by saying that although I did have Indian blood, a full one-fourth of my blood was French; therefore I did have some value. I said that often and even believed it. It was shameful.

Other times when the taunts became overwhelming, I would burst into tears and run home. My mother would say that the kids were just ignorant and that I should forgive them. Periodically, my reservoir of forgiveness became exhausted, and when I was next belittled because of my dark color, name, or race, I would bust the offender in the mouth. This action did not really help my situation, but it made me feel a whole lot better, at least for a while.

Beyond the Reservation

In spite of our reservation origins and the inferiority complexes we have because of them, many of us made it into adulthood. But age never makes a difference among racists. As we tried to blend into the larger world, the taunts continued to plague us. Whenever we got our hair cut, people would ask if we had been scalped; when the spring rains lasted too long we were asked if we had been rain dancing. Our babies were often called papooses and our wives, squaws. We were never left free to develop unhindered but were constantly under some sort of attack. We learned that all racial quips are destructive, whether delivered in jest or in evil. And as my children grew, they were not allowed to remain color-blind and were in turn hassled. When one of them was called a "prairie nigger," I knew we had to make changes.

With the new racial sensitivity and an increasing awareness of Indian needs, I knew that my job was untenable. Because of the limited resources of Indian people, it seemed essential that I commit the remainder of my life to working toward bettering their condition. Originally I thought I was alone on this quest. But as time passed, a whole generation and more were influenced by these same forces, and we traveled the same course.

With some regret, I quit my job and returned to school. This changed my status from the youngest state steel inspector to one of the oldest students. After a few general courses to get the gray matter functioning on a college level, I earned high enough grades to meet university requirements, and, assisted with an educational opportunity grant, I entered the University of California at Berkeley.

What a world of excitement! The campus teemed with beautiful people of all types, and everyone seemed to care about the world and each other. The courses were so stimulating, provocative, and free from restraint. The sheer energy and intellectual activity carried you along and forced you to think and respond and get involved in life as well.

I followed a formal academic course to gain skill and knowledge in those areas, anthropology and history, where I could work with Indian people. The Center for Native American Studies stimulated us to initiate many Indian community projects,

Waatyanath, Horse Capture (great-grandfather) and *Neakana,* George P. Horse Capture

such as Indian dance classes, music classes, all-Indian summer camps, and many more.

One quarter I enrolled in a bibliography course. We were to select a subject, then research it and write a formal report with annotated citations. My subject had to focus on my tribe—the Gros Ventre Indian people of Montana—or, failing that, on the more general subject of American Indian people. By the time the course ended, what I had learned once again altered my life, for I had found more printed information on my tribe in monographs, articles, and rare publications than any of us knew existed. I photocopied it all and sent it home in the hope that those tribal members who followed this interest would not have to start at the absolute bottom again.

Continuing this discipline, I expanded my focus to include visual materials, and for the first time, I met my great-grandfather—Horse Capture—among the materials of E. S. Curtis's *North American Indian.* What a wonderful moment it was, for in these publications I discovered not only a language text, tribal musical scores, tribal history and myths, but beautiful, classical visuals of our tribe's most prominent men. Since then I have learned that Horse Capture was of the Frozen Clan, one of the select tribal groups that produced a number of chiefs. As a special, devoted person, he was a warrior; and he sponsored our last recorded Sun Dance and was honored to be chosen the final keeper of our Sacred Flat Pipe. A community park named in his honor was to be dedicated in the summer of 1990.

In the aftermath of the American Indian demonstrations at Alcatraz, the author went back to school to study anthropology and history, concentrating especially on the history of his own tribe, the Gros Ventres. In the works of photographer Edward S. Curtis, he came face to face with his own great-grandfather, Horse Capture. An album of Horse Capture's kin shows the procession of an American Indian family, some of whose living members are circling back to recoup what they can from their past.

Joseph Horse Capture (father),
Leo Horse Capture (uncle), Paul
Horse Capture (grandfather),
Singing Rock or Clementine
Horse Capture (grandmother),
and Rosie Horse Capture.

These monumental discoveries at the university were mind-boggling to me, because they clearly defined my tribe as great and quite active in history; we had even burned down three forts.

Frequently while searching the records we would discover accounts that would fill us with horror, urgency, and tears: the Indian people must do something that will never allow these dreadful actions to happen to them or anyone ever again. The following—from Major Anthony's testimony before the committee appointed by Congress in 1868 to investigate Colonel John Chivington's 1864 massacre of Cheyennes and Arapahos in Colorado—is such an account:

A little baby, not more than three years old, emerged from one of the lodges after the flight of the Cheyennes from the village. Plump, brown, perfectly naked, it toddled down the pathway where the Indians had fled, crying a little, but not much in the cold. It was a sight which should have stirred compassion in a wolf, but it stirred none in the men who were sacking the village. A soldier saw the child and fired at seventy-five yards, missing. Another dismounted and said: "Let me try the little———," and fired and missed also. A third, with surer aim, shot and this time the innocent child crumpled up, dying.

Coming Daylight (maternal
great-grandmother) and Daylight
Horse Capture (daughter)

205

The Real Discovery

Now, as I look back at these enlightening times, starting with Alcatraz and strengthened by the other Indian movements since then, with deep appreciation, my gratitude is without measure. For no longer is our history locked away in isolation. Today we are familiar with our past, and it fills us with pride and stabilizes our journey into the future. My family is real and from a strong stock that produces chiefs, and my ancestors played a major role in our tribal history and religion. The Gros Ventres are a great tribe. No longer am I a bashful child, hiding away in shame. As the oldest male and the product of the traditions in our family, I have a tribal and family responsibility to guide my life and to carry on these customs. Most other Indian individuals and families have discovered similar points of pride. Someday this knowledge will be taught to our children in our schools, for we have our own George Washingtons.

This knowledge formed a foundation for me, a solid, firm one that extends to bedrock and gives me the intelligence and strength to withstand anything. Once this foundation had set, confidence emerged, allowing me to encounter new frontiers and to be successful. Now I stand out in the bright sunlight as an American Indian, filled with pride and armed with confidence and accomplishments.

Full of this pride in our glorious past, I realize that no sensible Indian person can celebrate the arrival of Columbus. As the earliest significant European to set foot in the Americas and the very symbol of the New World itself, Columbus initiated the trend of treating the native peoples as less than human. He and his race must be held responsible for the horrors and injustices that were inflicted upon native peoples and for the racism that runs rampant in Indian country today. We tragically learned that he was not from Heaven. Therefore, several Indian leaders believe that the Indian people should wear black armbands and mourn this commemoration and boycott all activities dealing with the Columbus Quincentenary.

I heartily disagree with this view. History has clearly shown us that the Indian people cannot withdraw and let the world go by without them. No celebrant is going to hold a roll call and find that the Indian people are not taking part. We have too much at stake to become invisible again. We must step out into the sunshine and use this historic point to celebrate, too.

Our celebration will not be like the celebration of the white man. We must celebrate our survival over the last five hundred years. To date we have outlasted the Spaniards, Dutch, Russians, French, and maybe even the Americans. We have much to be thankful for, because, in spite of everything the white man and his legacy did to rub us out, we still survive. We do better than survive. Our children are earning diplomas and college degrees like never before, even in spite of the recent federal cuts in Indian education, and our buttes and Sun Dance lodges fill each year with devout Indian people praying and fasting in the ways of their great-grandparents. We must take part in life and politics and fight to preserve our few remaining acres of land, water, minerals, and treaty rights. We cannot pity ourselves. We must be strong and lead our children along the right way—the Indian way—and tomorrow will be better.

American Indians are returning to the spiritual sites of their tribes and to old ways of worship. Bearing sprigs of spruce, the White Mountain Apaches trek to the summit of Sacred Mountain to give thanks to the Beautiful Land.

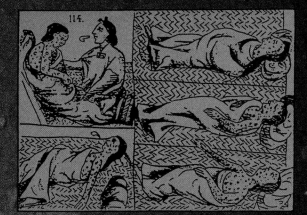

Health and Disease in the Pre-Columbian World

John W. Verano and Douglas H. Ubelaker

> Smallpox was the captain of the men of death in that war, typhus fever the first
> lieutenant, and measles the second lieutenant. More terrible than the conquistadores
> on horseback, more deadly than sword and gunpowder, they made the conquest
> . . . a walkover as compared with what it would have been without their aid. They
> were the forerunners of civilization, the companions of Christianity, the friends of
> the invader. (Ashburn 1947)

Since the publication in 1947 of P. M. Ashburn's classic study, *The Ranks of
Death*, scholars have become increasingly aware of the important role disease
played in the European conquest and colonization of the New World. The past
several decades have witnessed a significant increase in research in this area by
historians, demographers, and anthropologists. Using a variety of sources,
including early travelers' accounts, colonial-period documents, Native American

oral histories, archaeological excavations, and the study of human skeletal remains, a substantial new corpus of data has been generated. As a result of this research, it has become increasingly clear that the dynamics of infectious disease among European, African, and Native American populations had a major effect on patterns of colonization, economic development, and social interaction in the New World for centuries following Columbus's initial contact with the Americas. In addition, recent research by archaeologists and physical anthropologists has provided important new information on patterns of health, disease, and demography in New World populations before 1492.

The Isolated New World

Living on a continent largely isolated from biological exchange with the Old World for some ten thousand years, native peoples of the Americas had a unique history of both cultural development and disease experience. Although specific dates continue to be debated by archaeologists, it is generally accepted that the first humans to enter the New World were hunters and gatherers who traveled in small bands across the Bering land bridge from Siberia. The passage into North America—across the cold arctic steppe—and the small size of the groups that crossed the land bridge probably limited the number of infectious and parasitic diseases these people brought with them to the New World. In fact, physical anthropologist T. Dale Stewart has suggested that the arctic steppe may have served as a "cold filter," which discouraged the survival and propagation of many common infectious organisms and parasites that normally thrive in warm climates.

Settlement Pattern, Diet, and Disease

The first immigrants to the New World had no knowledge of agriculture or animal husbandry, although they may have brought the domesticated dog with them. Population densities were low and human settlements widely dispersed in much of the New World for thousands of years. With the development of agriculture, which had its origins as early as 5000 to 8000 B.C. in South America, population densities increased substantially in many regions. While subsistence agriculture did not spread to some areas of the New World until quite late in prehistory, and was never adopted by many Native American cultures, in Mesoamerica and the central Andes intensive irrigation agriculture eventually supported large, crowded urban settlements. In other parts of the New World, however, population densities probably never reached levels necessary to sustain and spread many of the infectious diseases, such as influenza, typhoid, measles, and smallpox, that were common ailments in Europe and West Africa in the late fifteenth century.

Travel, Trade, and Conquest

One of the important distinctions between the Old and New Worlds before their collision in 1492 was in the relative amount of population movement and contact between widely separated regions. On the eve of contact, western Europe, particularly the Iberian Peninsula, was a veteran of centuries of long-distance trade, exploration, and military adventurism. Spain and Portugal had suffered numerous invasions by the Romans, Germanic tribes, and Moors. Lisbon had been a principal port of call for ships departing or returning from the crusades. As William McNeill has argued

Human skeletal remains (previous pages) and Aztec codices (inset) are clues to our understanding of patterns of health in the New World before 1492 and the effects of Old World infectious diseases on Native American populations. Contrary to the suppositions of some historians, the New World was not a disease-free paradise.

While the Incas, Aztecs (opposite, top left and bottom), and Ecuadorian sea traders (opposite, top right) were given to long-distance trade, travel experience among New World peoples paled in comparison to the denizens of the Old World, veterans of centuries of trade, exploration, and military adventures. Since disease travels with people, the Old World had a long history of spreading and sharing pathogens. The relative isolation of New World peoples made them all the more vulnerable to the diseases brought by Europeans and Africans.

in his book *Plagues and Peoples,* history has shown repeatedly that human population movements and long-distance contacts lead to the spread of disease as well.

The New World, with the exception of the expansive Aztec and Inca empires (and Ecuadorian sea traders who sailed up and down the western coast of South America), had little to compare with the degree of population contact and movement that characterized the Old World. Thus, both the continental and regional isolation of New World populations made them especially vulnerable to the diseases brought by Europeans and Africans.

Was the New World Once a Disease-free Paradise?

Historical descriptions of the devastating effect of European and African diseases on New World populations have led some historians to suggest that the Americas were once a "disease-free paradise," free of the numerous infectious and parasitic diseases that continually tormented Old World populations and occasionally broke out in major epidemics. A Maya Indian compared conditions before and after the Spanish conquest: "There was then no sickness; they had no aching bones; they had then no smallpox; they had no burning chest; they had then no abdominal pain; they had then no consumption; they had then no headache. At that time the course of humanity was orderly. The foreigners made it otherwise when they arrived here" (Newman 1976).

Such assertions have stimulated medical researchers and anthropologists to examine in more detail the nature of health and disease in precontact New World populations. In the absence of medical histories for this period, most research has focused on the study of human skeletal remains from pre-Columbian contexts. Additional evidence of New World disease is suggested by artistic depictions of pathological individuals in pre-Columbian art.

Of all the pre-Columbian cultures, the Moche of Peru left the most numerous representations of physical maladies. Their ceramic artifacts depict such afflictions as missing limbs (opposite), skin problems, blindness, cleft palate, and clubfoot. This seemingly defaced visage probably was intended to illustrate leishmaniasis, an insect-borne disease that causes the sufferer's lips and nose to decompose.

Disease in the Precontact New World: Artistic Depictions

Most New World societies lacked a written language. With the exception of Aztec codices that recount epidemics and famines, little descriptive information is available on health and disease of native peoples before the contact period. However, some cultures, such as the Moche of Peru and the Nayarit and Colima of Mexico, created ceramic representations of deformities and pathological conditions.

The most numerous and diverse representations of pathologies were created by the Moche, whose culture flourished on the north coast of Peru around A.D. 100 to A.D. 750. These realistic ceramic depictions include easily recognizable malformations, such as individuals with missing limbs, as well as a variety of other conditions that have been interpreted as skin diseases, blindness, cleft palate, clubfoot, and intentional mutilation. Depictions of healers and patients, as well as certain medicinal plants, such as San Pedro cactus, are also known from Moche art. Representations of pathological individuals are also known from several other South American native cultures, as well as the Colima and Nayarit cultures of Mexico.

Although artistic depictions provide a rare glimpse into the pre-Columbian world of disease and healing, in most cases one can only hypothesize as to the disease being represented. There is general agreement, however, on the interpretation of certain representations, such as cleft palate. There is also general agreement that a common Moche depiction of individuals with erosive damage to the lips and nose probably represents infection with leishmaniasis (uta), an insect-borne fungal disease endemic in parts of Peru and Brazil today.

Analysis of Human Remains

More direct evidence of disease is provided by human skeletal and mummified remains from precontact cultures of the New World. Unfortunately, only a relatively small number of diseases that affect humans leave any trace of their presence in the skeleton, and some diseases affect bone in similar ways, making an accurate diagnosis difficult. Diseases that affect the skeleton are most commonly long-term ailments such as arthritis, chronic infections, and certain dietary deficiencies. Most illnesses that kill people quickly, particularly acute infectious diseases such as influenza, smallpox, typhoid, and measles, do not leave their signature on the skeleton.

In examining ancient New World skeletal remains for evidence of disease, paleopathologists are therefore limited to a relatively narrow field of inquiry. There are some exceptions to this rule, however. In arid regions such as the American Southwest and the west coast of South America, naturally and artificially mummified human remains have been found at a number of archaeological sites. Studies of mummified human remains from the coastal desert of southern Peru and northern Chile have provided conclusive evidence for the presence of infectious diseases such as tuberculosis and pneumonia. Coprolites, fossilized fecal material, from archaeological sites in the same areas have also produced substantial evidence of intestinal parasite infestation in precontact populations of the New World.

Diet, Disease, and Population Density

Recent studies of skeletal and dental stress indicators in New World remains have shown that health problems were common. Furthermore, morbidity seems to have increased through time in many areas of the New World with increased dependence on agriculture.

For example, studies of human remains recovered from archaeological excavations in Ecuador document that eight thousand years ago, populations who lived in coastal Ecuador had low levels of infectious disease, anemia, dental caries, and various measures of nutritional stress. Samples of human remains from more recent time periods in Ecuador show regular temporal increases in the frequencies of these problems, apparently resulting from a more sedentary way of life and a less varied diet. As populations grew larger and with a shift in subsistence began to live in more permanent settlements, sanitation problems inevitably developed, leading to an increase in infectious disease.

This pattern has now been detected in various parts of the New World. In areas where population density was high, New World peoples apparently were suffering from many of the crowd-related health problems that burdened Old World urban populations (polluted water supplies, sanitation and waste-disposal problems). A

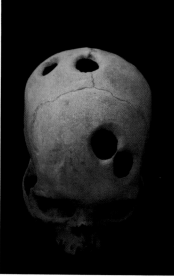

Trephination is a surgical treatment for skull fractures in which a portion of the bone of the skull is removed. Old and New World peoples developed the procedure independently, and it was widely practiced by the Inca (top right) and other Andean cultures. New World trephiners demonstrated a higher rate of success: 50 to 60 percent of their patients survived the procedure while in the Old World 90 percent died.

well-developed agriculture may have reduced seasonal shortages, but, at least in some communities, it limited variability in the diet, leading to nutritional problems.

Recent studies of coprolites preserved in some archaeological sites demonstrate that a variety of parasites that previously were thought to have been Old World introductions in fact plagued pre-Columbian New World populations. These include at least one species of hookworm, *Ancylostoma duodenale*, and the whipworm *Trichuris trichiura*. Research also has identified from pre-Columbian samples *Ascaris lumbricoides*, *Diphyllobothrium* spp, *Enterobius vermicularis* (pinworm), *Strongyloides* spp (hairworm), *Pediculus humanus* (louse), *Trichinella spiralis*, and *Echinococcus granulosis*. Also likely present were *Entamoeba* spp and *Moniliformis clarki* (a thorny-headed worm).

Some of the parasites show great antiquity. Eggs of *Enterobius vermicularis* and acanthocephalans have been found within deposits of caves in Utah that date as early as 8000 B.C. Most of the parasite evidence, however, originates from more recent samples representing large populations living in sedentary villages.

Tuberculosis

Over the years, many examples of pathological changes similar to those produced by tuberculosis have been found in pre-Columbian human skeletal remains in the New World. Proof positive came in 1973 when study of the mummified remains of a child of the Nazca culture of southern Peru showed not only symptoms of the disease in the skeleton and soft tissue but also revealed the acid-fast bacilli diagnostic of terminal miliary tuberculosis.

Numerous other well-dated pre-Columbian human remains have been found with tuberculosis-type lesions; these findings suggest the disease was a major health problem in densely populated areas during the last millennium. Like so many other health problems, the frequency of tuberculosis apparently increased through time with the development of sedentary agricultural communities.

Other Diseases

Without question, respiratory diseases, dysentery, and other ailments joined tuberculosis and perhaps treponemal disease to produce considerable morbidity in the pre-Columbian New World. Although the patterns of disease seemed to vary considerably in different regions and through time, they combined to generate a high mortality rate and reduced life expectancy. In some regions, mortality, especially infant mortality, was increasing through time, presumably in response to increased infectious disease resulting from more crowded and less sanitary living conditions.

Several well-controlled demographic reconstructions from archaeologically recovered samples suggest that life expectancy at birth for aboriginal populations in the New World was between twenty and twenty-five years, reflecting high rates of infant mortality. Adult age at death averaged in the mid-thirties. Figures for different times and places varied considerably, but they are quite similar to those estimated or recorded for European cities during comparable periods.

Clearly, the Americas were not a "disease-free paradise" in 1492. Significant mortality existed, but obviously New World populations had no immunity to diseases introduced from Europe during the sixteenth century. Smallpox was the major cause of rapid depopulation, but other diseases were also devastating. Measles, influenza, bubonic plague, diphtheria, typhus, cholera, yellow fever, and other diseases followed smallpox outbreaks, creating tremendous mortality among some groups. Preexisting diseases such as tuberculosis, dysentery, and parasitism continued during the historic period as well. During the last century, alcoholism, drug abuse, and occupational accidents have become important factors as epidemic disease has run its course or come under medical control.

Disease and Medical Practices in 1492

In their approach to disease treatment and medical intervention, fifteenth-century Europeans and New World peoples appear to have had many similarities. In both

L'ESPAIGNOL AFFLIGÉ DV MAL DE NAPLES.

A Spanish soldier taking a treatment for syphilis (left) and a pamphlet illustration warning of syphilitic infection (top) attest to the staggering dimensions of the disease in Europe in the years shortly after Columbus and his men returned from the New World. The timing of the epidemic in relation to the voyages of Columbus, combined with the apparent absence of syphilitic skeletal remains from the Old World before 1500, lend weight to the argument that the disease had a New World origin. Nonetheless the early epidemiology of syphilis remains a controversial topic among scholars.

Native Americans used guaiacum, derived from the wood of a West Indian tree, as a treatment for syphilis. In the wake of the epidemic, Europeans seized upon the diaphoretic as a miracle cure. In this engraving, ca. 1590 (right), the afflicted, lying allegorically in the bed of a prostitute, sips guaiac broth, while in the kitchen servants prepare more brew from the tropical wood.

Europe and the New World the *materia medica* consisted primarily of herbal preparations, and there was little understanding of the cause or treatment of infectious disease. Fifteenth-century Europe could boast of few medical advances since Greek and Roman times. Diseases were commonly attributed to imbalances in bodily humors, to "bad air," or to the position of the stars. Bloodletting was considered the appropriate treatment for a wide range of ailments. Fortunately for European patients at that time, surgical intervention was limited to extractions of teeth, amputation of limbs, and trephination of the skull. Antiseptic techniques were unknown, and the loss of a patient due to operation-induced infection was very common. Not until the sixteenth century did Europe see substantial advances in medical knowledge, due to a renewed interest in human anatomy among Renaissance artists and the invention of the printing press, which opened the door to more rapid diffusion and exchange of medical and anatomical knowledge.

Beginning with Columbus's first voyage to the New World, explorers began searching for plants of possible medicinal value to take back to the courts of Europe. In the late sixteenth century, Francisco Hernández and Bernardino de Sahagún compiled lists of many hundreds of medicinal plants used by the native populations of Mexico. The Aztec ruler Montezuma is reported to have had a royal garden devoted exclusively to medicinal plants. In both Mexico and Peru, the Spanish conquistadores were so impressed with native doctors that they frequently consulted them in preference to their European barber-surgeons. Gradually, a number of native New World medicinal plants, such as cinchona bark (the source for quinine) and coca, became important additions to the medical pharmacopoeia of Western physicians. In some of their medical practices, native New World peoples clearly outshone their European contemporaries. An example is trephination, a surgical procedure in which a portion of bone is removed from the skull of a patient, usually as a therapeutic treatment for depressed skull fracture. Curiously, trephination evolved independently in both the Old and New Worlds and was being practiced on both sides of the Atlantic Ocean in 1492. In the Americas, trephination was practiced extensively by some central Andean cultures. Trephination first appeared on the south coast of Peru around 400 B.C. and continued to be practiced in some areas of Peru and Bolivia until the sixteenth century A.D. What is most impressive about New World trephinations is the rate of survival. While trephinations performed in Europe had mortality rates averaging 90 percent until the late nineteenth century when sterile surgical techniques were first widely adopted, success rates among prehistoric South American trephiners averaged 50 to 60 percent, even in patients who had suffered severe skull fractures.

The Great Syphilis Debate

Given all the diseases that Europeans and Africans brought to the New World, it would not be surprising if some illness unique to the Americas was taken back to the Old World in exchange. Syphilis has long been the most popular candidate. Debate about the origin of syphilis has been running now for some 450 years. Ever since some Europeans began blaming it on the New World in the mid-sixteenth century, medical historians and scholars from other disciplines have been actively discussing the issue. Four major theories have grown out of this controversy. They can be referred to as the Columbian theory, the pre-Columbian theory, the mutation/virulence theory, and the unitary theory.

For centuries the collection and preparation of herbs formed the cornerstone of disease treatment in the Old and New World alike. On Columbus's first voyage, searchers looked for plants with possible medicinal value to take back to Europe.

According to the *Columbian theory,* Christopher Columbus and crew brought syphilis from the New World to Europe in 1493. This traditionally has been the most popular theory of the origin of syphilis, and it appears to be the most strongly supported by historical documents. Within two years of Columbus's return from his first voyage there are descriptions in Europe of the appearance and rapid spread of a new venereal disease. Contemporary Spanish historians Bartolomé de las Casas and Gonzalo Fernández de Oviedo y Valdés both claimed that Columbus brought syphilis from the New World, and the Spanish physician Ruy Díaz de Isla described treating some of Columbus's crew for a terrible disease they had contracted in the New World that he later claimed was syphilis.

Medical historians have repeatedly noted the absence of any unequivocal descriptions of syphilis in the medical literature of Europe, the Arab world, or China before A.D. 1500, and so far no convincing evidence of syphilitic skeletal remains are known from the Old World before 1500. Additional evidence sometimes marshaled in support for the Columbian theory is the knowledge among native Americans of guaiacum, a remedy derived from the wood of a West Indian tree, which was claimed to be effective for the treatment of syphilis. Guaiacum caused the patient to sweat freely and presumably purge himself of the malady; it was a popular treatment for syphilis in Europe in the 1520s.

According to the *pre-Columbian theory,* syphilis was present in Europe long before Columbus's voyage—it was simply misdiagnosed or confused with other diseases such as leprosy. Supporting evidence for this includes descriptions from thirteenth and fourteenth centuries of "venereal leprosy" and, later, "hereditary leprosy" (leprosy is neither venereal nor hereditary). Descriptions of the syphilis epidemic of 1500 in Europe include symptoms in some individuals that are more characteristic of acute infectious diseases such as typhus, typhoid, cholera, dysentery, and influenza than syphilis. In fact, few of these diseases had been distinguished from one another at that time, and it is quite possible that several distinct diseases were lumped together under the term "syphilis." Some historians have noted that the Chinese and Arabs used mercury rubs and inhalations for many centuries as treatments for "leprosy." The crusaders brought this "Saracen ointment" back with them from the Holy Land in the twelfth and thirteenth centuries. Apparently, mercury is useless for the treatment of true leprosy, but it was the most effective treatment for syphilis until the discovery of Salvarsan and antibiotics.

Spain and Portugal had been importing slaves from Africa for centuries before Columbus's voyage. Both nonvenereal syphilis and yaws were endemic to Africa, and the importation of slaves would have provided a continuous source of new infection to Europe. Several events that coincided with the syphilis epidemic in Europe have also been noted as possible contributing factors to its rapid spread. Papal proclamations of 1490 and 1505 abolished all leper asylums of the Order of Saint Lazarus, releasing these individuals throughout Europe. If some of the internees in these asylums were infected with syphilis, as some medical historians have suggested, the disease may have spread with them. The army of King Charles VIII of France, which contracted syphilis following its siege of Naples in 1494, was partially disbanded as a result of the epidemic, and infected soldiers then dispersed throughout Europe.

According to the *mutation/virulence theory,* syphilis was present in both the Old and New World before contact, but Columbus's crew exchanged different strains with Native Americans and brought back a more virulent strain, which quickly spread through Europe. There is little supporting evidence for this hypothesis. Critics have argued that if a form of syphilis was already present in Europe before 1492, previous exposure to the local strain should have provided some immunity to any new strain introduced, making an epidemic outbreak unlikely.

The mutation theory represents another epidemiological model for the 1500 epidemic in Europe. In its simplest form it does not concern itself with the question of Old/New World contact. It suggests that the epidemic of syphilis in Europe at the end of the fifteenth century was caused by a mutation in *Treponema pallidum* (the infectious agent in syphilis) that changed it from a relatively benign disease to a more virulent one. This theory cannot really be either supported or refuted by historical or medical evidence.

According to the *unitary theory,* syphilis and the other three known treponemal syndromes—pinta, yaws, and nonvenereal or endemic syphilis (bejel)—are not separate diseases but are caused by a single organism. The different syndromes reflect adaptation of the organism to different ecological conditions such as temperature and humidity and to cultural variables such as sanitation and amount of physical contact between individuals. Treponemal diseases are and have long been present in both the Old and New World. Supporting evidence for this model includes the observation that treponemes associated with the various syndromes cannot be distinguished from one another on morphological or antigenic grounds, and the fact that one form of infection (e.g., yaws, pinta) provides some cross-immunity to other forms of infection (e.g., syphilis). Although the treponemes responsible for each of the syndromes have been given different species names (*T. pallidum* for syphilis, *T. carateum* for pinta, *T. pertenue* for yaws), it is still unclear how they differ from one another, and some researchers do not accept the three-species division.

Despite 450 years of debate, there is still no consensus on the origin of syphilis. It remains a fact that no unequivocal cases of syphilis have been identified in Old World skeletal remains dated before A.D. 1500. This is true despite excavations at a

Syphilis and the other three known treponemal diseases—pinta, yaws, and nonvenereal syphilis—are caused by spirochete bacteria. An electron photomicrograph of *Treponema pallidum,* the spirochete that causes venereal syphilis, demonstrates the advances in knowledge about the disease since the 15th century. Despite this progress, researchers do not wholly understand the taxonomy of *Treponema* bacteria.

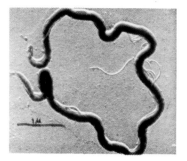

number of leprosarium cemeteries in Europe in recent decades in search of possible cases of syphilis. Careful examinations of these skeletal remains have yet to produce a good case suggestive of treponemal disease. The only argument for the presence of syphilis in the Old World before 1492 is based on documentary sources, which are often vague, contradictory, and subject to differing interpretations.

In contrast, there are an increasing number of cases highly suggestive of treponemal infections in pre-Columbian New World skeletal remains. Most of these specimens appear to represent yaws or endemic syphilis; several cases, however, have been interpreted as more suggestive of venereal syphilis. Will the issue ever be resolved? Some new experimental laboratory techniques hold promise. Several researchers are currently experimenting with the extraction of immunoglobulins (antibodies the body produces to fight specific diseases) from bone. If immunoglobulins specific to treponemal infection can be successfully isolated from bone, perhaps the debate can be resolved.

Disease and Population Decline Following 1492

While there is no disagreement among modern scholars that cycles of epidemic disease devastated native New World populations during the colonial period, estimates of the number of inhabitants of the New World at the time of contact have varied widely. Debate over the size of the population of the Americas at the time of contact has been active for the last twenty-five years and particularly intense in the last decade. While historians generally agree on New World population figures fifty to one hundred years after Columbus, there is substantial disagreement over population size at the time of initial contact and depopulation rates during the next five decades.

Estimates of population size of the New World in 1492 range from just over eight million to one hundred million. Similarly, estimates for North America range from nine hundred thousand to eighteen million. Such wide-ranging estimates reflect variability in the available information as well as the methodology used to estimate the numbers. Most scholars agree, however, that numbers for native populations declined rapidly during the first fifty years following initial European contact. Native population in North America reached a nadir in the early 1900s and has increased steadily since, reflecting diminished impact of disease, improved medical care, and, in recent years, shifting definitions of group membership.

"Two Faces of Love" is the not-too-surprising title of this 19th-century portrayal of syphilis. The illustration fits squarely within the tradition in arts and letters that over the centuries has dressed disease in metaphorical garb.

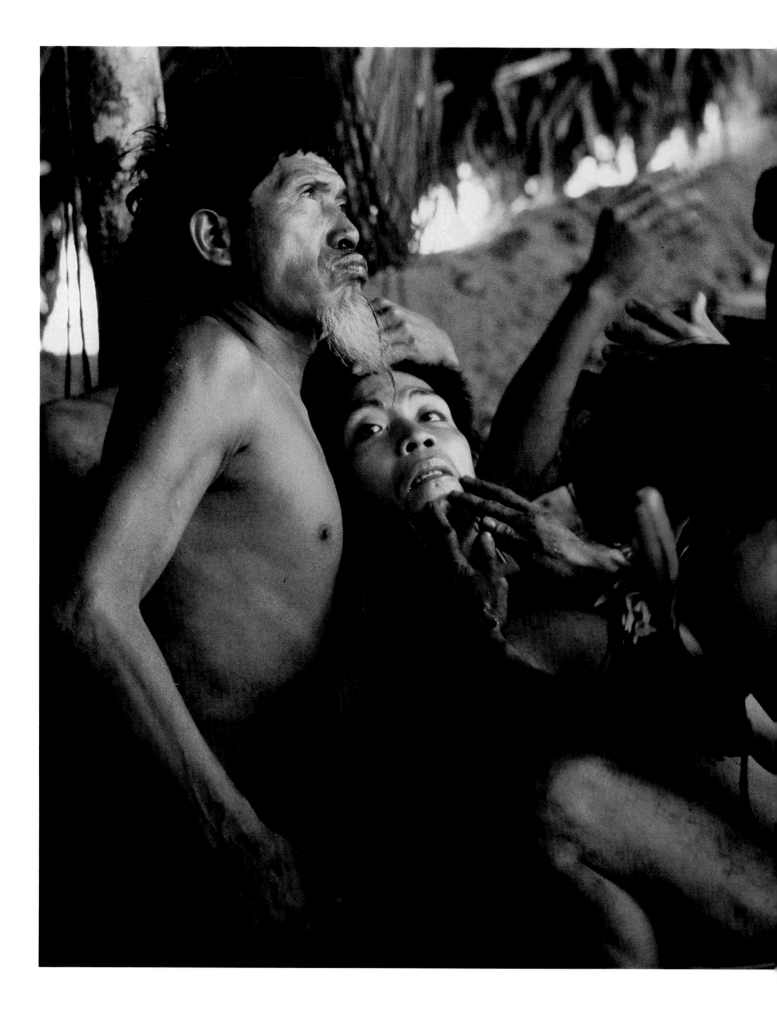

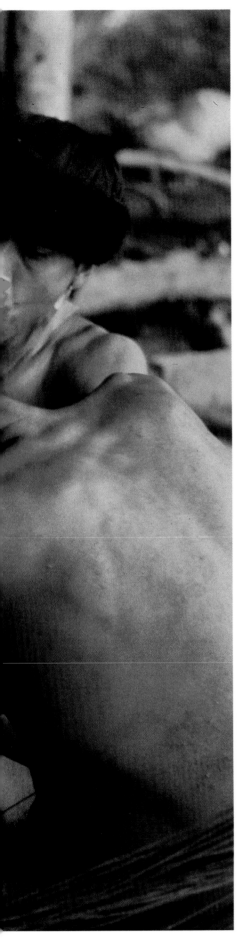

On the Eve of Contact

A New World observer looking eastward over the Atlantic Ocean in the year 1492 could not have imagined the powerful forces of change that were about to be unleashed by Columbus's voyages of discovery. Peoples and cultures of the Americas were about to end their long experiment of isolation and face an onslaught of explorers, conquerors, and colonists, who brought with them strange animals and plants, new customs, and frightening diseases.

The New World, however, was by no means simply a passive recipient of the changes brought from Europe and Africa, nor was it culturally homogeneous. On the eve of 1492, the Americas were inhabited by a complex mosaic of human societies, with an incredible diversity of languages, customs, and life-styles. Many of these societies already had long-term experience with the health challenges presented by rapid population growth, reliance on intensive agriculture, and urban living. In this regard, New World peoples had much in common with the health history of Europe. Certainly one of the important lessons we have learned from the study of health and disease in the precontact Americas is that human populations the world over share a long and fascinating history of adaptation to the challenges of changing environments, food resources, and disease.

As inroads are made into the last New World wildernesses, the decimation of Native Americans continues. Among the latest victims of alien pathogens are the Yanomamo Indians of Venezuela, one of whom is here attended by a tribal healer.

OTEZVMA
DALL'ORIGINA
DAL MESSICO
DI TOSCA

Health Profiles

An Aztec Warrior

An Aztec male was eligible for military service at age fifteen. In Aztec society, success on the battlefield was a principal vehicle for social advancement, and most young men were eager to become warriors. The battlefield was a hazardous place, however, and the standard weapons of war—arrows, darts, slings, and clubs with razor-sharp obsidian edges—could inflict terrible wounds. To treat its wounded the Aztec army maintained specialists who set fractured bones, realigned dislocated joints, and cleansed and sutured lacerations.

Common health complaints included intestinal disorders, headaches, coughs, and fevers. It was widely believed that disease was sent by the gods or was the result of sorcery, hence the advice of a professional healer was often sought—both to cure a disease and to divine its source. There were many healers in Aztec society who specialized in particular ailments, and treatment frequently combined ritual activities and herbal remedies. Some twelve hundred plants were used by the Aztecs for medicinal purposes. Most of these plants and plant preparations could be purchased in the marketplace from a vendor who specialized in herbs, medicines, and curing paraphernalia.

The Aztec people were meticulous about personal hygiene. They bathed regularly in streams and lakes, and took frequent sweat baths as well. Most dwellings in Tenochtitlán had a bathhouse, a small, circular structure that was heated by a fire built against the outer wall. The bather entered the structure and threw water against the wall to produce steam. Steam baths were used for personal cleaning, as well as to treat coughs, fevers, and joint problems. The Aztecs also recognized the importance of dental hygiene and cleaned their teeth regularly with powdered charcoal and salt.

As for general health and appearance, a sixteenth-century Spanish conquistador observed: "The people of this land are well made, rather tall than short. They are swarthy as leopards . . . skilful, robust, and tireless, and at the same time the most moderate men known. They are very warlike and face death with the greatest resolution" (Bray 1968).

A Spanish Conquistador

The Spanish conquistadores who made their way to the New World were survivors of a long and harsh process of selection. Infant mortality was high in fifteenth- and sixteenth-century Europe. One out of every three children died in the first year, and less than half survived to age fifteen. Poor nutrition and infectious disease were major contributors to this high mortality. Vitamin deficiencies were common, and scurvy was a familiar companion of sea voyagers. Recurrent outbreaks of bubonic plague, smallpox, measles, typhus, and other infectious diseases periodically winnowed the population of Europe, as did drought and famine. In terms of personal hygiene, the Spanish conquistador had much to learn from his Aztec adversary. Bathing was a seldom-practiced ritual in sixteenth-century Europe, and cities of this period were not renowned for their sanitary conditions.

While Europeans had a vague notion of the contagious nature of some diseases, illness more commonly was attributed to astrological phenomena, curses, personal and moral dissoluteness, and, above all, divine retribution upon sinful man. Medical treatments, which might include bleeding of the patient and treatment with herbal remedies, were aimed at restoring the balance of bodily humors—blood, phlegm, yellow bile, and black bile. While a wealthy individual might consult a university-trained physician for treatment of an illness, the common man generally relied on barber-surgeons, apothecaries, and self-taught practitioners. Barber-surgeons were the medical personnel who accompanied the Spanish conquistadores and early colonists to the New World. A general lack of confidence in their medical skill is suggested by the fact that conquistadores frequently sought out Aztec practitioners for health complaints, in preference to their fellow countrymen.

The Spanish who came to the New World in the early sixteenth century were tough, wiry, battle-scarred adventurers. Many showed the characteristic pockmarks left by a bout with smallpox during childhood, as well as wounds sustained in previous military campaigns. While they had little understanding of how to protect their health or to treat their illnesses, they were survivors, nevertheless. And like their Aztec opponents on the battlefield, they had little fear of death.

Three Faces of Eden

Stanwyn G. Shetler

Thirty minutes from the concrete and marble forest of offices and shrines in the heart of Washington, D.C., is a rocky headland of the Potomac River where one can look upriver for a mile through a wild and rugged gorge and sense the power and pleasure of nature much as the first Indians to stand here. Or, one can look downriver and glimpse human intrusion, the irrevocable infiltration of modern civilization with its culturally refined yet environmentally alien emplacements. To be sure, from this solitary Potomac promontory nature appears little disturbed. The natural environment has been artfully appeased, with the structures molded to the landscape and nestled largely out of sight. But make no mistake, our intrusions are permanent and ubiquitous. We are not only perched on the ramparts of the river but encamped everywhere else across the land. We long since have invaded the innermost sanctums of the American wilderness, from seashore and plain to highest pinnacle, and pushed beyond to the limits of the hemisphere, pole to pole.

Thus the view from this Potomac headland is metaphor for the past and present of the American wilderness. Two faces of Eden, two kinds of nature. In one direction is the First Eden, nature primeval, pristine; in the other, the Second Eden, nature modified, disturbed, and despoiled. The first nature is natural, the second unnatural, not because of human presence but because of human domination and destruction. There is a Third Eden, the totally artificial or synthetic nature that man creates. Here nature survives only by the perpetual intervention of man. This third kind of nature might be called postnatural. The remaking of Eden is the "unnaturalizing" of America.

Consider America's First Eden. When Christopher Columbus reached Caribbean shores in 1492 he reported the plant life to differ from Europe's as night from day. Those who followed outdid each other in telling big tales about the exotic American flora and fauna. It was not an empty and uninhabited land nor one untouched by human activity. The first seed for the Second Eden was sown, in fact, when the first human walked across the Bering land bridge and set foot in what is present-day Alaska. In some infinitesimally small way, the unnaturalizing of the American wilderness began at that moment. But, measured by our world five hundred years later, pre-Columbian America was still the First Eden, a pristine natural kingdom. The native people were transparent in the landscape, living as natural elements of the ecosphere. Their world, the New World of Columbus, was a world of barely perceptible human disturbance.

"When the first Europeans came to our shores," wrote naturalist Donald Culross Peattie, "our virgin forests, stretching from ocean to ocean and from arctic strand to tropic, staggered belief." Trees were everywhere, clothing all but 5 percent of the land in eastern North America, in forms, sizes, and virtues to surpass anything the rest of the earth had to offer in its temperate regions. America had the "tallest and the mightiest," as Peattie put it. In account after account, early sojourners wrote with awe and incredulity about the majestic American forests. We know from these early accounts that, although the modern forests of North America are but shreds of the once-continuous cloak, the distribution of tree species is much as it was in the time of Columbus, at least in the East.

We also know from reports and by inference from the odd tree or grove still managing to reach old age, something of the grand scale of the major eastern forest species as the earliest explorers and settlers found them. Towering giants presided over the forests. White pines commonly to 150 feet high, with records to well over 200 feet. Red and white oaks to 100 feet or more, with a diameter of 6 feet at breast height. American elms to as much as 140 feet high and 5 feet in diameter. Hickories, maples, and ashes to 4 feet or more in diameter. Atlantic white cedars to 100 feet and 6 feet in diameter.

The trees and forests of the Rocky Mountains and Pacific Coast were even more glorious. Pines, firs, spruces, hemlocks, cedars, the giant sequoia, the redwood, the world's tallest tree, known to reach nearly 400 feet—they defied imagining. Cathedrals of the vaulting trees dwarfed all previous notions of forest.

In the heart of the North American continent was an ocean of grass—the prairie. From the shortgrass shallows in the west to the tallgrass depths in the east, this prairie sea covered the immense Great Plains. So deep was the tallgrass prairie that early explorers could not see over the top from horseback in some places without standing up. The first Europeans to lay eyes on the prairie were Spanish conquistadores from Mexico searching for gold in 1541 under Francisco Vásquez de Coronado's command. He wrote incredulously of reaching grassy plains without limit (maybe in Kansas). What they found was a green gold, a renewable treasure

Wild, rugged gorges of the Potomac River (previous pages) give us a glimpse of the First Eden, the pristine natural world of the Americas before Columbus. Europeans laid claim to a continent that seemed a paradise, like that imagined by the 17th-century artist Theodore de Bry (below). Exploiting this apparently inexhaustible wealth of resources transformed nature into the disturbed and unnatural

Second Eden. Today we live in the Third Eden, an artificial, post-natural America where nature survives only where managed. The hallmarks of our progress have been gross over-consumption and widespread disregard for a sustainable future. Will they be replaced by a new ethic of stewardship?

"When the first Europeans came to our shores," one naturalist has written, "our virgin forests, stretching from ocean to ocean and from arctic strand to tropic, staggered belief." Today only scattered patches of these great North American forests remain (following page).

that for millennia had sustained a unique fauna of herbivores, from hordes of bison and pronghorns to prairie dogs and pocket gophers. To Coronado, the bison were numberless, and some now think that as many as sixty million roamed the plains in his day. The burrowing prairie dogs also occurred in unbelievable numbers. Social creatures, they live in subterranean "towns." Thousands of towns once riddled the prairie, and a single town could cover many square miles and include millions of individuals.

The Second Eden—Unnatural America

Columbus set into motion a cycle of human-dominated transformation in the New World Eden, the likes of which it had never seen. The primeval ecological balance slowly but surely was irreversibly challenged. He and the explorers and colonists who soon followed him planted seeds of change that would progressively destroy, degrade, or otherwise unnaturalize the wilderness and forever transform the First American Eden. The Europeans were so awed by the continent's seemingly boundless natural wealth that they took no thought for the consequences of their creeping conquest of the land and its riches. No sooner did they discover the New World than they began to subdue it: claim and settle it, till and harvest it, exploit and export it.

Every crop of changes sows new seeds that multiply these changes manyfold. Eventually, the native peoples and their cultures are extinguished, displaced, assimilated, or forever compromised. The native wealth—minerals, forests, wild game and fish, furbearers—is extracted without regard for a sustainable future; the fertile soils are exhausted, desertified, blown away, or flushed into the sea, as the priceless mantle of continent itself dissolves away; the air is polluted; and the water is poisoned or squandered.

Rapid, geometric, if not exponential, change has occurred mainly during the last two centuries, with the exploding of population and the coming of industrialization and mechanization, ever-improving transportation, and all of modern technology. Thus the systematic, all-pervasive unnaturalizing of the American landscape is relatively recent. The native American prairie, for instance, was little affected by the foreign immigrants before the first half of the nineteenth century. Massive invasion, contamination, and destruction of natural habitat is really a phenomenon of the last fifty years, especially of post–World War II America.

The systematic unnaturalization of America, which has occurred mainly in the last two centuries, is the result of an exploding population, industrialization, faster transportation, and a culture that equated success with wealth.

Exploitation

The agents of change have been legion, triggering never-ceasing cascades of unnaturalizing forces and influences. The musket (and all its descendants) in the hands of generations of immigrants was no respecter of creatures; it decimated and subdued the American Indians and decimated American wildlife. Through the years an awesome arsenal of catching and killing weapons has been used to assault the American fauna. But for the final dawn of a conservation ethic and principles of wildlife management, every species worth eating or wearing would have long since been exterminated. At the zenith of unbridled exploitation, greedy market hunters blasted birds from the skies, roosts, lakes and waterways, marshes, and shores by

Big, beautiful, delectable, and marketable, the wild turkey was first a casualty and is now a symbol of the exploitive habits of the colonizers of North America. By the early 1800s, commercial hunting had brought the wild turkey to virtual extinction. Last-minute conservation efforts saved the species and returned it to sufficient numbers that wild turkeys can be hunted in certain parts of the United States. A 15th-century Aztec rendering, a 16th-century drawing by a German artist, and the 19th-century painting by John James Audubon demonstrate that the wild turkey captured the attention of all cultures that encountered it.

the millions, even using cannons of sorts. Before the mass killing stopped, many species of waterfowl, shorebirds, and upland game birds were on the threshold of extinction. The passenger pigeon never made it back from the brink, nor did the less celebrated Eskimo curlew.

Even the wily all-American wild turkey, Benjamin Franklin's choice for a national emblem, was brought low. Once roaming over the territory of thirty-nine states from the East and Midwest to the Southwest, it probably would be extinct in the wild today except for the vigorous campaigns of latter-day sportsmen to reintroduce it for regulated hunting. The Aztecs tamed the noble bird long before Columbus arrived, and Hernán Cortés probably introduced it to Spain about 1519. It spread quickly to the tables of Europe, reaching England about 1541. The Pilgrims brought it back to America as a domestic food, only to find its wild relative abundant in the forests. Already in John James Audubon's time, in the early 1800s, when turkeys commonly sold in the markets for as little as three cents each, commercial hunting was raising concern. By 1851, the turkey was gone from New England, by 1900, from Ohio; Pennsylvania, once a stronghold, had few turkeys left by 1930. Significantly contributing to the disappearance of this bird were the destruction and fragmentation of its habitat and the loss of a principal food staple, the mast of the American chestnut.

"Furs, fish, and forests were the three resources that shaped the history of northern Europeans in the New World," wrote George Reiger in his essay "Hunting and Trapping in the New World." The trapper, with his simple gear and free spirit, could penetrate the wilderness in any direction at will. The trapper has been an important player in American history from 1500 until well into the twentieth century, and the first great exploitation of North America's natural wealth was the over-zealous harvest of furs. Before the end of the sixteenth century, a veritable navy of ships was transporting furs to Europe. Beaver fur was especially prized;

naturalist William J. Hamilton has suggested that no single factor was more consequential in early exploration and settlement than the beaver, even overshadowing the influence of the buffalo in the West. Today, scarcely more than a vestigial trade in wild furs remains, largely for sport.

Close on the heels of the fur trade came the next great harvest, the fishing of American waters. A sidelight of the rise and fall of the American fisheries is provided by one of the New World's caviar fish, the Atlantic sturgeon. At the time of Captain John Smith's colony, this anadromous fish was abundant in the Chesapeake Bay and, during spawning, in all its tributaries; at one point his settlement depended on the sturgeon for survival. In 1632, traveler Henry Fleet found the Indians taking as many as thirty a night from the Potomac at a narrows near present-day Washington, D.C. Atlantic sturgeons were shipped to Europe from New England as early as 1628. A major market, centered in New York City, developed along the eastern coast in the second half of the nineteenth century, but it crashed just before the turn of the twentieth century. Although a few may still be caught, the Atlantic sturgeon is almost extinct, and Captain Smith's band would surely starve if it were trying to survive on this fish today.

Of all the seeds of change that have transformed Natural America into Unnatural America, none surpasses the axe or the plow. Cutting down the forest fastness started from the day the Europeans first set foot on the continent, and it has never ceased, only accelerated. It took two centuries to catch on, but by the eighteenth century Europe had begun to exploit the American forests. Since then, waves of lumbering have felled most forests at least once, leaving only token patches of virgin timber. The American forest has shrunk like a drying lake bed, only isolated puddles of its former expanse still remaining. Today, it is highly fractured and fragmented almost everywhere except in its northern reaches.

The plow was not far behind. The vaunted American agriculture of our time has come at the expense of forest and prairie. The plow brought death to the natural prairie, transforming it into America's breadbasket. An acre of tallgrass prairie that once harbored as many as three hundred kinds of grasses and wildflowers now is likely to be an acre of hybrid corn or soybean monoculture. It is sustained only through perpetual care, going beyond unnatural to the postnatural Third Eden. Each step of care—plowing, irrigating, fertilizing, spraying—has unnaturalizing consequences that ricochet through the ecosystem, multiplying seeds of change.

The first massive exploitation of North America's natural wealth was the unrestrained harvest of furs; the second was the profligate fishing of its waters.

An anonymous 19th-century painting entitled *He That Tilleth His Land Shall Be Satisfied* celebrates one of the basic tenets of American settlement policies. That agrarian goal was achieved at the cost of the forest and prairie.

Introduction

The decline of the First Eden and rise of the Second Eden have been catalyzed through the years by countless introductions of exotic species that then diffuse throughout the land, sometimes extremely slowly, sometimes with devastating speed and epidemic proportion, as in the case of many diseases. Individually, each introduced plant, animal, or pathogen may be beneficial, innocuous, or harmful. Collectively, their cumulative effects have been overwhelming in the natural estate, variously contaminating, infecting, displacing, or destroying the native species and thus blending the species of continents toward an ever more homogenized global biota.

Wherever on earth man has gone, he has surrounded himself with the useful and familiar plants and animals of home, starting with his domestic crops and animals. Many fascinating stories can be told about exotic introductions to North America, intentional and unintentional. Nearly all of our common roadside weeds and hay grasses have come from Eurasia. Some cases are infamous. The notorious kudzu has overgrown the Southeast since it was brought in from Japan in 1911 to control erosion and fix nitrogen in the soil. Japanese honeysuckle, a pernicious weed, strangles trees and shrubs and smothers the indigenous herbaceous flora wherever it grows. The introduced Asiatic bittersweet is much more common in many parts of the East than the native bittersweet. Two aggressive Eurasian aliens have progressively been choking out the native plants of our freshwater marshes. They are the pretty purple loosestrife and the plumy reed or reedgrass. Both quickly form dense monocultures over vast acreages and exclude everything else. In California, very successful Australian eucalyptuses have become not altogether welcome. In Florida, it is the Australian pine (*Casuarina*). Both states are overrun in parts with foreign elements, such that it is difficult to separate the native from the alien.

Many animals have become weedy pests, too. The house, or English, sparrow and the European starling were introduced from Europe to New York in the nineteenth century, the latter by some romantic who wanted to have in America all of the birds in Shakespeare's writings. Both are extremely aggressive birds that have spread throughout the East in rural as well as urban settings. The sparrow sticks to the environs of dwellings, where the males chirp incessantly, but the starling also invades natural habitats, especially bottomlands with big dead or partially dead elms, sycamores, and other trees that provide abundant holes for nesting. Here, their cacophony of wheezing and screeching, especially in spring, is a sickening reminder of the unnaturalization of America. Both drive out such native hole-nesting species as the eastern bluebird and redheaded woodpecker. Although vigorous recent efforts to provide nesting boxes have slowed or reversed the decline, the bluebird population has dropped precipitously in this century.

Insect introductions have been numerous, often with harmful consequences. The present scourge of the European gypsy moth sprang from a deliberate importation that got out of hand. About 1869, a naturalist studying the ability of the caterpillars of various moths to produce silk brought the gypsy moth from Europe to his laboratory in Medford, Massachusetts. But some escaped into the nearby woodlands, and the pest has been spreading in every direction ever since.

The caterpillars are the devastators. In the outbreak zones where they reach astronomical numbers, they noisily devour the entire new foliage crop, denuding

The Lackawanna Valley, painted by George Inness in 1855 as a commission for the then-new Delaware, Lackawanna and Western Railroad, is an innocent-appearing landscape to which hindsight appends ominous overtones. The advent of the railroad changed farming from a small-scale subsistence practice to a booming commercial enterprise by opening the vast interior of the continent to distant markets. The prairies, plains, savannahs, wetlands, and woods, which supported incredible biodiversity, made way for monocultures of hybrid corn and soybeans.

Kudzu as a farm crop

Introductions of exotic flora and fauna into North America, whether by design or by accident, often have had dismaying results. About 1869 a biologist brought the European gypsy moth to America to study its silk-producing capabilities. A few escaped the laboratory and have run rampant ever since. The caterpillars, with audible voracity, devour new foliage and turn forests from spring green to winter brown. Oaks are particularly vulnerable to gypsy-moth infestations and often never recover. Kudzu was brought from Japan in 1911 as a livestock forage that would also combat erosion and fix nitrogen in the soil. Instead, the exotic legume outcompetes the native flora and now blankets parts of the Southeast.

whole mountainsides and abruptly turning back the forest from spring green to winter brown. The voracious caterpillars are no respecters of species, feeding on virtually any tree in the forest, deciduous or evergreen. But the oaks obviously are the most delectable, because they are always the first and the hardest hit, especially the white oak. The forest is resilient and usually survives a single hit, though with sapped vigor and diminished beauty and diversity. Most trees are capable of producing a second flush of leaves in a given season. But trees already weakened by other causes or subjected to repeated hits are likely to die. The oaks are the most vulnerable and often never recover. An oak-dominated forest after a gypsy moth invasion can be a scene of desolation, as one can witness on some mountain ridges of south-central Pennsylvania.

Insidious consequences can flow from accidental as well as deliberate introductions. Since Columbus, many unwelcome pathogenic seeds of change have made their way from the Old World to the New World as silent hitchhikers. Inoculating defenseless native fauna or flora, they have brought down entire species and devastated whole populations, forests, or biomes, forever changing their character. This is a tale of a thousand chapters. The eastern forests have been thrown into pitched biological warfare on many fronts, as one tree species after another is beset by uninvited aliens. Of all these chapters, perhaps none is so poignant and celebrated as the chestnut story, the passing of the great Appalachian forest monarch, which for some Americans still living is an etched memory.

A more perfect tree than the American chestnut could hardly have been imagined by the first Europeans to settle on these shores, and they thanked Providence for this gift. A whole economy in one tree. The bounty of its virtues has rarely been surpassed in a single wild species. Wood for any purpose that wood could be made to serve. Sweet, juicy nuts, long used by the Indians in a variety of foods, for a roasted delicacy, staple starch, or substitute for coffee or chocolate. Prodigious annual mast crops to fatten the wild turkeys and other game so vital to the tables of the colonists. Tannin for tanning. And magnificent proportions and a gracious, spreading beauty to inspire poets and place it in the top ranks of the continent's sylvan hall of fame.

With wood of superior indoor and outdoor quality, the chestnut was a timber tree of top commercial importance in the United States for more than a century. Its beautiful grain, durability, and ease of working made it ideal for furniture and all kinds of millwork. Fence posts outlasted fence-makers, barn beams supported generations of farmers, and somewhere trains may still be running the rails over chestnut ties. The tree touched even the social life of rural America, sheltering the village blacksmith and beckoning families and friends to the annual fall outing to gather chestnuts to eat, raw or roasted, or sell in the city markets and streets.

No one noticed or could have known, but the fate of the American chestnut was sealed when a well-meaning soul introduced the Chinese chestnut to the New York Zoological Gardens. Hitchhiking just inside its bark, in an evolutionary truce with its Chinese host, was a microscopic fungus that was soon to prove universally deadly to a new American host. When the first native chestnut trees in the gardens withered and died in the summer of 1904, some suspected nothing more than the hard winter of 1903. But about 1950, less than a generation later, the monarch had fallen throughout its stronghold. Already by 1940, healthy mature trees had virtually disappeared from the hardwood forests of eastern North America. Struck down by a killer blight that ripped with lightening speed through ever-widening circles of forest, the American chestnut was infected across New York State within seven years, and the species' doom was certain by 1920. Within twenty years the lethal radius extended a thousand miles, to the very portals of the southern Appalachian heartland.

Every attempt at control or quarantine proved futile. Pennsylvania tried desperately to save its vaunted forests. But the virulent fungus, *Endothia parasitica*, with its wind- and animal-borne spores, quickly made a mockery of the state's Maginot Line, a clearcut swath through the forest intended to halt the blight's westward and southward spread. We were to learn eventually that a single woodpecker, flying from tree to tree, might carry as many as 750,000 infectious spores at a time. The spores germinate under the bark, and the fungus causes cankers that kill the cambium, until the tree dies branch by branch. Because the roots are not killed, many of the stumps continue to this day to send up vigorous shoots. Some saplings may reach the flowering stage briefly, but infection soon strikes. Rarely does a tree survive long enough to produce a crop of chestnuts.

The scale of the ecological transformation that followed is hard to fathom. Scarcely a patch of eastern deciduous forest went unscathed. The American chestnut dominated many extensive forests and constituted almost the whole canopy of others. Its disappearance was further hastened by lumbermen rushing to salvage the remaining trees. From this devastation the eastern deciduous forest rebounded remarkably quickly, with oaks, hickories, and aspens commonly taking over the dominant roles in the canopy. Today the First Eden of the American chestnut would seem to be gone forever, though hope that science or nature will one day give birth to a blight-resistant strain is perennial. Cast down from the canopy, this majestic tree seems to be consigned forever to immaturity in the understory, to remind us perpetually of what we have wrought.

The American chestnut provided valuable timber unmatched for durability, ease of working, and the beauty of its grain. Its mast fattened the game so vital to the tables of rural America. But by the 1940s the chestnut had disappeared from the eastern forests. Earlier in the century a virulent fungus was inadvertently carried into this country under the bark of the Chinese chestnut, and rapidly spreading blight proved lethal to the American chestnut.

Other plagues are on the march in the North American forest, perhaps toward similar ultimate tragedies. The American elm is within sight of the vanishing point. Pines, spruces, oaks, maples, sycamores, dogwoods, aspens, and various other original species have fallen into the grip of assorted pathogenic blights that threaten decimation if not extinction. Indeed, one day, spring in the forest may be not only silent but leafless. Most of these plagues have been caused or hastened by the unwitting interventions of humans since the time of Columbus.

Pollution

Of all the human influences that have been seeds of change in the unnaturalizing of America, none has been more insidious, unpredictable, or illimitable than the pollution of our environmental commons, the air and the water. Pollution, often inadvertent and only belatedly recognized, is an unwelcome but largely uncontrolled effluent of our agricultural and industrial success.

The miracle story of recent American agriculture is in large measure the story of huge dosages of soil- and water-polluting chemicals. A mind-boggling arsenal of fertilizers, pesticides, and herbicides, compounded largely since World War II, has been dumped on the breadbaskets of North America year after year. The leaching residues already have caused some dramatic, unwanted, and multiplying effects, yet it is doubtful that the consequences have really begun to show. The latest chapter is being written by the countless lawn-care entrepreneurs saturating the suburbs of America with chemicals, in endless promise of sterile green monocultures.

The most dramatic testimony to the threats of pollution came first from the bird world. Rachael Carson's alarms, forever branded on our consciousness by her *Silent Spring*, shocked America and the world, consolidating concerns, galvanizing public opinion, and jump-starting a whole new era of environmentalism. Pesticide use would never be the same. Stunning case studies unfolded, most strikingly the bald eagle and the peregrine falcon stories.

For 150 years after the Continental Congress in 1782 designated it as the national emblem of the new American republic, the bald eagle survived without national protection despite shameless bounty hunting. Then along came the manic pesticide explosion of the 1950s and 1960s. Soon, persistent chlorinated hydrocarbons accumulated in the waters from the heavy use of DDT and its chemical relatives and poisoned the food chain. In many populations, the reproductive capacity dropped to zero in a few years, and soon the numbers of mature adults dropped precipitously.

Populations of the peregrine falcon also began to nose-dive suddenly in the 1950s. The peregrine, whose very name means wanderer, was one of the most widely distributed birds in North America and across the globe. Stooping in power dives to speeds of 175 miles per hour or greater, it probably is the fastest creature on wings. But in fifteen short years (1950–65) the Appalachian race of this majestic falcon was brought down by DDT in the food chain; it had folded its wings and made its last stoop—into oblivion. Nearly everywhere else in North America also it was in trouble.

The pesticide chain of death is now a familiar story. The chlorinated hydrocarbons were interfering with the ability of the bald eagle, peregrine falcon, osprey, and other raptors to reproduce, because their eggs were infertile or hopelessly thin-shelled. Only extraordinary, eleventh-hour efforts at protection and restoration, by

Of all the various ills that derive from the petroleum-driven cultures of the late 20th-century, oil spills are the most tangible and viscerally repulsive because of the speed with which they kill wildlife and the long-term damage to ecosystems.

In 1782 the Continental Congress designated the bald eagle as the emblem of the new republic. By the 1960s the majestic bird, at the brink of extinction, had become instead the symbol of a pesticide-poisoned earth. Since DDT was banned in 1972, the bald eagle has made a slow but steady recovery.

means of captive breeding in the case of the falcon, rescued both species from the brink and reversed the slide. The only redeeming feature of the bald eagle and peregrine falcon stories is that these two premier lords of the First Eden became flagship symbols of an entire environmental revolution to slow the unnaturalizing of America, even to restore some semblance of Natural America.

The ultimate weapon in the transformation of the First Eden surely is air pollution. Since the day when that first smokestack poked a hole in the skies and that first automobile hit the road, industrial and mobile America has poured pollutants into the atmosphere over the continent. The cumulative effects only now are becoming apparent, as we see a vivid continental, indeed global, example of the adage "what goes up must come down." Various pollutants are acidifying the precipitation, and others are warming the atmosphere, such that the situation seems out of control. Like a suffocating cloud of poison gas, acid rain has settled over the forests and waters, noiselessly and invisibly sowing killer seeds of change. It has acidified lakes and streams until the fish and amphibians can't breed, and it has begun to vanquish whole forests. The Applachian forests are dying from the top down, while we stand helplessly by. The beautiful, pyramidal red spruce, one of nature's great gifts to North America, evolved through the ages to cope with the harsh subarctic conditions of the northern and central Appalachian summits, where only patches of boreal forest cling. Once the sentinel of these rarified summit patches, with trees in favorable spots reaching four hundred years of age and a hundred feet in height, it now is making its last stand, declining everywhere and almost certain to make a final exit as a species in the not too distant future. This is only the beginning. The acidifying blight is making its way down the mountain slopes, and other tree species, most notably the American sugar maple, are already in deep trouble, especially in New England.

Air and water pollution strike at the very heart of primeval nature, starkly reminding us of the ultimate oneness of the ecosystem. The poison of one place soon becomes the poison of all, making all creatures of the earth vulnerable. Future generations will doubtless point the finger at the pollution of land, sea, and sky as the final and most pernicious force in the transformation of Natural America.

Extirpation and Extinction

The sorriest and most alarming chapter in the American story, surely, is the one being written by the declining and disappearing species. The North America of Columbus was endowed with a rich variety of plants and animals—thousands, perhaps millions, of species, if we but knew. Many of the species proved to be unique—endemic—to the continent, often to a single region or locality or two. Indeed, the novel wild garden and menagerie of this First Eden endlessly amused and bemused the dilettantes and savants of Europe. Slowly but relentlessly, species began to slip away, some to invisibility at the point of vanishing, others to extinction. Sometimes the causes were direct, as in harvesting for sport or commerce, exterminating pests, or unleashing rapacious and displacing pets, such as cats and dogs; sometimes they were quite indirect, as in the unintentional introduction of exotic competitors and pathogens, pollution, or destruction of habitat, even seasonal habitat in faraway places.

Of the case histories of disappearing species that have been documented and told, none has been so indelibly impressed on the American memory as the passing of the passenger pigeon or the near annihilation of the thundering hordes of American bison. The buffalo of the First Eden has come through the unnaturalizing eye-of-the-needle of the Second Eden to emerge in expanding but managed populations in the Third Eden. A less celebrated but intriguing case is the documented extirpation in the wild of the Franklin tree. It, too, is a tale with a ray of hope, because the species was brought into cultivation, where under perennial husbandry it has survived as a species of the Third Eden.

No one knows how many thousands of years this strange and wonderful small tree, a relative of the camellia in the tea family, may have existed or how far and wide it may have ranged. We only know that by the time it was discovered in 1765 by John and William Bartram, father and son botanists, the entire species population was confined to a few acres of swampy thicket along the Alatamaha (now spelled Altamaha) River in coastal Georgia. In 1803, less than forty years later, it was seen in the wild for the last time, the population now reduced to six or eight full-grown trees. This was less than two decades after it was formally described to science in the first botanical book to carry an American imprint, Humphrey Marshall's *Arbustrum Americanum*, published in 1785. He named it *Franklinia alatamaha*, honoring Benjamin Franklin and its only known habitat.

For the last century, industries in America, combined with ever more automobiles on the nation's highways, have lofted pollutants into the air that are returning to afflict the earth. Acid rain kills trees and poisons lakes. Ozone emissions make the air in many American cities unfit to breathe. Global warming threatens to alter the climate of the entire planet.

Thanks to the Bartrams, the Franklin tree was saved for posterity as a cultivated plant. William returned to the wild population in 1773 and found a blooming tree with the previous year's seeds, which he collected. One tree survived in the Bartrams' famous botanical garden near Philadelphia, and this tree became the chief seed source for the horticultural trade for years to come. While the Franklin tree, as a wild plant, became a lost camellia, its creamy white, orange-scented blossoms, blooming from midsummer to frost, and crimson fall foliage can still be enjoyed in parks and gardens across America and widely abroad. Thus its gene pool lives on, something that cannot be said for the passenger pigeon. Almost without doubt, its extirpation within twenty years of formal scientific description was caused by the collecting of greedy plantsmen, often for selling abroad.

John James Audubon was among the many who did not realize for years to come that the Franklin tree was extinct. In his painting for *Birds of America*, published in 1833, he posed the Bachman's warbler on a branch of *Franklinia*. In a twist of fate, the Bachman's warbler is now on the threshold of extinction. The warbler,

John James Audubon's painting of the Bachman's warbler is a portrait of the different routes toward extinction. The tiny bird, which nests in bottomland hardwoods of the southeastern United States and winters in similar habitat only in Cuba, is unlikely to pull out of its progression toward extinction. Eighty percent of its nesting habitat has been converted to rice and soybean cultivation and much of its wintering ground is now in sugarcane. Audubon perched the warbler on *Franklinia alatamaha*, a camellia that became extinct in the wild by 1803, probably because of rapacious collecting. The Franklin tree does exist as a horticultural species as a result of the survival of one specimen in the botanical gardens of the naturalists John and William Bartram.

painted by Audubon, was named in honor of John Bachman, a Charleston physician and naturalist collaborator, and the *Franklinia* was painted by Bachman's sister-in-law, Maria Martin.

Extinction begins with local extirpation, and for local endemics extirpation is extinction. Though the reality of general extinction usually is not perceived until it is too late, the tragedy accrues in increments, and a species may die a thousand deaths across its range before disappearing. The pace of extinction is continuing to quicken and is likely to steepen to catastrophic proportions in the next decade or early twenty-first century, as viewed on the grand scale of the Americas as a whole, including the highly vulnerable, species-rich tropics.

The biotic bleeding that began as a trickle will almost certainly become a hemorrhage, draining away the biodiversity and thus the lifeblood of continents.

Hardly a species of Natural America is secure. The chilling plight of the Neotropical migrant birds is a well-worn case in point, yet concern about a coming silent spring is more urgent than ever. Every new study raises new alarms about the precipitous decline of these species, which every year must overcome the triple threat of a shrinking and ever more hostile breeding range, wintering range, and migratory gauntlet. To the birds and large mammals must now be added the fish, the frogs, the butterflies and moths. And the plants. Some think that several hundred of North America's plant species will be extinct or face the imminent threat of extinction by the end of this century. The list of endangered fauna and flora goes on and on, always growing, never shrinking, its length constrained only by our elementary ignorance of the state of the American biota.

The Third Eden—Postnatural America

Today, we are living in the Third Eden, a nature of synthetic landscapes, fabricated biomes, and remade ecosystems. There are no sharp boundaries, only a progressive attenuation of nature primeval and a growing human tyranny as Eden inexorably shifts from natural to disturbed (unnatural) to artificial (postnatural). Today little if any of the original wilderness of the Americas remains truly original, untrammeled and untainted. The Third Eden brings us to what Bill McKibben calls "the end of nature," a planet so dominated by the human species that unadulterated nature has no place to hide, no realm beyond the reach of man; even the weather and the seasons are no longer tamperproof.

Of course, Natural America has been transformed in numerous positive ways into the modern synthetic Edens that today's inhabitants have come not only to cherish and depend on but also to demand. My opening Potomac River vignette distills the eternal tensions of the Edens: on the one hand, the progress that we have achieved with the amenities that we prize; on the other hand, the naked force and beauty of the natural wilderness to which we would retreat without our fabricated environments and our cultural crutches. We do try to make peace with our natural environments. To our credit, the natural shores of many Potomacs remain, and in the midst of our urban estates certain easements, "parks" in the vernacular, have been set aside to preserve surpassing parcels of nature for present and future generations to enjoy, albeit in a managed, window-shopping sort of way. Little patches of Eden under perpetual care, they are. The parks and wilderness areas across the land are as close as we come in Postnatural America to the First Eden, but in truth most are so highly engineered and managed as to be more typical of the Third.

Sometimes we love these preserved landscapes to death. Even as recently as twenty-five years ago one could still have my wild Potomac headland and its river view all to oneself even on fine days. To be sure, rock climbers and other urban braves had long since spooked the majestic peregrine falcons from their lonely aeries in the gorge. But nowadays the gorge crawls with human creatures even in winter. On warm days the rocks sprout variously clad bodies everywhere, virtually clothing the gorge with a garish rainbow. And such is the story of the parks and preserves throughout the America of the Third Eden. Too many people pursuing too little nature.

Under the circumstances, the keepers of the parks can never resist the urge to *develop* their preserves, improving them to meet the whims and wishes of the visiting pilgrims. Some miles up the Potomac from the headland, for instance, is Algonkian

Regional Park, a once lovely four hundred acres of river bottom. But the native habitat has been engineered out of naturalness to include, successively, a golf course, parking and picnic areas, boat-launching ramp, swimming pool, miniature golf course, chalets, storage compounds for RVs, and soccer fields, with more to come, including a conference center and millionaire housing on its immediate flanks. Poor nature. Not a chance. Even the apparent nature is deceptive, partly contrived and sustained through human intervention. Bluebirds, purple martins, and tree swallows that thrive only because of tended birdhouses. Mallards and Canada geese too comfortable with the managed environment to migrate in age-old fashion. Unnaturally herded white-tailed deer, with no guns and carnivores to fear and nothing more deadly to elude than a golfer or exuberant picnicker. Only ducks and grebes on the river that can endure the roaring of pleasure launches or hunting and fishing boats. And if all else fails to unnaturalize, over the momentary stillness or the natural sounds much of the year may come the pop, pop, pop of hunters blazing at ducks or upland game in the regulated preserve across the river. The Algonkian story is not unique; it is the life cycle of parks throughout the land.

The public mind of Postnatural America, conditioned by the triumphs of science and the self-conscious attempts of modern environmentalism to recapture or restore the First Eden, all too readily accepts as real the many forms of counterfeit nature synthesized or reconstituted by the well-intentioned of our time. Increasingly, we have no choice. The great natural commons of our past—the forests, prairies, mountains, waterways, swamps and marshes, coasts—are being destroyed, desecrated, or privatized. Too often, the natural wealth of the First Eden has turned to waste and the wilderness to wasteland, as wetlands and meadows have become dumps and landfills; forests, subdivisions; and rivers, open sewers. More and more we must turn to the artificial, managed commons of our future—the parks, botanical and zoological gardens and their hybrids; restored or reconstructed forests, prairies, wetlands, and other ecosystems; roadsides and meadows consciously planted with wildflowers; regulated shooting grounds and fishing streams; Disney Worlds and theme parks; bird feeders and butterfly gardens. They all thwart and falsify historical process and cut us off from the roots of Natural America.

Probably nothing epitomizes the American dream like home ownership or the American landscape like the modern subdivision and tract home. Likewise, probably nothing epitomizes better than subdivision sprawl Natural America at the limit. In our devotion to the dream, we have submitted to a new feudalism of property, a right—really a rite—of ownership in which we are little more than modern-day vassals of money lords, whose maximum-density parcels require totally external life-support systems to ensure the occupants' survival. The native Eden, whatever its original values, is digested by big machines, stripped of all natural virtues, and spewed out as postage-stamp parcels, tiny wedges in a totally artificial landscape. The original habitats are cleared, fragmented, attenuated, or bastardized until little natural diversity remains. Vicarious titles to such midget patches of Eden are conferred for the unending payment of various tributes. In many ways, the tract home is unfit at any price.

The American dream of home ownership is in many ways the quest to possess a little piece of Eden, but on these parcels the idea of nature has been compromised and misconstrued.

Yet millions of us manage to find happiness on a lot with a juniper and a silver maple, to find Eden in miniature in the subdivision, and we cling tenaciously to these personal preserves and whatever remnants of natural values they hold. It is generally a depressing struggle, because these little Edens almost always lose rather than gain in natural values as time goes on. It is the more depressing because they usually are indicators in microcosm of what is happening in macrocosm. Owners

of little Edens quickly learn that they are powerless to affect the fate of the larger ecosystem in which they are set. They live at the mercy of the keepers of the surrounding lands, helpless even to preserve their original vistas. Adding to the feeling of helplessness is the plague of free-roaming household fauna. Unrestrained cats and dogs displace natural carnivores in the ecosystem and destroy many native species. They are constantly at work silencing spring in the subdivision, menacing any birds and animals that one may succeed in attracting to a little corner of the man-made Eden.

The Third Eden has spawned the age of plastic biomes, of green concrete, fake turf, and plastic plants for office and home. None has much redeeming virtue as a synthetic surrogate for nature. Surely the ultimate cynicism in perpetual, loving care is a bouquet of plastic flowers on the grave. The Third Eden also has spawned many other postnatural rituals. Some modern pioneers, for instance, attempt to live off the land in a kind of throwback to hunting and gathering. They gather edible

While the use of chemical pesticides and fertilizers can produce significant increases in crop yields, their long-term effects on the human and natural environments can be pernicious.

wild foods, fish in put-and-take waters, or hunt in naturalistic shooting galleries that are stocked and managed game parks.

Such natural-living chic is, of course, a delusion that has nothing to do with the sustainable life of the First Eden. Natural living is largely an affectation, a virtual contradiction of terms in Postnatural America. But it is a token life-style with wide currency and shrewd, far-reaching exploitation in the marketplace. So-called natural foods and other products abound, and one can hardly tell the hope from the hype.

The Third Eden is in many ways a desperate scene. Once desperation reaches a critical level, some measure of restraint, recycling, or restoration is attempted, but only after circumstances force it. Civilization goes on but not without resorting to such self-destructive interventions as saturating the land with petrochemicals to fertilize the soil or subdue the pests, nor without building up artificial life-support systems and life-styles at the expense of someone else's resources and culture in other ecosystems of the biosphere. The precious natural estate of the First and Second Edens disappears in direct proportion to the growth of the precarious artificial estate until life itself becomes tenuous and the pristine Eden of the earth becomes little more than a vicarious Eden of the mind.

The First Eden nurtured and sustained the Native Americans in relative harmony with their environment. Man lived directly off the land in comparative balance with nature's other species. Unnatural America, by contrast, has not been a self-sustaining Eden. Indeed, the America of the Second Eden has been living ever more beyond its native means, reaching out and taxing the carrying capacities of many other lands. The America of the Third Eden is so intoxicated and imprisoned by its artificial life-support systems and simulated natural amenities that much of the population lives almost completely detached from the immediate natural environment and oblivious to it, isolated in frail man-made cocoons that are serviced and sustained by tenuous supply and disposal lines. The natural environment is, if anything, an irritating or intimidating nuisance to overcome or neutralize. The growing dominion of artificial nature has been devastating to the original heritage.

Scientific achievement is one of the great positive chapters in the story of the Edens. From the rugged early naturalists who took to the wilderness with collecting gun or sack and Latin grammar, to the host of scientists in the mighty modern enterprise of research and publication, the entrepreneurs of science have been pushing back frontiers at an ever-accelerating pace. The intellectual seeds sowed by those first explorers have been flowering and changing America and the world ever since. As the original wilderness has been shrinking, knowledge and mastery of the wilderness have been growing, along with our ability to synthesize alternative resources. The seeds of exploration and discovery sow seeds of description; the seeds of description sow seeds of explanation; explanation sows analysis and interpretation; and these sow synthesis, understanding, and action. The whole process builds slowly at first, and New World science did not begin to achieve significance until the eighteenth and nineteenth centuries. The pitfall of science in the Third Eden is that it can engender blind faith and utopian expectations. To society at large, science all too easily becomes a paradigm or philosophy for manipulating nature to achieve directed ends.

The postnatural era is America's Age of Environmentalism. If orchestrated or concocted nature is the hallmark, the prime legacy of the Third Eden is the far-reaching environmental revolution. Our unnaturalizing excesses of the Second Eden that have savaged the original wilderness have brought us to our senses in the Third Eden, giving birth to a national (and global) environmental conscience from which emerges a pervasive and ever-growing activism. From the ashes of abuse arises a new, hopeful ethic of stewardship. The timeless, unconscious stewardship of the American aborigines gives way, for centuries, to the conscious environmental conquest of the colonizers and now, at the eleventh hour, to the conscious stewardship of our time. Environmental heresy has become environmental ortho-doxy, as the ecofreaks of the fringes have become the ecological sages and seers of the mainstream.

The hazard of environmental concern is the facile solution. Profound ecological crises are trivialized with gesture and symbol. Life-style tokenisms of all sorts are promoted as patent medicines for saving the environment, but they seldom address the root cause, greedy materialism and gross over-consumption. Mankind has always worshipped the womb, the environmental envelope that nurtures us. The ancients had their gods and goddesses of fertility; the American Indians worshipped the nurturing womb of nature; and, today, we worship the womb of the material environment and the technological life-support systems that sustain us. We try to use it all, yet save it all, and slick hucksters in the marketplace would have us believe that we can have it both ways. Even while we are told that we are

contributing to the solution, often we are merely adding to the problem, as when we take actions that increase or at least do not decrease consumption of natural resources. The deceptive ambiguity of the market hype is epitomized by the "green product" fad of business and industry. The superficial notion of the green product that is environmentally sound begs more questions than it answers, and it completely distracts from the core issue, how to cut consumption.

Even our best efforts at conservation often are confused and artificial. Plant rescues, greenbelts, buffer zones, amenity landscaping, captive breeding, gene banks, rehabilitative and restorative ecology—they all are telling features of the engineered nature of our prefabricated lives in the Third Eden.

Cynicism aside, the environmentalism of our time is our only hope. It begins with an attitude but can become a conviction that leads to genuinely mitigating action, as capsulized in the watchwords of Earth Day 1990—recycle, reuse, and reduce. The wilderness of the First Eden was a many-splendored thing, and what is left of it can continue to inspire our lives, whether in reality or metaphor, as physical and intellectual frontier, fortress and retreat, storehouse and playground. The Third Eden is but a burlesque of the First, but it soon will be all that we have if we do not rally to the cause of saving the remnants that have survived the Second. Will the unnaturalizing of America be the undoing of the earth or the battle cry for its rescue?

Conservation projects such as reforestation are a feature of the engineered Third Eden, but environmental efforts may be our best hope.

Far from public view are the landfills overflowing with the mounting wastes of a throw-away culture.

247

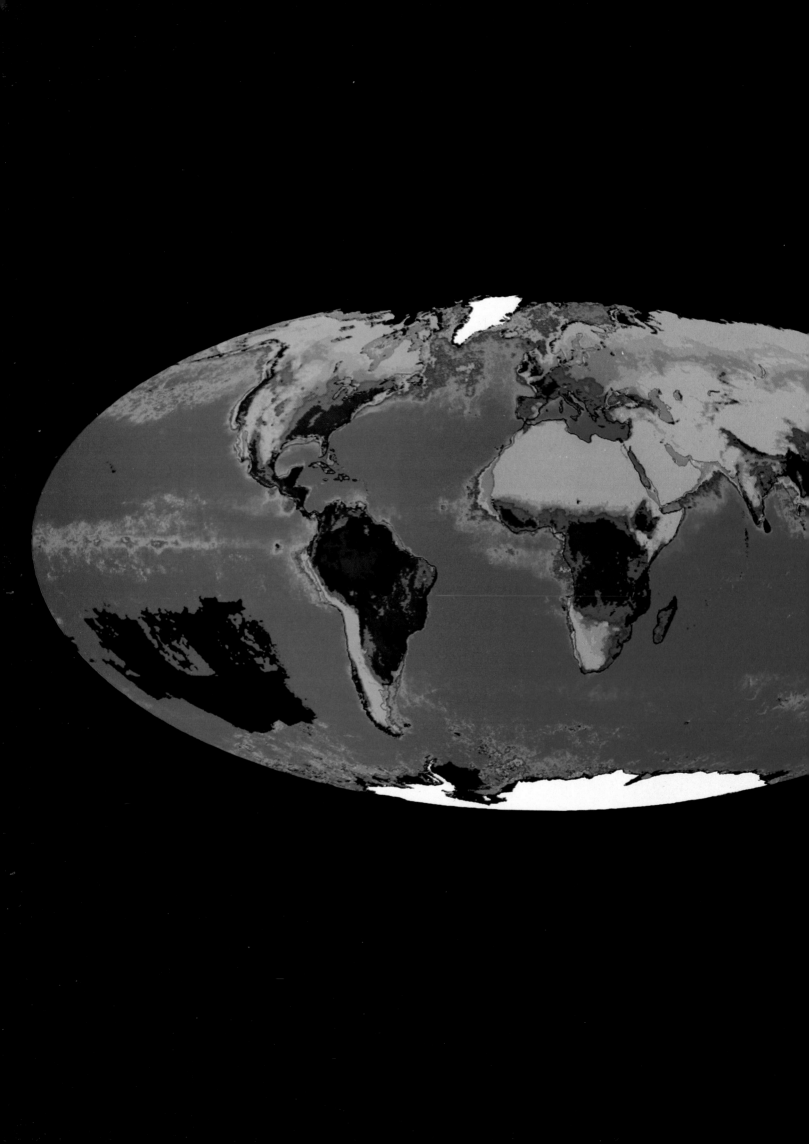

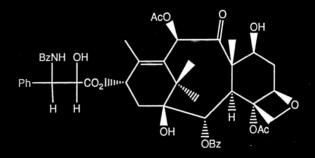

Nature's Future

Steven King and Liliana Campos Dudley

At sunrise 12 October 1992, a group of ecologists will meet on the beach in the Bahamas where Columbus is believed to have first landed. They will conduct a funeral ceremony for the natural environment of the Western Hemisphere. They will mourn the demise of the New World's natural heritage and the eradication of entire groups of indigenous Caribbean people. Nature's future, as envisioned by this group, is likely to be dismal.

The Legacy of Conquest

The ideas and attitudes of Columbus and many of the explorers and settlers who followed him can be described as a conquest mentality. The Europeans believed that the land and resources of the New World were limitless and that the indigenous people were primitive. Unfortunately, the colonizers frequently ignored knowledge native peoples had about their environment and dismissed their more appreciative relationship with the natural resources that sustained them. Exploitative attitudes have influenced choices made about the New World for five centuries and are still embraced by many. The resulting harm is alarmingly apparent.

Economic need, population growth, unsound land use, and destructive nationalism continue to devastate nature in the New World, particularly in the Andes and tropical forests. In the United States, a nation in which each citizen, on the average, accounts for more toxic wastes discharged into rivers and oceans than one thousand Asians, wilderness like none other on earth lies in jeopardy. Viewed by some as the most advanced nation in the world, the United States pursues a high-consumption life-style that, if it continues, will be significantly responsible for exhausting the earth's raw materials and life-support systems.

European colonizers in the New World believed its resources were unlimited and took an exploitative approach to nature, which is obvious in this 19th-century scene of deforestation in Brazil. Our very recent ability to view earth from space has helped put nature into proper perspective. The composite satellite image (previous pages) shows the planet's terrestrial chlorophyll resources and the phytoplankton in the oceans.

The Canadian Arctic, rich in resources but poor in diversity, has experienced more change in the past twenty-five years than at any other time since life on earth began. One must surely ponder the impact that large-scale development and settlement could have not only on its biota but on its people, the Indians and Eskimos, who share an uncommon reverence for life and nature. As a Canadian has asked: "If Canada—an industrialized and affluent country with a high material standard of living and natural resources far in excess of immediate needs—cannot 'afford' to slow down development in one of its frontier areas, what country on earth can?" (Woodford 1972).

Latin America is increasingly burdened with ecological disasters and dilemmas. Through mismanaged development, Central America and Mexico have lost areas of incalculable aesthetic, material, and scientific value. Only inaccessible and forbidding regions have escaped widespread and ruthless exploitation.

Rates of population growth in the Andean countries, with the exception of Chile, are among the highest in the world. The movement of many Andean people out of the mountains has led to environmental stress and new social problems. The tropical rain forest of the Amazon basin, unparalleled on earth for its biodiversity, faces destruction. In 1987, fifty-one million acres of the Brazilian Amazon were burned to make way for short-term farming ventures, cattle ranches, and roads. Losses in this incredible ecosystem are especially serious when we view the prospect of global warming.

We are seeing, because of changes in our global environment, that the ideas that accompanied Columbus now require revision if nature is to have a future. Our survival for the next five hundred years depends on our realization that natural resources are limited and must be managed with great care, especially in ways that safeguard biological diversity.

Knowledge about natural resources developed by the indigenous peoples of the New World was ignored or dismissed by ethnocentric Europeans, and destruction of native populations and cultures meant the loss of much expertise. Nevertheless, many food plants and agricultural techniques have survived and await rediscovery. In the highlands of Peru, Quechua-speaking people still grow and sell plant varieties unknown outside the Andes. The quinoa, pepino, babacos, and tubers pictured here may prove to have great value in other parts of the world.

Many solutions are offered by biotechnology, but our choices must reflect renewed scientific respect for the knowledge of the original inhabitants of the Americas and renewed political respect for their descendants. Cultural diversity is as important as biological and agricultural diversity.

Choices about the use of natural resources are subject to complex interactions of such human factors as population pressure, market economies, political systems, trends in international dominance, and ethical judgments. To ensure nature's future, we will have to devise new methods and technologies, new institutions and procedures, new global strategies and policies. This will be a continuing challenge to our science and philosophy.

Indigenous Knowledge

The acceptance of food crops and medicinal plants from the New World by the Old, as seen elsewhere in this volume, was a significant part of the post-Columbian exchange of resources. Potatoes and maize, first domesticated by native peoples of the Americas, now feed billions the world over. Cinchona bark, the source of quinine from the foothills of the Andes, has long been successful as a treatment for malaria and is now also being used as an antiarrhythmic.

Nevertheless, too often the ethnocentrism of the Europeans led them to ignore or dismiss native knowledge. The wide diversity of plants used for food, medicine, fuel, and shelter in the New World was not fully appreciated. For example, the Spaniards suppressed the crop plant amaranth in Mexico because of its powerful cultural and religious associations.

Sophisticated agricultural technology was also lost, as native understanding of land management was disregarded and, worse, inappropriate European systems imposed. Walsh and Sugiura mention the destruction of the floating gardens that supplied vegetables to Tenochtitlán. The raised-field agriculture of southern Peru was productive and capable of withstanding environmental extremes of drought, freezing, and flooding.

The drastic postconquest reduction of population in the Andes through war, forced labor, and disease contributed to the emergence of conditions quite unfavorable for land conservation in the following centuries. Huge European-owned estates, wastefully managed, were accompanied by overcrowded, fragmented land inadequate for the subsistence of their native cultivators. Unfortunately, decimation of the indigenous population and social order had brought about a disastrous loss of conservation ethics and know-how. No agrarian reform can completely restore such loss.

Still, many poorly known food plants and pre-Columbian agricultural systems are awaiting rediscovery. Revitalizing forgotten crops of the New World could expand the diversity and stability of agriculture around the globe (NRC 1989). Respect for indigenous knowledge could be a potent force in farming in the future, where creative approaches and productive, nonpolluting methods are required.

Medicine from Plants: AIDS and Cancer

With the advances of modern medicine, most persons in the developed world do not feel as susceptible to epidemic diseases as we did at the turn of the century. Certainly, our life spans continue to increase. Still, even in the United States, we

In the developed world, where epidemic disease seemed like a ghost of the past, the AIDS virus (left) has been a grim reminder of our vulnerability to new pathogens. As of February 1989, more than 42,000 people had died of AIDS in the United States. The toll is much higher in many countries in Africa, where 15 percent of some adult urban populations are affected by the virus.

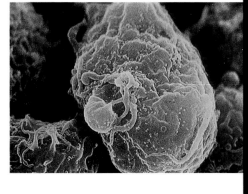

rely on plant-derived drugs on a daily basis. In the future, medicines from nature will continue to be extremely important in treating human illness.

Recently AIDS has reminded us that we are vulnerable to new diseases. As of February 1989, more than forty-two thousand people had died of AIDS in the United States, and no cure is known. Modern medicine is exploring all avenues to bring an end to this new disease, as well as various forms of cancer. Indeed, there are now large-scale programs under way to identify natural compounds that may help in the battle against terminal diseases. In 1986, the Developmental Therapeutics Program of the Division of Cancer Treatment in the National Cancer Institute (NCI) reinstituted the terrestrial plant, fungi, and marine organism collection. This program is concentrating on screening tropical species from central Africa, Madagascar, Latin America, and Southeast Asia. Rain forest conservation is urgent in this context; most plants of medicinal potential that Western pharmacologists have not tested are tropical.

Many methods are being applied to the search for plant compounds that may be effective against old and new diseases. Several of the scientists working with the NCI program are conducting ethnobotanical investigations, collaborating with people who still apply indigenous knowledge to determine the properties of plants in their native environments. Private industry is also beginning to return to the study of

The muralist Diego Rivera presents in rich detail Mexican medicinal preparations from pre-Columbian to modern times (right). Medicine from plants will continue to be important in the future. The U.S. National Cancer Institute (left) has been screening tropical species for natural compounds that may help fight disease. This evaluation has taken on an aura of urgency in the face of continued destruction of the world's rain forests; most untested plants with medicinal potential are tropical.

ethnobotanical information to target plant groups that have been used as medicine for centuries.

At this time several promising plant-derived compounds have been undergoing evaluation in the new NCI screening program. A toxin called 4-ipomeanol, produced by the common sweet potato (*Ipomoea batatas*) when infected with the fungus *Fusarium solani,* is under clinical investigation as a potential lung-specific antitumor agent. The roots of a Central American tree, *Phyllanthus acuminatus,* have yielded a terpene glycoside known as phyllanthoside that is showing selective activity against breast tumors in preclinical trials (Oldfield 1989).

In the drive to discover a cure for AIDS, a number of nature's compounds are already being closely examined. Castanospermine, extracted from the seeds of the Moorsestown Bay nut tree, *Castanospermum australe,* is one of these compounds. According to NCI laboratory tests, castanospermine interferes with the AIDS virus and its ability to damage other cells. The study of the novel mechanism by which castanospermine affects the AIDS virus will expand our capacity to stop the disease.

Should castanospermine prove effective in curing or arresting AIDS in humans, medical science may need large quantities of this substance. Although not common in its native habitat, the forests of New South Wales and Queensland, Australia, it has been cultivated to decorate avenues in South Africa, Hawaii, and California. Fortunately, the compound has also been discovered in several species of leguminous trees in tropical America. Trees in the genus *Alexa* could be tapped to yield castanospermine as part of extractive reserves in tropical forests (Duke 1989).

The Future for Potatoes and Maize

While previously unutilized plants can improve world health, improvements in previously known plants from the New World can reduce world hunger. Because potatoes are generally planted by using tubers or sections of tubers, large quantities of potential food are placed in the ground to obtain the next crop. Research conducted at the International Potato Center in Peru is focusing on developing and perfecting a true potato seed (TPS). To plant one hectare of the next year's crop in a developing country such as Nepal requires 1000 to 2000 kilograms of seed potatoes. By using TPS only 80 to 120 grams of seed would be needed for each hectare; all of the tubers can be eaten. Problems remain to be overcome, but with experiments with TPS being carried out in more than seventy-five countries around the world, a solution will soon be available.

Besides attempting to increase the yield, scientists are trying to improve the quality of the harvest. The quality of potato protein is the focus of research being conducted in collaboration with Louisiana State University. A synthetic gene, which produces high-quality protein, is being incorporated into the potato genome using *Agrobacterium* as the gene vector. As this technique is developed, the high-carbohydrate, low-protein potato will be transformed into a more nutritionally balanced food.

Scientists have already introduced genes to increase the disease resistance of potatoes. The Monsanto Company has successfully inserted two new genes into the Russet Burbank potato that make it resistant to two viruses—Potato X and Potato Y, which alone are responsible for several million dollars of damage a year. The imminent commercial availability of these gene-enhanced potatoes should be welcome news.

There are impressive examples of advanced biotechnology complementing traditional approaches in the hands of native farmers. In Vietnam, rural farmers have been taught a tissue culture technique of propagating promising potato varieties in the corners of their houses. With surprising success, these farmers are able to select and refine over generations specific varieties that work well in their fields.

Like the potato, maize was unknown outside of the New World before the arrival of Columbus. Today it is one of the four most important food plants. A dietary staple for 200 million people around the globe, roughly 300 million metric tons were produced in 1986 from 138 million hectares under cultivation. In the United States, more than 79 million acres are planted in maize for grain and fodder. Because of its worldwide importance, any improvement in the productivity of maize will affect vast segments of the earth's population.

Maize is one of the most photosynthetically efficient grain crops in the world: it transforms the sun's energy into food very effectively. In the future this characteristic may be enhanced. Research aimed at genetically increasing the photosynthetic efficiency of maize is being conducted, and, as techniques in molecular biology and biotechnology are enhanced, the productivity of maize may dramatically increase.

Like the potato, maize has the potential to be improved qualitatively as well as quantitatively. In 1963, researchers discovered a mutant maize that contained much higher levels of protein. The strain was called *opaque-2 maize*. It was estimated that by using opaque-2 maize ten million tons of quality protein could be added to the world food supply annually (NRC 1988). A group of dedicated maize breeders at the Center for Corn and Wheat Research in Mexico worked for a decade to improve the basic agricultural qualities of opaque-2 maize and developed a maize variety called *quality protein maize* or QPM. There are still problems to be overcome with

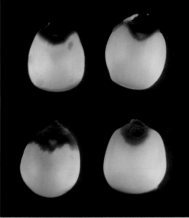

Scientists are pushing to improve the yield and nutritional value of the two most important New World food plants. Opaque-2 maize, discovered in 1963, is a mutant strain of corn with a high level of protein. Geneticists used it to produce nutritionally enhanced QPM, or quality protein maize (bottom). Other researchers are working to develop a true potato seed, or TPS, which would eliminate the age-old necessity of holding back parts of the tuber to produce the next crop.

To maintain crop diversity, plants must also be preserved *in situ*, in the places where they have evolved.

introducing a genetically stable QPM around the world, but it is one of the most exciting developments in the fight against world malnutrition.

For both potatoes and maize, emphasis on developing varieties that are tolerant to heat and drought and widely adaptable without needing fertilizer, insecticide, fungicide, and other petrochemicals or toxins will be of great importance. Two of the interconnected tools to achieve these goals will be biotechnological advances and *genetic resources,* that is, the genes of any organism that may have been or could be of use to human beings. Plant physiologists, agronomists, and botanists are debating how to preserve genetic resources and who should be the beneficiaries of the new agricultural technology. Decisions in these areas are some of the critical choices that have to be made in the last decade of this century.

Seeds of the Future: Germplasm Preservation

Farmers have always, of course, collected, exchanged, and selected crops for their specific agricultural conditions. It was the Russian N. I. Vavilov who in 1920 initiated a worldwide, systematic survey, the observation of the origins and evolution of crop plants and collection of those plants. In many respects the world's agricultural heritage that has evolved over the past ten thousand years is being cared for through a system of collections of crop diversity. Under the general oversight of the Consultant Group on International Agricultural Research (CGIAR), various regional and national organizations have collected from around the world farmer-selected crop varieties and less developed ancient cultivars or *landraces,* that is, those variations of a species cultivated in the same area over thousands of years within indigenous agricultural systems and specifically adapted to that region.

As the Green Revolution of the 1960s brought new and improved varieties of wheat, maize, rice, and potatoes around the world, predictably use began to diminish of less developed crop varieties, the older ones and the landraces. To cooperate with and to coordinate regional and national organizations that maintain varieties of crop plants, the International Board of Plant Genetic Resources was established in 1974 by CGIAR and based within the United Nations Food and Agriculture Organization in Rome. In most cases, seeds of the future are kept in gene banks, buildings that store thousands of seeds at varying temperatures to prolong their viability for many years. Some seeds are being experimentally frozen in liquid nitrogen at −160 to −196 degrees C. Only a tiny fraction of the natural biodiversity of crop plants can be conserved through this very expensive, high-technology cryogenic method.

Native peoples in North America practiced strikingly similar methods of seed preservation. Seeds were sealed in jars and stored in cool dark caves as insurance against crop failure (Nabhan 1989). Perhaps in the future, glaciers in the Andes or Himalayas will provide inexpensive long-term cold storage for seeds of crop plants the world over.

Expense is not the only reason why gene banks cannot be relied upon as the primary method for preserving our seeds of tomorrow. Not all seeds can be stored *ex situ,* and others only last until the next growing season. Many tropical seeds, both wild and crop, are short-lived in nature, and artificial conditions do not prolong their survival significantly.

Seeds of the future are stored in gene banks under optimum temperature and humidity. Some seeds are frozen in liquid nitrogen, but only a small fraction of crop plants can be preserved through this very expensive cryogenic method.

Furthermore, when a plant is taken out of its natural habitat it is no longer subject to the process of natural selection. The seeds of crops are the product of constant interaction between the plant and insects and other organisms, disease, climate, soils, and other conditions. The exchange of genes between wild species and crop plants over many years is one of the fundamental sources of diversity. These facts suggest that one of the critical methods for conserving seeds of the future is to preserve plants *in situ*, in the places where they have evolved.

Similarly, our specialists in crop plant evolution and preservation have overlooked the human dimension of selection. The landraces of our major food crops, such as maize and potatoes, were domesticated over millennia by people who developed a sophisticated knowledge of these plants. Descendants of the people who created these crops still successfully utilize information and techniques that have been part of their cultural heritage for several thousand years. Near Lake Titicaca, which spans the border between Peru and Bolivia, certain varieties of potatoes produce high levels of bitter, toxic glycoalkaloids, which make the plants insect-resistant and which may represent adaptation to the area's high altitudes. Natives of the region remove these bitter toxins by cooking the potatoes with three kinds of clay (Johns 1986). Plant specialists should learn to respect indigenous knowledge and draw routinely upon native farmers' knowledge of the qualities of seeds, the behavior of plants in different combinations and environments, and techniques for making plants palatable.

To guard and preserve our seeds of the future we will need to employ multiple strategies. Gene banks and cryopreservation are fine but should not be the primary methods. We will need national parks and reserves to conserve wild crop relatives *in situ*. We will also need to support the cultural values and knowledge of farmers around the world so that we will have networks of seed guardians to interact with the plant breeders of the next five hundred years.

Toward a Global Strategy: Sustainable Development

Many seeds of change in agriculture and medicine, as we have seen, were gifts from the people who inhabited the New World before the European arrival. What have we given them in return? Destruction of their bodies, souls, and culture. Now the remaining native peoples of the New World are witnessing, at the hands of Westernized development, the destruction of their natural environment. Although development is inevitable, humankind can choose whether future development will be the exploitative development that has wasted lands and peoples over the last five centuries or *sustainable development* that will protect natural resources and preserve the environment for the people who will inherit our planet five hundred years from 1992.

Decision makers are confronted with a complex political situation and thorny ethical issues. People in less developed countries are hungry for food and for an opportunity to live a good life, which is attained by many in America and the developed world. Advances in biotechnology and genetic engineering, in particular, raise concerns. The research programs of large international companies, national governments, and universities should be directed toward solving the food and health needs of people in developing nations. Appropriate technology that can be used by small farmers and producers throughout Latin America, Africa, and Asia is a reasonable, fair, environmentally sound goal. Profits derived from advanced new technologies should benefit the global community.

A modern martyr to the cause of sustainable development, Chico Mendez organized Amazonian rubber tappers to block destruction of the tropical rain forest. He was murdered in 1988.

Native peoples throughout the Western Hemisphere are struggling to regain title to their lands and to participate in decisions that determine the fate of their environment. "Debt for nature swaps," a promising financial mechanism for generating income in local currency and creating jobs focused on environmental protection, have yet to be used to support indigenous stewardship for certain ecosystems.

There are successful models for sustainable development, for stewardship. Chico Mendes organized rubber tappers and other Amazonian people to block destruction of large areas of rain forest, their primary source of income. Mendes gained international recognition for his efforts to bring nature and human needs into a harmonious balance. But the major landowners and cattle ranchers viewed him and the extractive reserve movement he led as a serious impediment to their continued acquisition of land and wealth. Chico Mendes was murdered in December 1988, but he proved sustainable development can work.

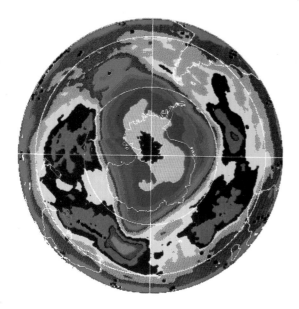

Scientists are strongly persuaded by the evidence that the skeletal trees on the summit of Mount Mitchell in North Carolina were destroyed by acid rain (right). Like ozone-layer depletion (left) and global warming, acid rain is a problem that is shared across state and national borders. It is also a concern that is not merely environmental, but one that calls into question traditional approaches to resource management, economic development, and population growth. Only global cooperation can provide solutions to these global problems.

People can earn a good living from the rain forest through managed extractive reserves, tapping rubber and collecting nuts and fruits, aromatic and medicinal plants, and other forest products for markets that are now being created. There is a growing international demand for rain forest products that are harvested by nondestructive methods. Cultural Survival, an organization based in the United States, markets Rainforest Crunch to generate financial support for Brazilian workers and for organizations that are striving to save the forest. A British firm, The Body Shop, produces soaps, oils, and cosmetics by methods that conserve rain forest resources.

Among the serious impediments to the implementation of sustainable development is tunnel vision in professional disciplines. Erik Eckholm observed that "when reading the analyses of economists, foresters, engineers, agronomists, and ecologists, it is sometimes hard to believe that all are attempting to describe the same country." For centuries the environment has been neglected by the social sciences, and natural scientists have tried to understand environmental change without the complementary methods and analytical tools for evaluating its social and economic implications. The conservation movement is opening paths of dialogue among specialties, agencies, countries, and social sectors.

It is time that environmental change is seen as a social process and environmental protection as a political objective. We can decide to make constructive changes. We can reduce the level of carbon dioxide released into the atmosphere. We can support community-based effort that conserves critical resources, such as agricultural topsoil, water, and forests, that sustain life on earth. We can support scientific action directed at rebuilding damaged ecosystems.

These are political choices. The deterioration of our natural world has been a historical process linked to economic and political structures. Change can result only from political action, a point emphasized in *Our Common Future*, the 1987 report of the United Nations Commission on Environment and Development. Under the energetic leadership of Norway's prime minister, Gro Harlem Brundtland, this commission explored the need for unified solutions to problems heretofore categorized narrowly. Environmental issues cannot be separated from development issues and pigeonholed under "conservation"; environmental problems cannot be addressed solely through their immediate causes; and international cooperation must be redirected to encourage positive change. Part of the answer will be found in exchanging nationalism for stronger awareness of the global human family.

Global warming and acid rain, which drifts across national borders degrading forest life and aquatic ecosystems, are problems that require international cooperation to solve. Food security is another. Our efforts here are unsuccessful even though much international assistance is geared to feed the hungry. Techniques to increase food production enter a system with deep inequalities and bring greater profit to the ones who already have power, land, money, and political influence. Land prices soar, export crops replace food crops, and poor farmers and tenants are forced out of rural areas into urban slums. The rich get richer and fewer, the rural poor, poorer and hungrier.

In *Our Common Future*, the Brundtland Commission urgently called for exploring new dimensions in international cooperation. Bilateral and regional arrangements must take place in a larger global framework, and international aid must cease to promote nonsustainable development. Projects must work within the constraints of local resources and should foster independence. Aid should support small-scale, environmentally appropriate projects aimed at making resource management and community development self-sufficient.

To realize sustainable development, we must redefine and redirect development itself, vigorously emphasize indigenous knowledge and experience, and take effective sociopolitical action on behalf of the environment. Only then will we have planted real seeds for change.

Sources and Suggested Readings

The Demise of the Fifth Sun

Bankes, George. 1977. *Peru Before Pizarro*. Oxford: Phaidon Press.

Barlow, Robert H. 1949. *The Extent of the Empire of the Culhua-Mexica*. Ibero-Americana, no. 28. Berkeley and Los Angeles: University of California Press.

Borah, Woodrow, and Sherburne Cook. 1960. *The Population of Central Mexico in 1548*. Ibero-Americana, no. 43. Berkeley and Los Angeles: University of California Press.

Díaz del Castillo, Bernal. 1956. *The Discovery and Conquest of Mexico*. Edited by Genaro García. Translated by A. P. Maudslay. New York: Farrar, Straus and Cudahy.

Fagan, Brian M. 1987. *The Great Journey, The Peopling of Ancient America*. London: Thames and Hudson.

Garáy, Francisco de. 1888. *El Valle de México: Apuntes históricos sobre su hidrografía*. Mexico City.

Gibson, Charles. 1952. *Tlaxcala in the Sixteenth Century*. New Haven: Yale University Press.

———. 1964. *The Aztec Under Spanish Rule*. Stanford: Stanford University Press.

Léon-Portilla, Miguel, ed. 1962. *The Broken Spears: The Aztec Account of the Conquest of Mexico*. Boston: Beacon Press.

———. 1963. *Aztec Thought and Culture: A Study of the Ancient Nahuatl Mind*. Norman: University of Oklahoma Press.

Lumbreras, Luis G. 1974. *The Peoples and Cultures of Ancient Peru*. Translated by Betty J. Meggers. Washington, D. C.: Smithsonian Institution Press.

Paddock, John. 1966. *Ancient Oaxaca*. Stanford: Stanford University Press.

Pagden, Anthony. 1986. *Hernán Cortés: Letters From Mexico*. New Haven: Yale University Press.

Palerm, Angel. 1955. *The Agricultural Basis of Urban Civilization in Mesoamerica*. Pan American Union Social Science Monographs. Washington, D.C.

Sahagún, Bernardino de. 1950–82. *General History of the Things of New Spain: Florentine Codex*. Translated and edited by Arthur J. O. Anderson and Charles E. Dibble. 12 vols. Santa Fe and Salt Lake City: School of American Research and University of Utah.

Todorov, Tzvetan. 1984. *The Conquest of America*. New York: Harper & Row.

Vaillant, George C. 1944. *Aztecs of Mexico*. New York: Doubleday and Co.

Weaver, Muriel Porter. 1981. *The Aztecs, Maya and Their Predecessors*. New York: Academic Press.

Willey, Gordon R. 1966. *An Introduction to American Archaeology*. Vol. 1, *North and Middle America*. Englewood Cliffs, N. J.: Prentice-Hall.

Wolf, Eric. 1959. *Sons of the Shaking Earth*. Chicago: University of Chicago Press.

Zantwijk, Rudolph A. M. van. 1985. *The Aztec Arrangement: The Social Prehistory of Pre-Spanish Mexico*. Norman: University of Oklahoma Press.

Zavala, Silvio. 1935. *La encomienda indiana*. Madrid: Imprenta helénica.

American Food Crops in the Old World

Crosby, Alfred W. 1972. *The Columbian Exchange: Biological and Cultural Consequences of 1492*. Westport, Conn.: Greenwood Press.

———. 1986. *Ecological Imperialism*. Cambridge: Cambridge University Press.

Ho, Ping-ti. 1955. The Introduction of American Food Plants into China. *American Anthropologist,* 57 (April):191–201.

Langer, William L. 1963. Europe's Initial Population Explosion. *American Historical Review* 69 (October):1–17.

———. 1975. American Foods and Europe's Population Growth, 1750–1850. *Journal of Social History,* 8 (Winter):51–66.

McNeill, William H. 1947. The Influence of the Potato on Irish History. Ph.D. diss., Department of History, Cornell University.

Messedaglia, Luigi. 1927. *Il mais e la vita rurale Italiana*. Piacenza: Federazione Italiana dei Consorzi Agraria.

Miracle, Marvin P. 1966. *Maize in Tropical Africa*. Madison: University of Wisconsin Press.

Murray, Laura May Kaplan. 1985. New World Food Crops in China: Farms, Food and Families in the Wei River Valley, 1650–1910. Ph.D. diss., Department of Oriental Studies, University of Pennsylvania.

Rotberg, Robert I., and Theodore K. Rabb, eds. 1985. *Hunger and History: The Impact of Changing Food Production and Consumption Patterns on Society*. Cambridge: Cambridge University Press.

Salaman, Redcliffe. 1949. *The History and Social Influence of the Potato*. Cambridge: Cambridge University Press.

Stoianovich, Traian, and George C. Haupt. 1962. Le mäis arrive dans les Balkans. *Annales: Economies, Sociétés, Civilisations* 17:84–89.

Metamorphosis of the Americas

The author would like to thank Frances R. Karttunen, the Nahuatlist, for her help in writing this article.

Acosta, Joseph de. 1962. *Historia Natural y Moral de las Indias*. Mexico City: Fondo de Cultura Económica.

Alden, Dauril, and Joseph C. Miller. 1987. Out of Africa: the Slave Trade and the Transmission of Smallpox to Brazil. *Journal of Interdisciplinary History* 18:195–224.

Carrier, Lyman. 1923. *The Beginnings of Agriculture in America*. New York: McGraw Hill Book Co.

Chimalpahin Cuauhtlehuanitzin. 1963, 1965. *Die Relationen Chimalpahin's sur Geschichte México's*. 2 vols. Hamburg: Cram, De Gruyter and Co.

Columbus, Christopher. 1963. *Journals and Other Documents on the Life and Voyages of Christopher Columbus*. Translated and edited by Samuel Eliot Morison. New York: Heritage Press.

Cook, Noble David. 1981. *Demographic Collapse: Indian Peru, 1520–1620*. Cambridge: Cambridge University Press.

Cook, Sherburne F., and Woodrow Borah. 1971–79. *Essays in Population History: Mexico and the Caribbean.* 3 vols. Berkeley and Los Angeles: University of California Press.

Crosby, Alfred W. 1972. *The Columbian Exchange: Biological and Cultural Consequences of 1492.* Westport, Conn.: Greenwood Press.

———. 1976. Virgin Soil Epidemics as a Factor in the Aboriginal Depopulation in America. *William and Mary Quarterly,* 3d series, 33:289–99.

———. 1986. *Ecological Imperialism: The Biological Expansion of Europe, 900–1900.* Cambridge: Cambridge University Press.

Denevan, William M., ed. 1976. *The Native Population of the Americas in 1492.* Madison: University of Wisconsin Press.

Denhardt, Robert M. 1975. *The Horse of the Americas.* Norman: University of Oklahoma Press.

Dobyns, Henry F. 1966. Estimating Aboriginal American Population: An Appraisal of Techniques with a New Hemispheric Estimate. *Current Anthropology* 7:395–449.

Fernández de Oviedo y Valdés, Gonzalo. 1959. *Natural History of the West Indies.* Translated by Sterling A. Stoudemire. Chapel Hill: University of North Carolina Press.

Gibson, Charles. 1964. *The Aztecs under Spanish Rule: A History of the Indians of the Valley of Mexico, 1519–1810.* Stanford: Stanford University Press.

González, Julio V. 1957. *Historia Argentina.* Vol. 1, *La Era Colonial.* Mexico City and Buenos Aires: Fondo de Cultura Económica.

León-Portilla, Miguel, ed. 1962. *The Broken Spears: The Aztec Account of the Conquest of Mexico.* Boston: Beacon Press.

———. 1988. *Mesoamerica 1492, and on the Eve of 1992.* 1991 Lecture Series, Working Papers, no. 1. College Park: Department of Spanish and Portuguese, University of Maryland.

M'Clure, David, and Elijah Parish. [1811] 1972. *Memoirs of the Rev. Eleazar Wheelock, D.D.* New York: Arno Press.

Patio, Victor M. 1970. *Plantas Cultivadas y Animales Domésticos en América Equinoctial.* Vol. 5, *Animales Domésticos Introducidos.* Cali: Imprenta Departmental.

Sahagún, Bernardino de. 1950–82. *General History of the Things of New Spain: Florentine Codex.* Translated and edited by Arthur J. O. Anderson and Charles E. Dibble. 12 vols. Santa Fe and Salt Lake City: School of American Research and University of Utah.

Thornton, Russell. 1987. *American Indian Holocaust and Survival: A Population History since 1492.* Norman: University of Oklahoma Press.

Pleasure, Profit, and Satiation

The author wishes to thank Mr. G. B. Hagelberg for his invaluable assistance with the text and Ms. Sharon Bhagwan for her help in locating source materials.

Barbeau, M. 1946. Maple Sugar: Its Native Origin. *Transactions of the Royal Society of Canada,* 3d ser., sec. 2. 40:75–86.

Browne, C. A. 1933. The Origins of Sugar Manufacture in America. *Journal of Chemical Education* 10:323–30, 421–27.

Curtin, P. 1969. *The Atlantic Slave Trade: A Census.* Madison: University of Wisconsin Press.

Daniels, J., and C. Daniels. 1988. The Origin of the Sugarcane Roller Mill. *Technology and Culture* 29(3):493–535.

Forbes, R. J. 1966. *Studies in Ancient Technology,* vol. 5. Leiden: E. E. Brill.

Galloway, J. 1989. *The Sugar Cane Industry.* Cambridge: Cambridge University Press.

Hooker, R. J. 1981. *Food and Drink in America.* Indianapolis: Bobbs-Merrill.

Konetzke, R. 1946. *El imperio español.* Madrid: Nueva Epoca.

Mintz, S. 1985. *Sweetness and Power.* New York: Viking.

Nef, J. 1950. *War and Human Progress.* Cambridge, Mass.: Harvard University Press.

Plant, R. 1987. *Sugar and Modern Slavery.* London: Zed Books.

Rye, W. B. 1865. *England as Seen by Foreigners.* London: J. R. Smith.

Wilkinson, A. 1989. *Big Sugar.* New York: Alfred A. Knopf.

Winberry, J. J. 1980. The Sorghum Syrup Industry, 1854–1975. *Agricultural History* 54(3):343–52.

Antigua Slaves and Their Struggle to Survive

British Parliamentary Papers: Correspondence, Returns, and Other Papers Relating to the Slave Trade, 1801–1815. 1971. Shannon: Irish University Press.

Caines, Clement. 1801. *Letters on the Cultivation of the Otaheite Cane.* London.

———. 1804. *The History of the General Council and General Assembly of the Leeward Islands.* Vol. 1. Basseterre, St. Christopher.

Curtin, Philip D. 1969. *The Atlantic Slave Trade: A Census.* Madison: University of Wisconsin Press.

Frederickson, George M., and Christopher Lasch. 1967. Resistance to Slavery. *Civil War History* 13 (December):315–29.

Gaspar, David Barry. 1985. *Bondmen and Rebels: A Study of Master-Slave Relations in Antigua.* Baltimore: Johns Hopkins University Press.

———. 1988. Slavery, Amelioration, and Sunday Markets in Antigua, 1823–1831. *Slavery & Abolition* 9 (May):1–28.

———. 1989. Amelioration or Oppression? Slave Protest in Antigua on the Eve of Emancipation. Goveia Lecture, University of the West Indies, Cave Hill, St. Michael, Barbados.

Genovese, Eugene. 1976. *Roll, Jordan, Roll: The World the Slaves Made.* New York: Vintage Books.

Goveia, Elsa V. 1965. *Slave Society in the British Leeward Islands at the End of the Eighteenth Century.* New Haven: Yale University Press.

Laws of the Island of Antigua Consisting of the Acts of the Leeward Islands, 1690–1798, and the Acts of Antigua, 1668–1845. 1805–46. 4 vols. London.

Methodist Missionary Society Papers. Library of the School of Oriental and African Studies, London.

Mintz, Sidney W., and Richard Price. 1976. *An Anthropological Approach to the Afro-American Past: A Caribbean Perspective.* Philadelphia: Institute for the Study of Human Issues.

Pitman, Frank W. 1917. *The Development of the British West Indies, 1700–1793.* New Haven: Yale University Press.

Robertson, Robert. 1730. *A Letter to the Right Reverend the Lord Bishop of London.* London.

Wayne, Michael. 1983. *The Reshaping of the Plantation Society: The Natchez District, 1860–1880.* Baton Rouge: Louisiana State University Press.

Wentworth, T. 1834. *The West Indian Sketch Book.* 2 vols. London.

Galways Plantation, Montserrat

The Galways study, directed by Conrad "Mac" Goodwin and Lydia Pulsipher, began in 1981 under the auspices of the Montserrat National Trust. For the past ten years it has been funded by grants from the Center for Field Research/Earthwatch, the Skaggs Foundation, the Wenner-Gren Foundation for Anthropological Research, the University of Tennessee, Boston University, the Fulbright Program, the Montserrat Foundation, and other public and private donors.

Cooper, Thomas. 1824. *Facts Illustrative of the Condition of the Negro Slaves in Jamaica.* London: J. Hatchard and Son.

Equiano, Olaudah. 1814. *The Interesting Life of Olaudah Equiano or Gustavus Vassa, the African.* Leeds: James Nichols.

Gaspar, David Barry. 1989. Slave Life and Sugar Production in Antigua Slave Society. Paper presented at the conference, Cultivation and Culture: Labor and the Shaping of Slave Life, April 1989. University of Maryland, College Park, Md.

Great Britain. *Calendar of State Papers, Colonial Series: America and the West Indies.* Vol. 10, no. 741. London: Public Record Office.

————. Public Record Office. Slave Lists for Galways Plantation 1817 (PRO no. T71/447); 1821 (PRO no. T71/448); 1824 (PRO no. T71/449); 1828 (PRO no. T71/450); 1831 (PRO no. T71/451).

————. Public Record Office. List of Inhabitants, Whites and Blacks, of Montserrat, 1729, referred to in Col. Matthews letter of 28th May, 1730. (PRO B.T. Leeward Islands. Vol. 21).

Jesse, C. 1966. An Houre Glasse of Indian Newes: A Record of the Settlement of St. Lucia in 1605. *Caribbean Quarterly* 12:46–67.

Laws of Montserrat, 1668–1740. 1740. London: John Baskett.

Ligon, Richard. 1673. *A True and Exact History of the Island of Barbados.* London.

Mintz, Sidney. 1986. *Sweetness and Power: The Place of Sugar in Modern History.* New York: Elsabeth Sifton Books/Penguin Books.

Mountserrat Island, 1673. Manuscript map in the Blathwayt Atlas. Brown University, Providence, R. I.

Montserrat, 1677–78 [A Census]. 1910–20. In *Caribbeana,* edited by V. L. Oliver. 6 vols. London: Hughes and Clarke.

Pulsipher, Lydia M. 1986. *Seventeenth Century Montserrat.* Historical Geography Research Series. Norwich: Geo Books.

————. 1987. Assessing the Usefulness of a Cartographic Curiosity: The 1673 Map of a Sugar Island. *Annals of the Association of American Geographers* 77(3):408–22.

Siegel, Peter E., ed. 1989. *Early Ceramic Population, Lifeways, and Adaptive Strategies in the Caribbean.* Oxford: BAR International Series 506.

Thomas, Dalby. 1690. *An Historical Account of the Rise and Growth of the West India Colonies.* London.

Savoring Africa in the New World

Alagoa, E. J. 1970. Long-Distance Trade and States in the Niger Delta. *Journal of African History* 11(3):319–29.

Barbot, John. [1732] 1746. *Description of North and South Guinea.* London: Henry Lintot and John Osborn.

Birmingham, David. 1967. Central Africa and the Atlantic Slave Trade. In *The Middle Age of African History,* edited by Roland Oliver. London: Oxford University Press.

Brazelton, T. Berry. 1972. Child Development in Africa. *Science News* 102 (November 4):298.

Caillié, René. 1830. *Travels through Central Africa to Timbuctoo.* London: Colburn and Bentley.

Coursey, D. 1976. The Origins and Domestication of Yams in Africa. In *Origins of African Plant Domestication,* edited by Jack R. Harlan, Jan M. J. de Wet, and Ann B. L. Stemler. The Hague: Mouton Publishers.

Coursey, D., and J. Alexander. 1968. African Agricultural Patterns and the Sickle Cell. *Science* 160:1474–75.

Crosby, Alfred W. 1972. *The Columbian Exchange: Biological and Cultural Consequences of 1492.* Westport, Conn.: Greenwood Press.

Donnan, Elizabeth. 1930–35. *Documents Illustrative of the History of the Slave Trade to America.* 4 vols. Washington, D.C.: Carnegie Institution.

Falconbridge, Alexander. 1788. *An Account of the Slave Trade on the Coast of Africa.* London: J. Phillips.

Kaul, Lalita, et al. 1987. The Role of Diet in Prostate Cancer. *Nutrition and Cancer* 9(233):122–28.

Kiple, Kenneth F. 1986. Future Studies of the Biological Past of the Blacks. *Social Science History* 10 (Winter):501–06.

Kovi, J., et al. 1988. Large Acinar Atypical Hyperplasia and Carcinoma of the Prostate. *Cancer* 61(3):555–61.

Levtzion, Nehemiah H., and J. F. P. Hopkins, trans. and eds. 1981. *Corpus of Early Arabic Sources for West African History.* Cambridge: Cambridge University Press.

Livingstone, Frank B. 1958. Anthropological Implications of Sickle Cell Gene Distribution in West Africa. *American Anthropologist* 60:533–62.

Matthews, D. S. 1955. Ethnological and Medical Significance of Breast Feedings with Special Reference to Yorubas of Nigeria. *Journal of Tropical Pediatrics* 1:9–24.

Mintz, Sidney. 1975. History and Anthropology. In *Race and Slavery in the Western Hemisphere,* edited by Stanley L. Engerman and Eugene D. Genovese. Princeton: Princeton University Press.

Palmer, Colin. 1981. *Human Cargoes: The British Slave Trade to Spanish America, 1700–1739.* Urbana: University of Illinois Press.

Philips, John Edward. 1990. The African Heritage of White America. In *Africanisms in American Culture,* edited by Joseph E. Holloway. Bloomington: University of Indiana Press.

Portères, Roland. 1955. L'introduction du maïs en Afrique. *Journal d'agriculture tropicale et de botanique appliquée* 2:620–75.

————. 1959. Le maïs ou "blé des Indes." *Journal d'agriculture tropicale et de botanique appliquée* 6:84–105.

Posnansky, Merrick. 1969. Yams and the Origin of West African Agriculture. *Odu: A Journal of West African Studies,* n.s., 1 (April):101–07.

Purdue, Robert E., Jr. 1968. "African" Baskets in South Carolina. *Economic Botany* 22:289–92.

Royal African Company Papers, Records of the Treasury. Public Record Office, London.

Scarupa, Harriet Jackson. 1986. Cancer: Lowering the Odds for Blacks. *American Visions* 1(3):33–39.

Vlach, John Michael. 1978. *The Afro-American Tradition in Decorative Arts.* Cleveland: Cleveland Museum of Art.

Wiesenfeld, Stephen L. 1967. Sickle-cell Trait in Human Biological and Cultural Evolution. *Science* 157:1130–40.

Williamson, Kay. 1970. Some Food Plant Names in the Niger Delta. *International Journal of American Linguistics* 36:156–67.

Wood, Peter H. 1974. *Black Majority: Negroes in Colonial South Carolina from 1670 through the Stono Rebellion.* New York: Norton.

————. 1974. "It Was a Negro Taught Them," A New Look at African Labor in Early South Carolina. *Journal of Asian and African Studies* 9 (1974):159–79.

Hispanic American Heritage

Axtell, James. 1987. Europeans, Indians, and the Age of Discovery in American History Textbooks. *American Historical Review* 92 (June):621–32.

Bannon, John Francis. 1970. *The Spanish Borderlands Frontier, 1513–1821.* New York: Holt, Rinehart and Winston.

Juderías y Loyot, Julian. 1922. *Don Francisco de Quevedo y Villegas: la Epoca, el Hombre, las Doctrinas.* Madrid.

Lummis, Charles F. 1896. *The Spanish Pioneers.* Chicago: A. C. McClurg and Company.

McNeill, William H. 1986. Mythistory, or Truth, Myth, History and Historians. *American Historical Review* 91 (February):1–10.

Paredes, Americo. 1958. *With His Pistol in His Hand: A Border Ballad and Its Hero.* Austin: University of Texas Press.

Powell, Philip Wayne. 1971. *Tree of Hate: Propaganda and Prejudices Affecting United States Relations with the Hispanic World.* New York: Basic Books.

Sánchez, Joseph P. 1989. The Spanish Black Legend: Origins of Anti-Hispanic Stereotypes. *Encounters, A Quincentennial Review* (Winter), 16–22.

An American Indian Perspective

Collier, Peter. 1970. The Red Man's Burden. *Ramparts* (February), 26–38.

Ewers, John C. 1958. *The Blackfeet, Raiders of the Northwestern Plains.* Norman: University of Oklahoma Press.

Foreman, Grant. 1953. *Indian Removal.* Norman: University of Oklahoma Press.

Jane, Cecil, ed. 1988. *The Four Voyages of Columbus.* New York: Dover Publications, Inc.

Josephy, Alvin M., Jr. 1982. *Now That the Buffalo's Gone.* New York: Alfred A. Knopf.

McNickle, Darcy. 1973. *Native American Tribalism.* London: Oxford University Press.

Mooney, James. 1975. *Historical Sketch of the Cherokee.* A Smithsonian Press Book. Chicago: Aldine Publishing Co.

Spicer, Edward H. 1969. *A Short History of the Indians of the U.S.* New York: D. Van Nostrand Co.

Trennert, Robert A. 1975. *Alternative to Extinction.* Philadelphia: Temple University Press.

Thornton, Russell. 1987. *American Indian Holocaust and Survival.* Norman: University of Oklahoma Press.

Tyler, S. Lyman. 1973. *A History of Indian Policy.* Washington, D.C.: Bureau of Indian Affairs, Department of the Interior.

Washburn, Wilcomb E. 1975. *The Indian in America.* New York: Harper Colophon Books.

Health and Disease in the Pre-Columbian World

Allison, M. J., D. Mendosa, and A. Pezzia. 1973. Documentation of a Case of Tuberculosis in Pre-Columbian America. *American Review of Respiratory Disorders* 107:985–91.

Ashburn, P. M. 1947. *The Ranks of Death: A Medical History of the Conquest of America.* New York: Coward-McCann.

Baker, Brenda J., and George J. Armelagos. 1988. The Origin and Antiquity of Syphilis: Paleopathological Diagnosis and Interpretation. *Current Anthropology* 29(5):703–37.

Bray, Warwick. 1968. *Everyday Life of the Aztecs.* New York: Dorset Press.

Buikstra, J. E., and D. C. Cook. 1980. Paleopathology: An American Account. *Annual Review of Anthropology* 9:433–70.

Cockburn, T. Aidan. 1971. Infectious Diseases in Ancient Populations. *Current Anthropology* 12:45–62.

Cohen, M. N., and G. J. Armelagos, eds. 1984. *Paleopathology at the Origins of Agriculture.* New York: Academic Press.

Hrdlička, A. 1939. Trepanation among Prehistoric People, Especially in America. *Ciba Symposia* 1(6):170–77.

Keatinge, Richard W., ed. 1988. *Peruvian Prehistory: An Overview of Pre-Inca and Inca Society.* New York: Cambridge University Press.

Lastres, J. B. 1951. *Historia de la Medicina Peruana.* Vol. 1, *La Medicina Incaica.* Lima: Universidad Nacional Mayor de San Marcos, Imprenta Santa Maria.

Lastres, J. B., and F. Cabieses. 1960. *La Trepanacion del Craneo en el Antiguo Peru.* Lima: Universidad Nacional Mayor de San Marcos.

Lopez Austin, Alfredo. 1975. *Textos de medicina náhatl,* 2d ed. Mexico City: UNAM, Instituto de Investiagiones Históricas.

Newman, Marshall T. 1976. Aboriginal New World Epidemiology and Medical Care, and the Impact of Old World Disease Imports. *American Journal of Physical Anthropology* 45:667–72.

Omran, Abdel-Rahim. 1961. The Ecology of Leishmaniasis. In *Studies in Disease Ecology,* edited by Jacques M. May. New York: Hafner Publishing Company.

Ortner, D. J. 1986. Skeletal Evidence of Pre-Columbian Treponemal Disease in North America. In *VI European Meeting of the Paleopathology Association Proceedings,* edited by F. G. Bellard and J. A. Sanchez, 203–20. Madrid: Universidad Complutense de Madrid.

Ortner, D. J., and W. G. J. Putschar. 1981. *Identification of Pathological Conditions in Human Skeletal Remains.* Smithsonian Contributions to Anthropology, no. 28. Washington, D.C.: Smithsonian Institution Press.

Patrucco, Raul, Raul Tello, and Duccio Bonavia. 1983. Parasitological Studies of Coprolites of Pre-Hispanic Peruvian Populations. *Current Anthropology* 24(3):393–94.

Reinhard, Karl J. 1988. Cultural Ecology of Prehistoric Parasitism on the Colorado Plateau as Evidenced by Coprology. *American Journal of Physical Anthropology* 77:355–66.

————. 1990. Archaeoparasitology in North America. *American Journal of Physical Anthropology* 82:145–63.

Sahagún, Bernardino de. 1950–82. *General History of the Things of New Spain: Florentine Codex.* Translated and edited by Arthur J. O. Anderson and Charles E. Dibble. 12 vols. Santa Fe and Salt Lake City: School of American Research and University of Utah.

Shutler, Richard Jr., ed. 1983. *Early Man in the New World.* Beverly Hills: Sage Publications.

Steinbock, R. T. 1976. *Paleopathological Diagnosis and Interpretation.* Springfield, Ill.: Charles C. Thomas.

Stewart, T. D. 1958. Stone Age Skull Surgery: A General Review, with Emphasis on the New World. In *Annual Report of the Smithsonian Institution, 1957,* 469–91. Washington, D.C.

Three Faces of Eden

This essay is based in part on an earlier essay of mine, "Look What We've Done to Our Eden," published in the November 1987 issue of *Dial WETA* (now *WETA Magazine*) of the Greater Washington Educational Telecommunications Association. I am indebted to former editor Philip Kopper for permission to draw upon my words there for this article. I have also drawn in part from my series of articles under the heading "Bicentennial Glimpses of Audubon's Wilderness," published in the *Audubon Naturalist News* in 1975 and 1976, and from my book, *Portraits of Nature: Paintings by Robert Bateman* (Washington, D.C.: Smithsonian Institution Press, 1987).

Carson, Rachel. 1962. *Silent Spring.* New York: Fawcett Crest.

Elias, Thomas S. [1980] 1987. *The Complete Trees of North America: Field Guide and Natural History.* New York: Gramercy Publishing Company.

Fernald, Merritt Lyndon. 1950. *Gray's Manual of Botany.* 8th ed. New York: American Book Company.

Grasslands and Tundra. 1985. Alexandria, Va.: Time-Life Books.

Greller, Andrew M. 1988. Deciduous Forest. In *North American Terrestrial Vegetation,* edited by Michael G. Barbour and William Dwight Billings, 285–316. Cambridge: Cambridge University Press.

Hamilton, W. J., Jr. 1939. *American Mammals.* New York: McGraw-Hill.

Kastner, Joseph. 1977. *A Species of Eternity.* New York: Alfred A. Knopf.

Kimball, Thomas L., and Raymond E. Johnson. 1978. The Richness of American Wildlife. In *Wildlife and America,* edited by Howard P. Brokaw, 3–17. Washington, D.C.: U.S. Government Printing Office.

McKibben, Bill. 1989. *The End of Nature.* New York: Random House.

Mello, Robert A. 1987. *Last Stand of the Red Spruce.* Washington, D.C.: Island Press.

Peattie, Donald Culross. 1966. *A Natural History of Trees of Eastern and Central North America.* 2d ed. New York: Bonanza Books.

Reiger, George. 1978. Hunting and Trapping in the New World. In *Wildlife and America,* edited by Howard P. Brokaw, 42–52. Washington, D.C.: U.S. Government Printing Office.

Sims, Phillip L. 1988. Grasslands. In *North American Terrestrial Vegetation,* edited by Michael G. Barbour and William Dwight Billings, 265–86. Cambridge: Cambridge University Press.

Terres, John K. 1980. *The Audubon Society Encyclopedia of North American Birds.* New York: Alfred A. Knopf.

West, Meredith J., and Andrew P. King. 1990. Mozart's Starling. *American Scientist* 78(2):106–14.

Nature's Future

Duke, James A. 1989. Castanospermum and Anti-AIDS Activity. *Journal of Ethnopharmacology* (Elsevier Scientific Publishers) 25:227–28.

Eckholm, Erik P. 1976. Losing Ground: Impending Ecological Disaster. *The Humanist* (March/April), 7.

Johns, Timothy. 1986. Detoxification Function of Geophagy and Domestication of the Potato. *Journal of Chemical Ecology* 12(3):635–46.

Nabhan, Gary P. 1989. *Enduring Seeds.* Austin: University of Texas Press.

National Research Council. 1989. *Lost Crops of the Incas.* Washington, D.C.: National Academy Press.

National Research Council. 1988. *Quality-Protein Maize.* Washington, D.C.: National Academy Press.

Oldfield, Margery L. 1989. *The Value of Conserving Genetic Resources.* 2d ed. Sunderland, Mass.: Sinaur Associates Inc.

Woodford, James. 1972. *The Violated Vision: The Rape of Canada's North.* Toronto: McClelland and Stewart.

World Commission on Environment and Development. 1987. *Our Common Future.* Oxford and New York: Oxford University Press.

Index

Picture Credits

cover: photo courtesy of International Institute of Tropical Agriculture, Nigeria; back cover: Library of Congress; pp. i-1: Noel Hapgood/Tony Stone Worldwide; p. 1 inset: Library of Congress; pp. 2–3: Library of Congress; pp. 6–7: Guy Motil (c) Westlight; p. 7 inset: woodcut from *Estoria do emperador Vespesiano*, 1496, courtesy of the Science Museum Library, South Kensington, London; p. 8: from Christopher Columbus, *De insulis inventis Epistola*, Basel: J. Wolff, 1493, courtesy of the John Carter Brown Library at Brown University; p. 10: from Paolo Giovio, *Elogia vivorum bellica virtute illustrium*, Basel, 1575, courtesy of the John Carter Brown Library at Brown University

The Demise of the Fifth Sun

pp. 16–17: George F. Mobley (c) 1979 National Geographic Society; p. 16 inset: Museo Nacional de Antropología/INAH, Mexico, photo by Lee Boltin, Croton-on-Hudson, New York; p. 17 inset: from Diego Duran, *Historia de las Indias de Nueva España*, Atlas, 1880, courtesy of the Library of Congress; pp. 18–19: Museo Nacional de Antropología/INAH, Mexico, photo by Bob Schalkwijk, Mexico City; p. 18: Monument 1, San Lorenzo, Veracruz/INAH, Mexico, photo by Lee Boltin, Croton-on-Hudson, New York; p. 21: Alex Castro; p. 22 left: David Alan Harvey (c) 1975 National Geographic Society; p. 22 right: from Guamán Poma de Ayala, *Nueva Cronica*, courtesy of Det Kongelige Bibliotek, Copenhagen; p. 23: from *Borbonicus Codex*, courtesy of the Bibliothèque de l'Assemblée Nationale, Paris; p. 24 top: A. Moldvay (c) 1970 National Geographic Society; p. 24 bottom: from Jorge Hardoy, *Urban Planning in Pre-Columbian America* (c) 1968 George Braziller, reprinted by permission of George Braziller, Inc.; p. 25 top: from *Codex Telleriano Remensis*, 16th C., ms. mex. 385, courtesy of the Bibliothèque Nationale, Paris; p. 25 bottom: from *Codex Ixtlilxochtitl*, 16th C., ms. mex. 65–71, courtesy of the Bibliothèque Nationale, Paris; p. 26 left: Otis Imboden (c) 1974 National Geographic Society; p. 26 right: (c) 1989 Kenneth Garrett, Washington, D.C.; p. 27: (c) 1990 Victor Englebert, Cali, Columbia; p. 29 left: (c) 1972 Loren McIntyre, Alexandria, Virginia; p. 29 right: from Pedro de Cieza de León, *Parte primera de la chronica del Perú*, Seville, 1553, courtesy of the John Carter Brown Library at Brown University; p. 31 background: from *Matricula de Tributos*, ca. 1520, Biblioteca del Museo Nacional de Antropología/INAH, Mexico, photo courtesy of the Instituto de Investigaciones Estéticas, UNAM; p. 31 inset: from *Codex Ixtlilxochtitl*, 16th C., ms. mex. 65–71, courtesy of the Bibliothèque Nationale, Paris; p. 32 top: from *Histoire de la nation Mexicaine*, 18 C. copy, ms. mex. 35–36, courtesy of the Bibliothèque Nationale, Paris; p. 32 bottom: Museo Nacional de Antropología/INAH, Mexico, photo by Bob Schalkwijk, Mexico City; p. 33 left: from *Document sur l'Aperreamiento*, ca. 1540, ms. mex. 374, courtesy of the Bibliothèque Nationale, Paris; p. 33 right: from Antonio de Solis y Rivadeneyra, *Historia de la conquista de México*, 1783–84, courtesy of the Library of Congress; p. 35 top: Hernán Cortés [Cartas. Carta 2a] *Praeclara Ferdina[n]di, Nuremberg*, 1524, courtesy of the John Carter Brown Library at Brown University; p. 35 bottom: from Theodore de Bry, *Americae*, 1602, courtesy of the Library of Congress; p. 37: Museo Nacional de Antropología/INBA, Mexico, photo courtesy of the Instituto de Investigaciones Estéticas, UNAM; p. 39: Leandro Izaguirre, *Torture of Cuauhtémoc*, 1893, oil on canvas, 295 x 456 cm., Museo Nacional de Arte/INBA, Mexico, photo courtesy of the Instituto de Investigaciones Estéticas, UNAM; pp. 40–41: (c) 1990 David Hiser, Photographers/Aspen

American Food Crops in the Old World

pp. 42–43: photo courtesy of International Institute of Tropical Agriculture, Nigeria; p. 43 inset: from *Florentine Codex* (Med. Palat.

220, c. 400 v), courtesy of the Biblioteca Medicea Laurenziana, Florence, photo by Isabella Sansoni; p. 44: Brueghel the Younger, *Les Moissoneurs* (The Reapers), private collection, Brussels, photo courtesy of Giraudon/Art Resource; p. 45 left: from Guamán Poma de Ayala, *Nueva Cronica*, courtesy of Det Kongelige Bibliotek, Copenhagen; p. 45 center: National Museum of Natural History, Smithsonian Institution, photo by John Verano; p. 45 right: from John Gerard, *Herball*, 1597, courtesy of the Newberry Library, Chicago; p. 46: from J. Lagnvet, *Recueil de Proverbes*, 1657–1663, courtesy of the Bibliothèque Nationale, Paris; p. 47: from Denis Diderot, *L'Encyclopedie*, I: Planches, Paris, 1762, courtesy of Houghton Library, Harvard University; p. 48 left: courtesy of the International Potato Center, Lima; pp. 48–49: Vincent Van Gogh, *Aardappelpoters* (Planting Potatoes), 1884, oil on canvas, 66 x 149 cm., cat. no. 94, collection: State Museum Kröller-Müller, Otterlo, The Netherlands; p. 49 bottom left: from *The Illustrated London News*, 20 February 1847, p. 116; p. 49 right: from *The Illustrated London News*, 10 May 1851, p. 386, courtesy of Harvard College Library; pp. 50 and 51: from John Gerard, *Herball*, 1597, courtesy of The Newberry Library, Chicago; p. 52: from Giovanni Battista Ramusio, *Terzo volume delle navigationi et viaggi*, f 109v, Venice, 1606, courtesy of the John Carter Brown Library at Brown University; p. 53: from Fuchs, 1542, courtesy of Houghton Library, Harvard University; p. 54 left, top and bottom: from *Keng chih t'u*, complied by Lou Shou (1090–1162), Japanese edition of 1808, courtesy of the Harvard-Yenching Library; p. 54 right: James Stanfield (c) 1980 National Geographic Society; p. 55: from *Chich-wu ming-shih t'u-k'ao*, 1848, courtesy of the Harvard-Yenching Library; p. 56 top: from Francis Moore, *Travels into the Inland Parts of Africa*, London, 1738, by permission of the British Library, photo courtesy of Robert Harding Picture Library, London; p. 56 bottom: photo by George Schwab, ca. 1920, courtesy of the Peabody Museum of Archaeology and Ethnology, Harvard University; pp. 58–59: Gordon Gahan (c) 1981 National Geographic Society

New World, Vineyard to the Old

pp. 60–61: courtesy of the Wine Institute, San Francisco; p. 60 inset: "Vitis vinifera Linn," from J. Plenck, *Icones plantarum medicinalium*, 1784, v. II, 144, courtesy of the Botany Libraries, Harvard University; p. 61 inset: woodcut, from *Ordonnances de la Prévoste des Marchans et Eschevinaige de la Ville de Paris*, 1415, ed. dated 1500, courtesy of the Bibliothèque Nationale, Paris; p. 62: from Jacque de Beaune, *Missel romain à l'usage de Tours*, 16th C., courtesy of the Bibliothèque Nationale, Paris; p. 63: "How the Women of the Savages Make Their Drinks," from André Thevet, *La Cosmographie Universelle*, vol. 2, Paris, 1575, by permission of the British Library; p. 64 top left: from *Le journal illustré*, 1878, courtesy of the Musée National des Arts et Traditions Populaires, Paris, (c) photo Réunion des musées nationaux; p. 64 bottom left and right: from W.M. Davidson and R.L. Nougaret, *The Grape Phylloxera in California*, USDA Bulletin no. 903, 1921, courtesy of the Museum of Comparative Zoology Library, Harvard University; p. 65 top: Edge Hill vineyards, California, courtesy of the Wine Institute, San Francisco; p. 65 bottom: Beringer Brothers winery, California, 1895, courtesy of the Wine Institute, San Francisco; p. 66: "Les vendanges," miniature from *Heures è l'usage de Paris*, attributed to Rohan, c. 1418, courtesy of the Bibliothèque Nationale, Paris; p. 68: (c) 1991 Victor Englebert, Cali, Colombia; p. 69: Comstock Inc./Mike and Carol Werner

Metamorphosis of the Americas

pp. 70–71: (c) 1980 David Hiser, Photographers/Aspen; p. 70 inset: from *Titres de propriétés des terres de Santa Isabel Tola*, 18th C. copy, ms., mex. 94, courtesy of the Bibliothèque Nationale, Paris; p. 72:

from *Florentine Codex* (Med. Palat. 220, c. 406), photo by Isabella Sansoni, courtesy of the Biblioteca Medicea Laurenziana, Florence; p. 73: from *Florentine Codex* (Med. Palat. 220, c. 460v.), photo by Isabella Sansoni, courtesy of the Biblioteca Medicea Laurenziana, Florence; p. 75: photo by David Hiser, overlay by Ned Seidler (c) 1980 National Geographic Society; p. 76: Martínez Compañon, *Trujillo del Perú*, v.II, E70, courtesy of the Biblioteca del Palacio Real, photo by MAS Ampliaciones y Reproducciones, Barcelona, authorized by the Patrimonial Nacional, Madrid; p. 77: fresco, ca. 1550, Church of Ixmiquilpan, Hidalgo, Mexico, photo by Bradley Smith, courtesy of Laurie Platt Winfrey, Inc., New York; p. 78 left, top and bottom: courtesy of the Instituto de Investigaciones Estéticas/UNAM, Mexico; p. 78 right, top and bottom: anonymous painter, *The Castes*, c. 1775, Museo Nacional de Historia/INAH, Mexico, photo by Bradley Smith, courtesy of Laurie Platt Winfrey, Inc., New York; p. 79: from G.F. de Oviedo, *Cronica de las Indias*, 1547, by permission of the British Library; p. 80: from Francisco de Xerez, *Verdadera relación*, Seville, 1534, courtesy of the John Carter Brown Library at Brown University; p. 81: (c) 1973 Loren McIntyre; p. 82 left: engraving by J. Orr, *The Cultivator*, 1834–65, courtesy of the Library of Congress; p. 82 right: from de Ulloa, *Relación histórica del viaje a la América meridional (historia de los Inca del Perú)*, vol. I, courtesy of the Herzog August Bibliothek, Wolfenbüttel, Germany; p. 83: frontispiece by Johann Zwecker in George Chaworth Musters, *At Home with the Patagonians*, London, 1873, courtesy of The Newberry Library, Chicago; p. 84: courtesy of the Master and Fellows, Magdalene College, Cambridge, England; p. 85: Theodore de Bry, *Americae*, Frankfurt, 1593, pt. III, p. 39, courtesy of the Library of Congress; p. 87: portrait by Jodocus Hondius, courtesy of the Bancroft Library, University of California, Berkeley; pp. 88–89: Dick Durrance (c) 1970 National Geographic Society; p. 89 right: from Jim Harter, *Animals*, New York: Dover Publications, 1979, reproduced by permission Dover Publications, Inc.

Ranching in the New World

pp. 90–91: George F. Mobley (c) 1969 National Geographic Society; p. 91 inset: from Christophe Weiditz, *Das Trachtenbuch*, c. 1500–1550, courtesy of the Library of Congress; p. 92: Diego Rivera, *La era*, 1904, oil on canvas, 100 x 114.6 cm., Marte R. Gómez Collection, Museo Diego Rivera, Guanajuato, photo by Dirk Bakker, courtesy of the Founders Society Detroit Institute of Arts, reproduction authorized by the Instituto Nacional de Bellas Artes y Literatura, Mexico; p. 93 left: Pancho Fierro, *Juanita Breña*, watercolor, 19th C., collection of Sr. Fernando Berckemeyer, Museo Taurino, Lima, courtesy of Dr. Stanton Loomis Catlin and *Art of Latin America Since Independence*, Yale University Art Gallery and University of Texas Art Museum, 1966, photo courtesy of the Library of Congress; p. 93 right: by permission of the Archaeological Museum of Heraklion, Crete, photo by Ekdotike Athenon S.A., Athens; p. 94: Rochefort, *Histoire Naturelle*, Rotterdam, 1665, pp. 332–333, courtesy of the Library of Congress; p. 96: reproduced from *America Pintoresca*, 3d ed., Bogotá: El Ancora Editores, 1987, by permission of El Ancora Editores; p. 97: O. Louis Mazzatenta (c) 1980 National Geographic Society; p. 98: 1961.12, Frederic Remington, *The Stampede*, 1909 bronze, 22⅝ in. high, cast #5, courtesy of the Amon Carter Museum, Fort Worth; p. 99: Oriana Day, *Missión Nuestra Señora de la Soledad*, 37565, courtesy of The Fine Arts Museums of San Francisco, gift of Eleanor Martin; p. 100 left: James L. Stanfield (c) 1971 National Geographic Society; p. 100 right top: woodcut from *The Cultivator*, 1834–65, courtesy of the Library of Congress; p. 100 right bottom: woodcut by F.E. Fox, Boston, from *The Cultivator*, 1834–65, courtesy of the Library of Congress; p. 101: engraving by P. Maverick, 1804, courtesy of the Library of Congress; p. 102: from M. C. Saint Girons, *Les Mammifères de France et du Benelux*, Paris: Doin éditeurs, 1973; p. 104: Zuni Pueblo, New Mexico, 1879, photo by John K. Hillers, Bureau of American Ethnology, courtesy of the National Anthropological Archives, Smithsonian Institution; p. 106: from an 18th C. manual, courtesy of the Bancroft Library, University of California, Berkeley; p. 107: from *M. y P. Uniformes*, 81, courtesy of Archivo de Indias, Seville, photo by Fernando Suárez González; p. 108: James Walker, *Vaqueros in a Horse Corral*, 0126.1480, courtesy of the Thomas Gilcrease Institute of American History and Art, Tulsa, Oklahoma; p. 109: D'Orbignay, "Hierra en Rincón de Luna—Corrientes," lithograph, 1827, from Bonifacio del Carril, *Monumenta Iconográfica*, Argentina, 1536–1860, plate LV, courtesy of The Newberry Library, Chicago; p. 110–111: from Edward S. Curtis, *The North American Indian*, Supplement, vol. I, 9, courtesy of the Library of Congress

Pleasure, Profit and Satiation

pp. 112–113: (c) Martin Rogers, 1978/Woodfin Camp & Associates; p. 112 inset: from William Rhind, *A History of the Vegetable Kingdom*, 1865, courtesy of Sidney W. Mintz; p. 114: by permission of the British Library; p. 115: "Canamelle sucre," from M.E. Descourtilz, *Flore pittoresque et medicale des Antilles*, vol. IV, 283, 1883, courtesy of the Botany Libraries, Harvard University; p. 116 left: from John François Lafitau, *Moers des savages amériquains*, vol. 2, Paris, 1724, courtesy of the John Carter Brown Library at Brown University; p. 116 top right: Jan van der Straet, *Nova Reperta*, vol. f81, pl. 13, c. 1600, from the Art Collection of the Folger Shakespeare Library, Washington, D.C.; p. 116 bottom right: detail reprinted from *The Complete Book of Fruits and Vegetables* by F. Bianch and F. Corbetta, illustrated by Marilena Pistoia, by permission of Crown Publishers, Inc. (c) Arnoldo Mondadori, photo courtesy of the Botany Libraries, Harvard University; p. 117: rock painting from Cueva de la Araña, Bicorp, Valencia, Spain, photo by Douglas Mazonowicz, Gallery of Prehistoric Art, New York; p. 118 left: "Hindoo confectioner's shop," from Henry Pitman, *Indian Sketches*, 19th C., courtesy of Peter Kraus, Ursus Rare Books Ltd., New York; p. 118 right: "Preparation of Sweets for the Sultan of Mandu," from *Nimat Nama* (Book of Recipes), Mandu, Central India, c. 1500, by permission of the British Library; p. 119 left: from Guy de Cahuliac, *Chirurgia*, VIII, 4, ms. 6966 f154v, courtesy of the Bibliothèque Nationale, Paris; p. 119 right: anonymous woodcut, 16th C., courtesy of the Bibliothèque Nationale, Paris; p. 120: Brazil plantation from Blaue, *Atlas: America*, courtesy of the John Carter Brown Library at Brown University; p. 121 left: East Indian mill reproduced from Noel Deerr, *The History of Sugar*, London: Chapman and Hall, 1950, by permission of Chapman and Hall Ltd.; p. 121 right: from John Baptiste Labat, *Nouveau voyage aux isles de l'Amérique*, vol. 3, Paris, 1722, courtesy of the John Carter Brown Library at Brown University; p. 122 top left: from Robert Walsh, *Notices of Brazil in 1828 and 1829*, London: 1830, by permission of the British Library; p. 122 top right: "Insurrection on a Slave Ship," from W. Fox, *Brief History*, 1851, by permission of the British Library; p. 122 bottom: "Sugar Plantation of Don Eusebion Alfonso, Havana, Cuba, 1860," reproduced from Jacob Baxa and Guntwin Bruhns, *Zucher im Leben der Volker*, Berlin: Dr. Albert Bartens, 1967, by permission of Verlag Dr. Albert Bartens; p. 123: from William Clark, *Ten Views in the Island of Antigua*, 1823, by permission of the British Library; p. 124 left: reproduced from Jim Harter, ed., *Men: A Pictorial Archive from Nineteenth Century Sources*, New York: Dover Publications, 1980, by permission of Dover Publications, Inc.; p. 124 right: "Leclerc's Veterans Storm Ravine-à-Couleuvre, 1802," courtesy of Nancy G. Heinl, Washington, D.C.; p. 125 left: J.P. Davis, "Chinese Workers on a Sugar Plantation in Louisiana," 1871, reproduced from Jacob Baxa and Guntwin Bruhns, *Zucher im Leben der Volker*, Berlin: Dr. Albert Bartens, 1967, by permission of Verlag Dr. Albert Bartens; p. 125 right: reproduced from L.A.G. Strong, *The Story of Sugar*, London: George Weidenfield and Nicholson, 1954, by permission of George Weidenfield and Nicholson Ltd.; p. 126 left: John Greenwood, *Sea Captains Carousing in Surinam*, 1758, oil on bed ticking, 95.9 x 191.2 cm. (256:1948), courtesy of the Saint Louis Art Museum; p. 126 top right: from Sebastian Münster, *Kosmographie oder Bescheibung*, Basel, 1564, courtesy of the John Carter Brown Library at Brown University; p. 126 bottom: Alex Castro; p. 127 and 128: from the Warshaw Collection of Business Americana, courtesy of the Archives Center, National Museum of American History, Smithsonian Institution; p. 129: from the Bella C. Landauer Collection, courtesy of the New York Historical Society

Antigua Slaves and Their Struggle to Survive

p. 130: from John Gabriel Stedman, *Narrative . . .*, vol. 2, London: Johnson, 1794, courtesy of Tozzer Library, Harvard University; p

131 top: courtesy of the National Library of Jamaica, Kingston; p. 131 bottom: from William Clark, *Ten Views in the Island of Antigua*, 1823, by permission of the British Library; p. 132 top: from James Williams, *A Narrative of Events*, 1834, courtesy of the Library of Congress; p. 132 bottom: "Stocks for Hands and Feet" from Richard Bridgens, *West India Scenery . . .*, London: R. Jennings & Co., 1836, courtesy of the University of Texas General Libraries, Austin; p. 133 top: Nathaniel Jocelyn, *Cinque*, oil on canvas, 1839 (1971.205), courtesy of the New Haven Colony Historical Society; p. 133 bottom: engraving from Barber, 1840, courtesy of the Library of Congress; p. 134: "French Set Girls," courtesy of the National Library of Jamaica, Kingston; p. 135: St. John, Antigua, (c) 1902 H.C. White Co., Vermont, courtesy of the Library of Congress; p. 136: "Going to Market. Constant Spring Road," from A. Duperly and Son, *Picturesque Jamaica*, Kingston, 1902, courtesy of the Harvard College Library; p. 137: UPI Newsphoto, courtesy of the Bettmann Archive, New York

Galways Plantation, Montserrat

pp. 138–139: (c) 1991 Lydia Pulsipher; p. 138 inset: courtesy of the National Philatelic Collection, National Museum of American History, Smithsonian Institution; p. 140: Jacque Bellin, "Veue de Montserat," mid–19th C., courtesy of the John Carter Brown Library at Brown University; p. 141: courtesy the Department of Geography at the University of Tennessee, Knoxville; p. 143: (c) 1991 Lydia Pulsipher; p. 144: "Old North Sound Plantation," from *An Historical and Descriptive Account of Antigua . . . 1830*, photo by Mark Williams, Big Dog Photography, Milwaukee; p. 145: "Plymoth face of the island of Montserrat," map #30 from Blathwayt, *Atlas*, 1673, courtesy of the John Carter Brown Library at Brown University; p. 146: (c) 1991 Conrad M. Goodwin; p. 147: (c) 1991 Carol Watkins, courtesy of Lydia Pulsipher; p. 148 top: J.M. Da C. Velloso, *O fazandeiro do Brazil*, Lisbon: 1798–1806, courtesy of the John Carter Brown Library at Brown University; p. 148 bottom: from William Clark, *Ten Views in the Island of Antigua*, 1823, by permission of the British Library; p. 149: Barbara Tipson, *Galways Village*, courtesy of Conrad M. Goodwin; p. 150: from Trelawney Wentworth, *The West India Sketch Book . . .*, London, 1834, courtesy of the John Carter Brown Library at Brown University; p. 151 left, top and bottom: (c) 1991 Jean Howson, courtesy of Lydia Pulsipher; p. 151 bottom right: from Richard Bridgens, *West India Scenery . . .*, London: R. Jennings & Co., 1836, courtesy of the University of Texas at Austin General Libraries; p. 152 left: (c) 1991 Robert Gibson, courtesy of Lydia Pulsipher; p. 152 right: "After a Day's Work on a Banana Plantation," from A. Duperly and Son, *Picturesque Jamaica*, Kingston, 1902, courtesy of the Harvard College Library; p. 153: from Richard Bridgens, *West India Scenery . . .*, London: R. Jennings & Co., 1836, courtesy of the University of Texas at Austin General Libraries; p. 154: "On the Way to Market," courtesy of the National Library of Jamaica, Kingston; p. 155: "Sunday Morning in the Country," from Richard Bridgens, *West India Scenery . . .*, London: R. Jennings & Co., 1836, courtesy of the General Research Division, The New York Public Library, Astor, Lenox and Tilden Foundations; p. 156: George Robertson, "View in the Island of Jamaica," print published in 1778, courtesy of the Library of Congress; p. 157: from A. Opic, *The Black Man's Lament*, 1826, by permission of the British Library; p. 158: (c) 1991 Lydia Pulsipher; pp. 158–159 (c) 1991 Conrad M. Goodwin

Savoring Africa in the New World

pp. 160–161: (c) 1991 Elizabeth Hamlin, taken at Bob the Chef's Restaurant, Boston, Massachusetts; p. 161 inset: courtesy of the Trustees of the British Museum; p. 162 left: copy of rock painting from Tassili n'Ajjer, Henry Lhote Collection, Musée de l'Homme, Paris, photo (c) 1966 Eric Lessing, Magnum Photos, Inc.; p. 162 right: Alex Castro; p. 163: from George Eberhard Rumpf, *Herbarium Amboinese*, vol. 5, 1755, courtesy of the Botany Libraries, Harvard University p. 164 top: from Van der Aa, *La Galerie Agreeable*, c. 1729, courtesy of the Library of Congress; p. 164 center: "Negres a fond de calle," from Mortiz Rugendas, *Malerische reise in Brasilien*, Paris, 1835, courtesy of the Houghton Library, Harvard; p. 164 bottom: from Théophile Conneau, *Captain Canot . . .*, New York: Appleton,

1854, courtesy of the Library of Congress; p. 166 left top: *Hibiscus esculentus* (okra), from F. Tussac, *Flore des Antilles*, 1808, courtesy of the Botany Libraries, Harvard University; p. 166 left bottom: *Blighia sapida Koen* (ackee), from Engler and Drude, *Die Vegetation der Erde*, vol. IX, 1910, courtesy of the Botany Libraries, Harvard University; p. 166 right: courtesy of North Wind Picture Archives, Alfred, Maine; p. 167: James P. Blair (c) 1987 National Geographic Society; p. 168: (c) 1990 Greg Sims, taken in Louise Chase's restaurant Dooky Chase, New Orleans, painting by Richard Thomas; p. 170 top: Zaire, Azande, wood, from Lang Collection, Panga, 1914 (AMNH 90.1/3320), Neg./Trans. no. 3915, Courtesy Department of Library Services, American Museum of Natural History, New York; p. 170 bottom: (c) 1991 Victor Englebert; p. 171: courtesy of Centers for Disease Control, Atlanta, Georgia, 30333

Hispanic American Heritage

pp. 172–173: (c) 1990 Craig Aurness, Woodfin Camp & Associates, Inc.; p. 174: "Mother María de Jesús de Agreda preaching to Chichimec Indians in New Mexico," woodcut, 1631, courtesy of the Nettie Lee Benson Latin American Collection, University of Texas at Austin General Libraries; p. 175: from Georg Braun and Frans Hogenberg, *Civitates Orbis Terrarum*, 1572–1618, vol. 3, courtesy of the Library of Congress; p. 176: anonymous painter, *Casmiento de Loyola La Companía, Cuzco*, 17th C., photo courtesy of the Harth-Terré Collection, Latin American Photographic Archive, Tulane University, New Orleans; p. 177: A. Lara, portrait of Bartholomé de Las Casas, courtesy of the Biblioteca Capitular Colombina, Seville, photo courtesy of MAS Ampliaciones/Reproducciones, Barcelona; p. 178: from Bartolomé de Las Casas, *Narratio regionum*, Frankfurt, 1598, courtesy of the John Carter Brown Library at Brown University; p. 179: C.G. Bush, "Spain's 'Sense of Justice,'" from the *New York World*, 1898, reproduced from John J. Johnson, Latin America in Caricature, Austin: University of Texas Press, 1980, by permission of University of Texas Press; p. 180: film still from *The Ballad of Gregorio Cortéz*, Paravision ParaFrance, photo courtesy of the University of Southern California Cinema-Television Library, Los Angeles; p. 181 top: courtesy of the Library of Congress; p. 181 center: from Herrera, *Historia general . . .*, courtesy of the Library of Congress; p. 181 bottom: from *Retratos de Los Españoles Illustres*, Paris, 1791, courtesy of the Library of Congress; p. 182: courtesy of the Library of Congress; p. 183: handcolored etching, 1781, courtesy of Geography and Maps Division, Library of Congress; pp. 184–185: (c) 1988 Victor Englebert, Cali, Colombia

An American Indian Perspective

pp. 186–187: (c) 1991 Deven Shirkhande, courtesy of George Horse Capture; p. 188: (c) 1973 New York Times; p. 189: Wide World Photos; p. 190: from Drapper, 17th C., courtesy of the Bettmann Archive; p. 191: John White, "Indian Man and Woman Eating," 1585, courtesy of the Trustees of the British Museum; p. 192: from Theodore de Bry, *Americae*, 1602, courtesy of the Library of Congress; p. 194: portrait of Running Face (Mandan), attributed to C.M. Bell, Washington, D.C., 1874, courtesy of the National Anthropological Archives, Smithsonian Institution; pp. 194–195: Long Soldier, Winter Count (copy after buffalo robe by Lone Dog), Sioux, Fort Yates, South Dakota, 1798–1902, no. 11/6720, collected by Mrs. M.K. Squires, presented by Mrs. Thea Heye, courtesy of the Museum of the American Indian/Heye Foundation, Smithsonian Institution; p. 196 left: engraving, 1762, courtesy of the National Anthropological Archives, Smithsonian Institution; p. 196 right: woodcut, Antwerp, 1566, from the Department of Prints and Drawings of the Zentral-bibliothek, Zürich; p. 198: Brummet Echohawk, *Trail of Tears*, black-and-white wash (cat. no. 0227.1487), courtesy of the Thomas Gilcrease Institute of American History and Art, Tulsa, Oklahoma; p. 199: courtesy of the National Anthropological Archives, Smithsonian Institution; p. 200 left: Jesse Hastings Bratley, *Port Gamble Indian School*, Puget Sound, ca. 1894, courtesy of the National Anthropological Archives, Smithsonian Institution; p. 200 right: Alexander Gardner, *Sauk & Fox and Kansa representatives meet with U.S. Commissioner of Indian Affairs and chief clerk of the Indian Bureau*, Washington, D.C., 1867, courtesy of the National Anthropological

Archives, Smithsonian Institution; p. 204 left: Edward S. Curtis, *Horse Capture*, courtesy of the National Anthropological Archives, Smithsonian Institution; p. 204 right: courtesy of George Horse Capture; p. 205 all: courtesy of George Horse Capture; p. 207: Bill Hess, Running Dog Publications, Wasilla, Alaska, (c) 1980 National Geographic Society

Health and Disease in the Pre-Columbian World

pp. 208–209: courtesy of John Verano; p. 209 inset: from *Florentine Codex* (Med. Palat. 220, c.460 v), courtesy of the Biblioteca Medicea Laurenziana, Florence, photo by Isabella Sansoni; p. 211 top left: from *Florentine Codex* (Med. Palat. 220, c.123 v), courtesy of the Biblioteca Medicea Laurenziana, Florence, photo by Isabella Sansoni; p. 211 top right: engraving, 17th C., reproduced from Ferdinand Anton, *The Art of Ancient Peru*, London: Thames and Hudson, 1972, by permission of Thames and Hudson, London, and VEB E.A. Seemann Buch- und Kunstverlag, Leipzig; p. 211 bottom: from *Codex Azcatitlán*, ms. mex. 59–64, f. 5, courtesy of the Bibliothèque Nationale, Paris; p. 212: courtesy of the Countway Library, Harvard Medical School, photo by John Verano; p. 213: Neg./Trans. no. B4919, Courtesy Department of Library Services, American Museum of Natural History; p. 214 left: courtesy of the National Museum of Natural History, Smithsonian Institution, photo by John Verano; p. 214 right: mural by Alton Tobey, courtesy of the National Museum of Natural History, Smithsonian Institution; p. 215 left: popular lampoon, 16th C., courtesy of the Bettmann Archive, New York; p. 215 right: woodcut, 1497, courtesy of the Wellcome Institute for the History of Medicine, London; p. 216 left: from Valerius Cordus, *Annotationes in Pedacii Dioscoridis Anazarbei de Media materia libros*, f. 191v, Strassburg: J. Rihel, 1561, courtesy of the Wellcome Institute for the History of Medicine, London; p. 216 right: Jan van der Straet, *Nova Reperta*, plate 6, Antwerp, c. 1590, from the Art Collection of the Folger Shakespeare Library; p. 217: from Pseudo-Musa, *De herba vettonica*, German ms., ca. 1200, reproduced by permission of the Provost and Fellows of Eton College, Windsor; p. 218: courtesy of the Centers for Disease Control, Atlanta, Georgia, 30333; p. 219: Belin and Duchamp, "Les deux visages de l'Amour," from Auguste Marseille Barthelemy, *Syphilis*, Paris: Martinon, 1851, courtesy of the Bibliothèque Nationale, Paris; pp. 220–221: Robert Madden (c) 1975 National Geographic Society; p. 221 right: Santisteban, *Chinchona*, colored drawing, Linnean Herbarium, courtesy of The Linnean Society, London, photo by Eileen Tweedy; p. 222: from Antonio de Solis y Rivadeneyra, *Historia de la conquista de México*, 1783–84, courtesy of the Library of Congress; p. 223: Culver Pictures

Three Faces of Eden

pp. 224–225: M. H. Win/Washington Stock Photo, Inc.; p. 225: from G. Benzoni, *Historia del Mondo Nuovo*, 1563; p. 226: from Theodore de Bry, GV XIII, 1634, courtesy of the John Carter Brown Library at Brown University; p. 227: Kings Canyon National Park, photo (c) 1990 Larry Ulrich, Trinidad, California; p. 228: The Three Sisters, Sequoia National Forest, photo (c) 1990 Anacelto Rapping, Thousand Oaks, California; p. 229: Bowles and Carver, *Bowles' Moral Pictures*

(detail), courtesy of the Yale University Art Gallery, The Mabel Brady Garvan Collection, New Haven; p. 230 left top: Jost Amman, engraving, from Marx Rumpolt, *Ein New Kochbuch*, f. 788, Frankfurt, 1604, by permission of the British Library; p. 230 left bottom: Codex Mendoza, Ms. Arch. Seld.A1, f.16r (detail), courtesy of the Bodleian Library, Oxford; p. 230 right: from John James Audubon, *Birds of America*, courtesy of the Museum of Comparative Zoology Library, Harvard University; p. 231 left and right: from Duhamel du Monceau, *Traité général des pesches*, vol. 2, pt. 1, 1769–77, courtesy of the Library of Congress; p. 232: anonymous, *He That Tilleth the Land Shall Be Satisfied*, 22.5 x 29.5 in., no. 65–209–5, courtesy of the Philadelphia Museum of Art: Edgar William and Bernice Chrysler Garbisch Collection; p. 233: *The Lackawanna Valley*, George Inness, National Gallery of Art, Washington, Gift of Mrs. Huttleston Rogers; p. 234 top left: from Roland McKee and J.F. Stephens, *Kudzu as a Farm Crop*, USDA Farmer's Bulletin #23, October 1943, courtesy of the Botany Libraries, Harvard University; p. 234 top right: (c) William Christenberry; p. 234 bottom: Emory Kristoph (c) 1972 National Geographic Society; p. 235: "American Chestnut," from F. Andrew Michaux, *North American Sylva*, v.III, 1889, courtesy of the Botany Libraries, Harvard University; p. 236: (c) 1990 Gary Braasch, Woodfin Camp & Associates; p. 237 left: courtesy of the United State State Department; p. 237 right: (c) 1989 Alan Carey, Visual Resources for Ornithology (VIREO), Philadelphia; p. 238: (c) 1991 James Joern, New York; p. 240: from John James Audubon, *Birds of America*, courtesy of the Museum of Comparative Zoology Library, Harvard University; p. 243: David Alan Harvey (c) 1980 National Geographic Society; p. 244: Comstock, Inc./George Lepp; pp. 246–247: (c) 1990 James Joern, New York; p. 247: (c) 1990 Mary Ann Griggs, California Nature Conservancy

Nature's Future

pp. 248–249: courtesy of NASA; p. 249 inset: taxol chemical structure, courtesy of Steven R. King; p. 250: "Defrichement d'une forêt," from Mortiz Rugendas, *Malerische reise in Brasilien*, Paris, 1835, courtesy of Houghton Library, Harvard University; p. 251 all: (c) 1991 Steven R. King; p. 253 left: courtesy of Centers for Disease Control, Atlanta, Georgia, 30333; p. 253 right: photo (c) 1989 Joanna Pinneo/Foreign Mission Board/Southern Baptist Convention, courtesy of Black Star, New York; p. 254 left: (c) 1991 Steven R. King; p. 254 right: Diego Rivera, *El pueblo en demanda de salud*, mural (detail), Hospital de La Raza, 1953, photo (c) 1986 Bob Schalkwijk, Mexico City; p. 255 top: courtesy of the International Potato Center, Lima; p. 255 bottom: (c) 1988 Sergio Pastén, courtesy of Centro Internacional de Mejoramiento de Maíz y Trigo (CIMMYT), Mexico City; p. 256 left: (c) 1989 David Cavagnaro, Decorah, Iowa; p. 256 right: (c) 1972 Loren McIntyre, Alexandria, Virginia; p. 257 left: (c) 1989 Terrence Moore, Tucson; p. 257 right: (c) 1989 David Cavagnaro, Decorah, Iowa; p. 259 left: Randall Hyman/(c) 1990 Discover Publications, New York; p. 259 right: (c) 1991 Victor Englebert, Cali, Colombia; p. 260 left: courtesy of NASA; p. 260 right: (c) 1988 John Shaw, Greensboro, North Carolina; pp. 262–263: courtesy of NASA

Contributors

Deb Bennett: museum specialist in geology at the Office of Education, National Museum of Natural History; foremost hippologist; frequent contributor to *Equus* magazine.

Liliana Campos Dudley: coordinator for Peruvian programs at Conservation International; member of the South American Flamingo Specialist Group; working on developing sustainable development alternatives around the Amazon basin in Peru and Bolivia.

Alfred W. Crosby: professor of American studies at the University of Texas, Austin; author of *The Columbian Exchange* and *Ecological Imperialism*; former Guggenheim fellow.

David Barry Gaspar: professor of history at Duke University; author of *Bondsmen and Rebels*; currently working on the amelioration of the effects of slavery in the British Caribbean.

Robert L. Hall: professor of African-American studies at Northeastern University; author of an essay in *Africanisms in American Culture*; co-editor of *Holding on to the Land and the Lord: Kinship, Ritual, Land Tenure, and Social Policy in the Rural South*.

Henry Hobhouse: journalist, farmer, and educator; writer for the *Daily Express, The Economist, The Wall Street Journal*; author of *Seeds of Change* and *Forces of Change*.

Robert S. Hoffmann: assistant secretary for research, Smithsonian Institution; fellow, American Association for the Advancement of Science, honorary member, All-Union (U.S.S.R.) Theriological Society; author of eight books and over two hundred scientific articles.

George Horse Capture: developer of an arts and crafts cooperative and tribal museum with Fort Belknap Ventures at the Fort Belknap Reservation; former curator at the Plains Indian Museum Buffalo Bill Historical Center; producer and director of the film "I'd Rather be Pow-wowing."

Steven King: director of ethnobotany and conservation at Shaman Pharmaceuticals, Inc; contributor to National Academy of Sciences' *Lost Crops of the Andes*; former chief botanist for Latin America at the Nature Conservancy.

Carolyn Margolis: project coordinator for Quincentenary Programs at the National Museum of Natural History; organizer of exhibitions at the Anacostia Museum, Library of Congress, and the National Museum of Natural History; author of brochures, catalogs, and museum publications; co-editor of *Magnificent Voyagers: The U.S. Exploring Expedition, 1838–1842*.

William H. McNeill: professor emeritus in history at the University of Chicago; member of the Christopher Columbus Jubilee Commission; author of *Plagues and People*; former Woodrow Wilson Scholar.

Sidney W. Mintz: professor of anthropology at The Johns Hopkins University; author of *Sweetness and Power*; former Regents fellow.

Lydia M. Pulsipher: cultural geographer at the University of Tennessee; co-director of the interdisciplinary study of Galways plantation on the island of Montserrat; recipient of many awards, grants, and fellowships.

Joseph P. Sánchez: director of the Spanish Colonial Research Center, National Park Service at the University of New Mexico; author of *Spanish Bluecoats: The Catalonian Volunteers in Northwestern New Spain 1767–1810*; currently working on Spanish colonial frontiers in North America.

Stanwyn G. Shetler: acting deputy director and curator of botany, National Museum of Natural History; author of more than one hundred scientific, technical, and popular publications, including *The Komarov Botanical Institute—250 Years of Russian Research*, *Nearctic Harebells*, and *Portraits of Nature: Paintings by Robert Bateman*.

Yoko Sugiura: research scientist at the Institute for Anthropological Research at the National University in Mexico; extensive archeological field work throughout Mexico.

Douglas H. Ubelaker: curator and head of the Division of Physical Anthropology, National Museum of Natural History; forensic anthropology consultant to the F.B.I; co-editor of the forthcoming *Disease and Demography in the Americas: Changing Patterns Before and After 1492*.

John W. Verano: research associate in the Department of Anthropology, National Museum of Natural History; lecturer at George Washington University; co-editor of the forthcoming *Disease and Demography in the Americas: Changing Patterns Before and After 1492*.

Herman J. Viola: director of Quincentenary Programs at the National Museum of Natural History; founder and editor of *Prologue: The Journal of the National Archives*; curator of exhibitions at the National Archives, Corcoran Gallery of Art, and various Smithsonian Museums; author of numerous articles and books, including *The National Archives of the United States*, *Exploring the West*, *A Smithsonian Book*, *After Columbus: The Smithsonian Chronicle of the North American Indians*, and co-editor of *Magnificent Voyagers: The U.S. Exploring Expedition, 1838–1842*.

Jane MacLaren Walsh: research/museum specialist, Department of Anthropology, National Museum of Natural History; Ph.D. candidate at Catholic University with dissertation on first contact between Spaniards of Coronado's expedition of 1540 and the Pueblo Indians of the American Southwest.